ENERGY/WAR

Breaking the Nuclear Link

Amory B. Lovins and L. Hunter Lovins

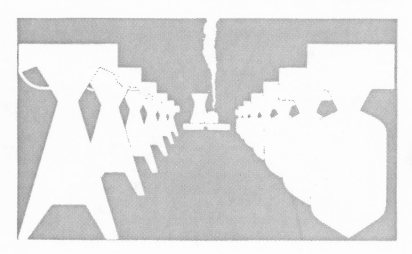

FRIENDS OF THE EARTH

San Francisco

Figure 2 is reproduced from A. B. Lovins' article "Soft Energy Paths" in the 1980 edition of *The Great Ideas Today,* and is reproduced by kind permission of the copyright holder, Encyclopaedia Britannica, Inc.

A condensation of this book, co-authored with Leonard Ross, was published as "Nuclear Power and Nuclear Bombs," *Foreign Affairs* 58:1137-77 (Summer 1980) published in New York by the Council on Foreign Relations, Inc.

Library of Congress Catalog Card No. 80-70178

ISBN: 0-913890-44-8

Trade Sales and distribution by Friends of the Earth, 124 Spear Street, San Francisco, CA 94105

Distributed in Canada by Hurtig Publishers, Edmonton.

Contents

Acknowledgments

A synthetic work relies foremost on the work of other analysts, many of whom have generously shared with us their unpublished insights and work in progress. We are further indebted for comments and corrections to Chip Bupp, Al Carnesale, Dick Falk, Jim Harding, Farley Hunter, Joe Nye, Walt Patterson, Paul Sieghart, Dick Speier, Vince Taylor, Don Westervelt, and many other reviewers. Greg Jones, Charlie Komanoff, and Randy Willoughby kindly helped us to track down elusive numbers and references. We, of course, are solely responsible for stated opinions and for any factual errors remaining, and we solicit further suggestions for improvement.

A condensation of this book first appeared in the Summer 1980 issue of *Foreign Affairs* (published and copyright by the Council on Foreign Relations, Inc.) thanks to the unfailing skill, patience, and faith of its Editor, Bill Bundy. His many refinements in structure and clarity have in turn enriched this rehydrated version. We benefitted further in that article from early discussions and (so far as geography and deadlines permitted) from useful editing, concepts, and language supplied by our coauthor, Lenny Ross. Some of his contributions, chiefly on financing soft energy for development, appear also, with our thanks, in this book. His range of experience in law, utility regulation, and the State Department was an invaluable leaven.

Finally, we take pleasure in ackowledging the unstinted hospitality and tolerance—during various stages of redrafting on the run—of Paula Quirk, Farley Hunter and Paul Sheldon, Gail Boyar Hayes, the Lindisfarne Association (which supported some of the writing), the Aspen Institute for Humanistic Studies (which lent a typewriter), Steve and Linda Conger, and Ken and Betty Moore.

Amory and Hunter Lovins

Bridgton, Maine
Hiroshima Day 1980

Dedicated to the memory of Lew Kowarski
(1907–1979)
and to the other nuclear pioneers
who changed their minds.

Prologue

Proliferation Is the Answer
(But What Was the Question?)

After the final no there comes a yes
And on that yes the future of the world depends.
Wallace Stevens

The nuclear proliferation problem, as posed, is insoluble.
As we near the end of the thirty-fifth year after Trinity, the
tenth year of the Non-Proliferation Treaty (NPT), and the fourth
of the Ford/Carter plutonium policy, the auguries are inauspici-
ous. The price and supply of oil become less predictable. Afghanistan falls. Tensions rise. The world financial system shud-
ders. The intellectual revelry of escape to outer space is in
vogue[1]. Nuclear hardware, knowledge, and expectations spread.
Undergraduates design workable fission bombs. The hydrogen
bomb goes public. A satellite announces the probable anonymous
entry of nuclear weapons state number seven or eight. Regional
military alliances become more frayed and less credible. The
world continues to spend over half a trillion dollars a year—a
million dollars per minute—on more efficient ways to kill people.
"Vertical" proliferation—the multiplication and refinement of
the more than fifty thousand atomic bombs now held by the nuclear weapons states—intensifies. Total nuclear firepower, well
over a million Hiroshimas, rises rapidly. The United States
quietly makes components for neutron bombs (which have no use
other than first use), adopts a first-strike-oriented targeting policy, seeks faster plutonium production, and continues to improve
the performance of its inventory of about thirty thousand bombs.
The USSR and (presumably) China follow suit as the latter tests
its first ICBM. The UK announces programs to make its own
tritium and highly enriched uranium (essential ingredients of hydrogen bombs), to MIRV its aging Polaris missiles, and to buy
Trident missiles from the US. France develops neutron bombs.
India wonders about affordable missiles and launches its first
earth satellite. As the weapons states maintain and even increase
their reliance on bombs as an essential instrument of foreign pol-

[1]L. J. Halle, "A Hopeful Future for Mankind," *Foreign Affairs* 58:1129–36
(Summer 1980), which proposes space colonization as a way to preserve the
species in an inevitable nuclear holocaust.

1

icy, other states and perhaps nongovernmental groups seek the same putative advantages via "horizontal" proliferation. A lucrative nuclear gray market[2] grows rapidly, and scientific mercenaries migrate. Reports spread of clandestine exports of key components for enrichment plants from two European countries to three aspiring weapons states. Ambiguous nuclear cooperation flourishes: Federal Republic of Germany-Argentina-South Africa, FR Germany-Brazil, Israel-South Africa, Italy-Iraq, France-Libya-Iraq, Iraq-Brazil, Brazil-Argentina, Argentina-India, US-Taiwan, France-Niger-Pakistan, Pakistan-Libya. The BBC's Reith Lecturer calls for a Black bomb. Pakistan pursues an Islamic bomb with advanced uranium centrifuge designs stolen (as predicted) from the Netherlands. At least two countries are believed to have built clandestine reprocessing plants to extract plutonium from spent reactor fuel. Some analysts believe a black market in bomb materials already exists. Missile and space technologies continue to be sold to countries known to seek them for potential nuclear delivery systems. US and European vendors export key non-nuclear technologies for making fission and fusion bombs, such as implosion systems and means of analyzing them: not being related to nuclear power, such dual-purpose items are not on the London Suppliers' Group "trigger list" of sensitive technologies, and controls on their export are haphazard. In at least one major non-weapons state, some of the directions being taken in the laser fusion research program seem more relevant to designing hydrogen bombs than to developing an energy source. Meanwhile, more conventional routes to bombs continue to multiply via nuclear power. New vulnerabilities are discovered in supposedly proliferation-resistant fuel cycles. Britain and France hasten to offer plutonium exports from reprocessing plants that do not yet exist. Japan joins the race. The US subsidizes more reactors for South Korea, pressures the Philippines to continue one, and seeks to send more fuel to India. The more cautious policy enshrined in a Nuclear Non-Proliferation Act notable for its opacity and prolixity starts to erode in 1979 and to crumble in 1980. Under commercial pressure, other suppliers backslide. Argentina, its nuclear bureaucrats now far ahead of Brazil's in pushing for bombs, openly pays an extra half-billion dollars for an FR German heavy-water reactor with loose safeguards and a Swiss heavy-water plant in preference to a better-proven Canadian reactor with stricter safeguards. Colonel Qadafi tries to purchase atomic bombs from several countries. France and Italy pre-

[2]L. A. Dunn, "Nuclear 'Gray Marketeering,'" *International Security* 1(3):107–118 (Winter 1977).

pare to ship bomb capability to Iraq. Iran (or, it is claimed, Israel, using planes with Iranian markings) bombs Iraq's nuclear research center. Irrational leaders and fanatical terrorists dominate the headlines. A senior official of the International Atomic Energy Agency (IAEA) says that terrorist acquisition of bomb materials is "becoming both possible and probable." In an era when the total explosive power released in World War II is encapsulated in single bombs that can fit beneath a bed, the conviction grows: We shall all blow each other up; the only question is when.

Perhaps in such an admission is to be found a semblance of equanimity—the release which accompanies abandonment to inevitability. Beyond the fear and denial of the syndrome of terminality is the enjoyment of the simple things left to us. Take that moment now—accept the absence of a future—for we have failed.

Or, if you would rather, explore with us a sudden cessation of stupidity[3]. In equanimity may be found an enhanced awareness: Stevens's courage to affirm. The problem of proliferation as it has been posed *is* insoluble: proliferation is the recurring answer. In our frantic provision of a terrible answer we have denied ourselves the space to realize that we have asked the wrong questions—creating a nuclear-armed crowd[4] by assuming its inevitability.

This book explores how different questions can lead to a different answer. The challenging of hallowed myths often excites intense emotions in persons who find those myths convenient or comforting. Some, hostile to the findings, may charge that we came to the proliferation problem in search of ammunition to support a doctrinaire anti-nuclear-power position. On the contrary, the search for practical ways to stop and even to reverse proliferation—the transcendent threat of our age—leads by inexorable logic to the necessity of phasing out nuclear power, as part of a coherent package of policies addressing both the vertical and the horizontal spread of bombs. We thus argue, with Jacques-Yves Cousteau[5], that

. . . human society is too diverse, national passion too strong, human aggressiveness too deep-seated for the peaceful and the warlike atom to stay divorced for long. We cannot embrace one while abhorring the other; we must learn, if we want to live at all, to live without both.

Such denuclearization may seem to some utopian and unachievable. We shall suggest that it is both achievable and intensely pragmatic. The immediate motive and justification for it is rooted in simple market economics; but the necessity for it springs from skepticism about reliance on the truly utopian fancy that the habits of thought and emotion which have shaped human societies through hundreds of generations will be abruptly jettisoned in the interest of mere survival.

Some problems have no solutions; indeed, the *cause* of many problems is solutions. But we have to try.

[3]This phrase is due to Edwin Land.

[4]This phrase, and many parts of our analysis, reflect our intellectual debt to A. Wohlstetter *et al.* for their pioneering work, notably *Moving Toward Life in a Nuclear Armed Crowd?*, ACDA/PAB-263, Pan Heuristics (Los Angeles, now Marina del Rey CA[8]) report to US Arms Control & Disarmament Agency, 22 April 1976.

[5]May 1976 UN speech, reprinted in R. N. Gardner, ed., "Nuclear Energy and World Order: Implications for International Organizations," Institute on Man & Science (Rensselaerville NY), 1976.

Chapter One

Introduction

Since nuclear bombs were invented some four decades ago, all policies to try to prevent or slow their proliferation into more hands have rested on three assumptions which emerged from obscurity during the 1950s, achieved their greatest credence in the 1960s, and became sharply controversial during the 1970s:

- that the rapid worldwide spread of nuclear power[5a] is essential for world energy supply (especially, of late, to reduce dependence on oil), economically desirable, and inevitable;
- that efforts to inhibit the concomitant spread of nuclear bombs must not be allowed to interfere with this vital reality; and
- that the international political order must remain inherently discriminatory, dominated by bipolar hegemony and the nuclear arms race.

The first of these assumptions rested on a tacit supposition that the backbone of energy supply must be additional large power stations. The second was consistent with the belief that US policy could not have decisive influence abroad and that only minimal, marginal adjustments within this assumed regime could be realistically contemplated. The third reflected a conviction that national security could rest only on the power of a centralized military apparatus. All these assumptions, explicit and tacit, artificially constrain the arena of choice and maximize the intractability of the proliferation problem. Yet they have remained, until now, largely unexamined and wholly unverified.

The influential Ford-MITRE report[6], among the first to state these assumptions clearly, argued from them that proliferation was inevitable but could be slowed by distinctions, in both domestic and export programs, between various nuclear fuel cycles that lent themselves more or less well to proliferation. These distinctions were embodied in initiatives by Presidents Ford and

[5a] In this book, "nuclear power" refers to the use of nuclear *fission* as an energy source. Nuclear *fusion*, if feasible, would have abundant fuel, probably greater complexity and higher total costs, less severe (but still unattractive) radioactive waste problems, significant proliferative potential[25], and the same fundamental economic and logistical irrelevance to the energy problems as any other central-electric system (Chapter Four).

[6] Nuclear Energy Policy Study Group, *Nuclear Power: Issues and Choices* (sponsored by the Ford Foundation and administered by the MITRE Corporation), Ballinger (Cambridge MA), 1977.

Carter to slow the spread of plutonium technologies, which were judged especially proliferation-prone; but the distinctions were soon fuzzed by euphemisms and, curiously, denied by plutonium advocates who argued that rival fuel cycles were nearly as dangerous.

Nonetheless, the nuclear industry and its friends in government, considering the proposed distinctions invidious, carefully orchestrated a chorus of international protest which led to the 1977-80 International Nuclear Fuel Cycle Evaluation (INFCE)[7]—a rival study to Ford-MITRE done largely by governmentally appointed nuclear technocrats with an undisguised fondness for plutonium cycles. During INFCE's two years of voluminous studies, the US refrained from inhibiting allies' haste to enter vast commitments prejudging it. Both before and during INFCE, US delegates compromised away a commanding position based on technical merits to acquiesce in conclusions driven by nuclear growth forecasts that seemed dubious at the start and risible by the end. During INFCE "...it is our allies who have stuck to their initial position in the face of evidence which supports the US position while [the US has] been weakening in spite of it."[8]

Today, INFCE's conclusions—largely unsympathetic to the Ford-Carter policies resting on the Ford-MITRE analysis— are being widely cited by INFCE's instigators as a political and technical rationale for dismantling what is left of the 1976-77 US reforms (whose later rapid erosion is examined in Chapter Six). Yet as in the Ford-MITRE report, with its quite different conclusions, INFCE's findings were generally mere unexamined *assumptions*—masquerading and often presented in the press as its *conclusions*, ostensibly resulting from a careful assessment of alternatives which never actually took place. All that did emerge was that neither INFCE nor its US counterpart—a government study called NASAP (Nonproliferation Alternatives System Assessment Program)[9]—had found the technical solutions to proliferation which the Ford-Carter policy required if it was to work

---

[7]The eight-volume INFCE report was published by the IAEA (Vienna) in February 1980. A concise summary volume gives an adequate flavor of the whole.

[8]H. Rowen and A. Wohlstetter, "US Non-Proliferation Strategy Reformulated," report to CEQ/DOE/NSC, Pan Heuristics (PO Box 9695, Marina del Rey CA 90291), 29 August 1979.

[9]The nine-volume NASAP report was published by the US Department of Energy in June 1980 as document DOE/NE-0001/1–9.

properly. The illusion that technical solutions could be found had meanwhile encouraged four years of worsening risks, deteriorating policy, and narrowing options.

This book rests on a different perception. Instead of debating the fine points of marginal reforms in a fatalistic regime that accepts proliferation as inevitable, this analysis reconsiders basic assumptions. It begins with the empirical fact that the global nuclear power enterprise is rapidly turning into a pumpkin. *De facto* moratoria on reactor ordering exist today in the United States, the Federal Republic of Germany, the Netherlands, Italy, Sweden, Ireland, and probably the United Kingdom, Belgium, Switzerland, Japan, and Canada. Nuclear power has been indefinitely deferred or abandoned in Austria, Denmark, Norway, Iran, China, Australia, and New Zealand, and is elsewhere in grave difficulties. Only in centrally planned economies, notably France and the USSR, is bureaucratic power sufficient to override, if not overcome, economic realities. The high nuclear growth forecasts that drove INFCE's endorsement of fast breeder reactors are thus mere wishful thinking. For fundamental reasons (Chapters Four and Five), nuclear power is simply not commercially viable, and questions of how to regulate an inexorably expanding world nuclear enterprise—the focus of present policy—are moot. The relevant question is rather how to manage, and turn to nonproliferative advantage, the gradual contraction and disappearance of nuclear power under the irresistible force of market economics.

This analysis further shows that the collapse of nuclear power in response to the discipline of the marketplace is to be welcomed, for nuclear power is both the main driving force behind proliferation (Chapters Two and Three) and the least effective known way to replace oil (Chapters Four and Seven). Indeed, nuclear investments *retard* oil displacement by the faster, cheaper, and more attractive means which new developments in energy policy now make available (Chapters Seven and Eight). Acknowledging and taking advantage of the nuclear collapse, as part of a coherent alternative program (Chapter Eleven), can offer not only an internally consistent approach to nonproliferation, but also a resolution to the bitter dispute over the rights of developing countries as reflected in Article IV of the NPT (Chapter Nine), and some hope of progress in nuclear disarmament (Chapter Ten).

In short, *both* present US proliferation policy *and* the watered-down version with which the nuclear industry seeks to replace it rest on analyses (Ford-MITRE and INFCE) which rely for their most basic assumptions on proof by vigorous assertion

and refutation by emphatic dismissal. We shall seek to replace
these assumptions with others that are demonstrably more consistent with reality. It is perhaps surprising that this has not been
done before; but a little reflection suggests why it is predictable.
As generals seek to refight the previous war, and arms controllers
to prevent it, technology outpaces them both. In energy policy,
technical facts have not only been changing with dizzying speed
of late; their changes also transform the *conceptual structure* of
the problem. Ford-MITRE's technological debates were and are
sterile, not only because the report's analysis of (say) solar
energy was sophomoric, but because, as Chapter Four shows, the
nature of the energy problem is not what that distinguished group
supposed. New information about both energy and nuclear matters, emerging worldwide with extraordinary speed, has made
anachronisms of basic structural premises.

From premises consistent with this new information we
shall argue that the benefits of nuclear power (especially in displacing oil) are illusory; that nuclear power is not exclusively
peaceful, economically or logistically attractive, necessary for
energy supply, or commercially sustainable; that nuclear power
and nuclear weapons reduce national security; that horizontal and
vertical proliferation are inextricably linked; that there is a con-
structive and equitable solution to developing countries' desire
for nuclear parity; and that an effective nonproliferation policy,
though impossible with continued commitments to nuclear
power, may become possible without them—if only we ask the
right questions.

Chapter Two

Nuclear Power and Nuclear Bombs

All concentrated fissionable materials are potentially explosive. All nuclear fission technologies both use and produce fissionable materials that are or can be concentrated. Unavoidably latent in those technologies, therefore, is a potential for nuclear violence and coercion which may be exploited by governments, factions, terrorist groups, criminal syndicates, lunatics, economic speculators, or their agents. Action by one group may be disguised as action by another, and a mere threat of action, if competent enough to be credible, may suffice to achieve the same political ends.

Little strategic material is needed to make a weapon of mass destruction. A Nagasaki-yield bomb can be made from a few kilograms of plutonium, a piece the size of a tennis ball[10]. A threat of having made such a bomb could be authenticated, or a formidable aerosol-dispersion weapon made, with a gram or less. (The amount virtually certain to cause lung cancer if inhaled by dogs is known to be less, and may be much less, than a millionth of a gram.) Yet these amounts are a minute fraction of plutonium flows in normal fuel cycles. A large power reactor annually produces, and an experimental "critical assembly" may contain, hundreds of kilograms of plutonium; a large fast breeder reactor would contain thousands of kilograms; a large reprocessing plant may separate tens of thousands of kilograms per year, or more than one bomb's worth per hour.

Nor is it only fissionable materials that lead to bombs. Though most of our analysis here is concerned with materials, it is at least equally important that most of the knowledge, much of the equipment, and the general nature of the organizations relevant to making bombs are inherent in civilian nuclear activities, and are "in much of their course interchangeable and interdependent" for peaceful or violent uses.[11] "Whoever achieves a high

---

[10]Or a slightly larger amount of uranium-233 (an artificial element derived from thorium), or about ten to twenty kilograms of uranium-235 in fairly concentrated form, or conceivably—subject to availability and some technical problems— broadly similar amounts of certain other isotopes, notably neptunium-237, which are created (and in some cases extracted) in present fuel-cycle operations but which are currently subject to no safeguards.

[11]"A Report on the International Control of Atomic Energy" (the Acheson-Lilienthal Report[73]), US State Dept. 2498, 16 March 1946.

level of civilian technology is almost automatically on the threshold of nuclear weapons."[12] The mere presence or planning of an apparently peaceful nuclear program thus carries an ambiguous threat which may motivate regional rivals to seek similar capabilities.

Peaceful use does not imply exclusively peaceful use, and currently peaceful intentions in no way diminish military utility; yet a habit early arose "of talking as if a civilian use automatically substituted for a military use, rather than complementing or supplementing it."[13] This sloppy thinking became a peril when physicists, having known sin, sought atonement by harnessing vice for virtue.[14] Politicians, starting with President Eisenhower in 1954, then spread these "peaceful" applications (spun off from Admiral Rickover's nuclear navy) worldwide with missionary fervor, even though this had only an "allusive and sentimental" rather than a "substantive and functional" link[15] with the nuclear disarmament to which they made rhetorical obeisance. Many world leaders were advised that the dangers were negligible or imaginary. Some of this wrong advice arose from honest mistakes and oversights, some from emotional distortions of logic, and some—"a chilling point—[was] clearly caused by malfeasance and deliberate suppression of facts."[16] But whatever the motives—humane liberalism, commercial avarice, guilt—Atoms for Peace was arguably "one of the stupidest ideas of our time"[17], conceived in a spirit of political daydreaming, commercial euphoria, and scientific amnesia. It embodied the hubris of the illusion that we could split the atom into two roles as easily and irrevocably as into two parts. Forgetting that ontology recapitulates philology, we forgot that atomic energy is a-tomic,

[12]J. Schwelein, "Heisses Geschäft mit dem Atomstrom," *Die Zeit,* 27 June 1975.

[13]F. C. Iklé, Foreword to A. Wohlstetter *et al., Swords From Plowshares,* U. of Chicago Press, 1979.

[14]While we do not intend to be drawn into theological disputations, some theologians feel that nuclear fission may be an inherently and irremediably evil technology, rather than a neutral or value-free tool that can be used for good by those with good intentions. The concept that there could be inherently evil technologies was evidently alien to most scientists within a Western tradition founded on the possibility of redemption from sin by virtue of grace and works.

[15]These phrases are due to J. R. Oppenheimer.

[16]Iklé, *op cit.*[13].

[17]D. M. Rosenbaum, quoted by J. G. Phillips, *National Journal Reports* 421, 22 March 1975. David Lilienthal Sr. has expressed similar views: *Atomic Energy: A New Start,* Harper & Row (NY), 1980.

indivisible[18]—and so institutionalized an extraordinary schizo-phrenia.

The Superpowers offered up their myriads of bombs to a strategic-deterrence doctrine whose very foundations they were eroding through reactor exports which made possible anonymous and hence undeterrable nuclear attacks on them. The nuclear power enterprise, meant to develop morally justifiable spinoffs from costly military programs (with the indispensable aid of their subventions), is in its turn spawning more military programs. If, as Samuel Butler said, "the hen is only an egg's way of making another egg," then perhaps a reactor is a bomb's way of making another bomb. The genotype reasserts itself in many complex ways. Making bombs requires both capability and intention, but these feed on each other. Intention seeks capability to fulfill it, while capability lowers the threshold—in time, money, and polit-ical initiative—for developing a matching intention (the process called "latent proliferation"). Thus separation of plutonium from spent fuel preceded and facilitated the British, French, and Indian decisions to build bombs. Nuclear power "provided the essential expeditor, and in many cases the necessary cover,"[19] for diffu-sion of bomb capabilities to and beyond India. Completing the circle, the nuclear weapons states dominate world affairs by the threat of exercising unique military power. They seek to appease other countries' natural desire to imitate their own domineering capacities by offering instead a supposed surrogate—"peaceful" nuclear technology—which in fact provides larval bombs. To these, their own visible power and the capability's latent threat add motivation. The "perverse logic of nonproliferation," as Richard Falk calls it, thereby requires proliferation to all and security for none.

Knowledge and organizations

President Eisenhower foresaw in his 1953 address to the United Nations that the knowledge of bombs then "possessed by several nations will eventually be shared by others—perhaps all others." He hastened this unhappy equilibrium through massive declassification—millions of pages, the fruits of a generation's secret research of a previously unprecedented scale and quality, including over eleven thousand papers on plutonium technology alone—and through training programs which suffused this

[18]Keith Critchlow suggests that the ancient Greeks' message in coining the word "atom" was moral, not physical: not that the atom *could* not be split, but that it *should* not be.

[19]Iklé, *op. cit.*[13]. See also note 22 below.

knowledge into thousands of scientists from eighty-four countries. That dual-purpose information, (propagated as irreversibly
as the political constraints on its use were reversible), is now
being diligently applied in every bomb laboratory.

Few instruments or theories used in civil nuclear power
have no military application. Such data as the criticality conditions and equation of state of plutonium are secret when applied
to bombs; some analyses of proliferation problems have come to
a dead end for lack of these data; yet precisely the same data are
published in civilian literature which reactor programs make
available to proliferators. And often they are the data on which
the training programs have focused. Probably half the key staff of
the Indian bomb program was US-trained at the expense of US
taxpayers[20]: the thirteen hundred sixty-seven US-trained Indian
nuclear scientists are equivalent to over half the total number at
the main Trombay nuclear research center. The one thousand
fifty-two Taiwanese, two hundred twenty Argentinians, and two
hundred seventy-two South Koreans must similarly form the bulk
of their nations' expertise. By 1972, the US had trained one
hundred sixty-nine foreign nationals in Purex reprocessing[21] (the
process designed to extract military plutonium of maximum purity), and far more in enrichment, plutonium chemistry and metallurgy, fast reactor theory, and other essentials of bomb-making.
Recently, exchange students from Taiwan and South Korea reportedly continued their work in US weapons laboratories at the
very moment when the US was trying to stop their governments'
drift toward bombs. Even today, disproportionate numbers of
Libyan and Palestinian students are showing disproportionate
interest in US nuclear curricula.

Capabilities and intentions may merge in dedicated, elite
cadres of nuclear scientists, especially those whose intellectual
critical mass invites exploratory thinking and the subordination of
personal to group values. As Herbert York has emphasized, such
a group is statistically likely to contain a few members
susceptible—as thousands of ordinary, decent Americans proved
susceptible—to the seductions of secrets and of weapons physics
(perhaps the most fascinating kind of physics there is). Such
people tend to attract the like-minded. For prestige or mere

[20]H. M. Agnew, *Bulletin of the Atomic Scientists* 22, May 1976, reprinted at 23 in
US Senate Committee on Governmental Affairs, *Reader on Nuclear Nonproliferation* (USGPO, 7 December 1978), an invaluable sourcebook.

[21]J. Fialka, quoted by L. Weiss, *Bulletin of the Atomic Scientists* 27 March 1978,
reprinted at 454 in *Reader*[20]. For an analytic summary of US training programs,
see C. D. Long, *International Security 1* (4):52 (Spring 1977), *Reader*[20] 272–96.

curiosity, they may then want to play with bombs. Selected politicians can be told this is desirable—to "keep national security options open" or to develop a "peaceful" excavation tool—and, for reasons of their own, may agree. If not, they can be ignored or bypassed; sooner or later, a clientele can be found. Politicians come and go, bureaucracies stay and grow. While three French Premiers declared against developing bombs, the technologists nominally under their control continued doing so unabated, justifying all their programs for other purposes.[22] A bigger nuclear program increases opportunities—exports, prestige, cooperative research, indigenous fuel cycles—for attracting resources that can encourage and conceal military sidelines. A military nuclear community then develops, its activities and its possibly pathological personalities concealed from public view and political control by a hermetic wall of secrecy. Or a semipermeable wall—all too permeable to outward leaks as some scientists seek to display their ingenuity to a wider audience.[23] Metastasis begins as the tools of nuclear science corrupt the weaknesses of the human psyche and exploit the potential for people in groups to do things that they might not dream of doing individually.

Fissionable materials

All commercial nuclear fuel cycles are fueled with uranium.[24] The 7.1 kilograms of fissionable uranium-235 in each 1000 kg (metric ton) of natural uranium as mined are about enough for a bomb but far too dilute. The few percent of uranium-235 present in "low-enriched uranium" (LEU) is also

[22]The French bomb advocates shunted aside the anti-bomb head of the Atomic Energy Commission, Joliot, and bullied his successor, Perrin, into expanding plutonium production. In both Britain and France, the formal decision to build a bomb was taken after the apparently unstoppable technologists were nearly through doing so on their own, as noted by Gowing, Scheinman, H. York (*Reader*[20] 498–504), and other historical commentators. The programs' inherent momentum (W. W. Lowrance, *International Security 1*(2):147, Fall 1976) bulldozed through or around all political control mechanisms in the two countries with perhaps the world's greatest experience in exercising them—not a good omen for states less politically mature.

[23]As, for example, by Lawrence Livermore Laboratory's museum exhibits and open seminars (by e.g. Edward Teller), available even to nominally "cleared" casual visitors with no need to know.

[24]Experimental fuel cycles based on thorium differ only in detail, not in conclusions: A. B. Lovins, "Thorium cycles and proliferation," *Bulletin of the Atomic Scientists* 16–22, February 1979, and discussions *id.* 50–54, May 1979, and 57–59, September 1979. See also E. Beardsworth, reports 76-823-04 and 78-832-01 to ACDA from Pan Heuristics[8] re re-enrichment.

too dilute to sustain an explosion. Practicable bombs require concentrations of tens of percent; highly efficient bombs, about ninety percent ("highly enriched uranium" or HEU). A few minor types of commercial reactors, notably the Canadian CANDU, are fueled with natural uranium. The dominant world type, the US-designed light-water reactor (LWR), is fueled with LEU. One prospective commercial type (the high-temperature gas-cooled reactor or HTGR), naval reactors, and many research reactors are fueled with directly bomb-usable HEU.

The irradiation of uranium fuel in any reactor produces the artificial element plutonium, which is a bomb material regardless of its isotopic composition or chemical form. Its main isotope, plutonium-239, and that isotope's product of radioactive decay, uranium-235, together last essentially forever. Once created, they must be guarded with exquisite care, continuously and indefinitely. But the only practical source of plutonium (or of the almost equally explosive artificial isotope uranium-233, made by irradiating thorium) is spent fuel discharged from a reactor[25]. In spent fuel, the plutonium is highly diluted and intimately mixed with fission products whose intense radioactivity makes it essentially inaccessible for about the first century or more.[26] The plutonium is thus a proliferation risk only[27] if it is extracted by

[25]Or fertile isotopes (uranium-238 to make plutonium-239, or thorium-232 to make uranium-233) exposed to a strong neutron flux from some source other than a reactor. Such sources could be based on powerful particle accelerators, though these are so few, costly, and conspicuous that preventing this abuse by safeguards does not seem unduly difficult. Fusion and near-thermonuclear reactors would also produce copious, cheap fast neutrons which could also be used for breeding fissionable materials—one of the arguments against developing such devices. (Another argument is that laser fusion—which Edward Teller, among others, would like to be largely declassified—spreads key knowledge about how to design fusion bombs: J. P. Holdren, *Bulletin of the Atomic Scientists* 4, March 1978.) Both methods, however, are only future possibilities. See A. Gsponer, "Implications of Particle Accelerators and Fusion Technologies on Horizontal and Vertical Proliferation of Nuclear Weapons," GIPRI (41 rue de Zürich, 1201 Geneva), 8 August 1980, submitted to *Science*.

[26]B. J. Snyder of the US Nuclear Regulatory Commission (NRC) provides a good quantitative assessment in "Non-Proliferation Characteristics of Radioactive Fuel," May 1979 paper to the European Nuclear Conference (Hamburg).

[27]Since most of the penetrating radioactivity from spent fuel has decayed after about a half-millenium (Snyder[26]), its plutonium could be relatively easily extracted if the fuel had not by then been irretrievably disposed of. Further, if the fuel has been reprocessed, one or two percent of its plutonium remains in very weakly radioactive alpha-emitting wastes from which it may be extractable with special "chelating" chemicals like those used in agriculture to promote the uptake of trace metals. The US Atomic Energy Commission even proposed to build the world's first plutonium mine (fully automated) to recover several hundred kilo-

"reprocessing" the spent fuel—chopping up and dissolving the fuel bundles and chemically separating the purified plutonium. It is then in a concentrated, homogeneous, and divisible form that can be safely handled, is hard to measure precisely, and is therefore much easier to steal undetected. Extracted plutonium can be made into bombs so quickly (in days, hours, or in some conceivable circumstances minutes) that even instant detection cannot provide "timely warning," the cardinal principle of safeguards since the start of the nuclear age.[28]

US nonproliferation policy since 1976 has rested on distinctions between proliferation-prone fuel cycles and fuel cycles thought to be proliferation-resistant. LWRs were considered highly proliferation-resistant so long as technologies or services which could further enrich the LEU fresh fuel or extract plutonium from the spent fuel were not available to non-weapons states. It was considered possible for such states to obtain these technologies on their own, but only at high cost, with great technical difficulty, and with a large risk of timely detection. Reprocessing spent LWR fuel in conventional large plants, for example, is so difficult that no country, despite intensive efforts by several nations of great technical ability, has yet succeeded in doing it on

---

grams selectively adsorbed onto a clay layer through which low-level liquid wastes had been poured in Trench Z-9 at Hanford. Such potential recovery routes need to be considered, but this should not divert attention from the far more likely and dangerous routes described in the text. Such a diversion has been persistently advanced by Walter Marshall of the UK Atomic Energy Authority (UKAEA) in the form of decrying spent fuel storage or disposal as the creation of future "plutonium mines." His preferred solution—reprocessing and re-use of the plutonium—would create a vast "plutonium river" instead, turning much of the world into a "plutonium flood plain."

[28]The concept is explicit in the IAEA's technical criteria, most principal documents back to Baruch (and some even earlier, such as Szilard's 1945 call for one or two years' warning), the 1969 report to the IAEA Director-General by Consultants on Criteria for Safeguards Procedures Under the NPT, etc. What amount of time is timely depends on the gap between detection and effective sanctions—which is imponderable but (judging by such precedents as the Cuban missile crisis) at least weeks and preferably months—and on how long it takes to make stolen material into a bomb. On the basis of at least Trinity-style bomb designs requiring metallic cores, the IAEA assumes a typical requirement of about 1–3 weeks starting with unirradiated or 1–3 months with irradiated materials.[40] But these estimates, the result of political compromise, are not minima: the then Inspector-General's personal planning basis (R. Rometsch, personal communication, 9 February 1977) is twelve hours or less, recognizing the possibility of simpler designs and fuller advance preparations. The UNAEC's report to the Security Council, 31 December 1946, said "a few days"—curiously less than current IAEA values—and it is now known that by the direct use of oxide powder, a crude bomb might be improvised on the spot in minutes.

a reliable commercial basis.[29] (It must be noted that this argument considers only the availability of fissionable materials, and ignores the proliferative effects of knowledge, expectations, latent threats, infrastructure, and organizations.)

Consistent with this technological line of reasoning (encapsulated in the Ford-MITRE report), the United States sought to defer as long as possible domestic and foreign commitments to widespread use of fuel cycles requiring reprocessing—recycling plutonium in LWRs and breeding it in fast reactors[30]. "Once-through" (no-reprocessing) LWRs, on the other hand, were encouraged for domestic use and for export because of their alleged proliferation resistance. But this reversed a long-standing official US policy of encouraging reprocessing, plutonium recycle, and fast breeders. Prior US proclamations that these were essential to our nuclear, hence energy, hence economic future had taken root at home and abroad.

In particular, Britain and France, late in the 1970s, had embarked on ambitious construction programs to expand their existing, rather unsuccessful reprocessing plants (which handle almost exclusively the relatively weakly radioactive metallic fuel from gas-cooled graphite-moderated reactors[31]). The expansion

[29]The dismal status of reprocessing technology was reviewed in detail in a lucid 1500-page report to the Governor of Lower Saxony by the independent Gorleben International Review, published in German by the Niedersächsisches Sozialministerium (Hannover, April 1979), and summarized (along with adversarial hearings on it[151]) H. Hatzfeldt et al., eds., *Der Gorleben-Report*, Fischer (Frankfurt/M), 1979. Its critique on grounds of policy, economics, routine public and occupational exposures, accidents, sabotage, safeguards, technical maturity, and long-term stability had a powerful effect (Chapter Seven). As another illustration, the French plant at La Hague has operated at only about a tenth of planned capacity, and its unit costs (current francs per kg output), having risen tenfold in six years, show no signs of stabilizing. Other valuable discussions of reprocessing are the California Energy Commission's exhaustive 1976-77 hearings; C. Conroy, *What Choice Windscale?*, Friends of the Earth Ltd (9 Poland St, London W1V 3DG), 1978; G. Rochlin et al. (Institute of International Studies, U. of California at Berkeley), *Non-Proliferation and Nuclear Waste Management*, Report AC6AC725 to USACDA, 1977; G. Rochlin, *Plutonium, Power, and Politics*, U. of California Press (Berkeley), 1979; and a survey in preparation by J. Harding, Friends of the Earth Inc (124 Spear St, San Francisco CA 94105), 1980.

[30]What is "fast" is the neutrons, not the breeding. Ordinary "burner" reactors, which do not produce more plutonium than they consume, normally slow ("moderate") their neutrons to "thermal" speeds and hence are called "thermal reactors."

[31]The first reactor programs in both countries used these "Magnox" or "gaz-graphit" reactors, originally meant for military plutonium production. Magnox reactors, so called from the magnesium alloy that clads their natural-uranium fuel, were also exported on a small scale (one each to Italy, Spain, and Japan). The fuel is about ten times less radioactive than LWR fuel, and, being metallic, is easier to cut and dissolve than the ceramic (oxide) fuel of LWRs.

would be dedicated to export services for LWRs—in return for an open-ended fee with no guarantee of performance, doubtless reflecting a lack of technical confidence in the success of the process. But the offer of reprocessing services, vigorously peddled worldwide, would at least relieve other countries of any need to try to solve the technical difficulties of reprocessing oxide fuel[32]. Such export services would offer three further signal advantages to potential customers:

• getting spent fuel (a thorny political problem) out of one's own country for the next decade or two, and so removing an inhibition to reactor licensing;
• providing an appearance of progress on the waste problem in a country (France) where "a nearly complete lack of data makes it essentially impossible for any outsider to assess the technical validity of official statements on the status of nuclear development"[33]; and
• providing bomb-usable separated plutonium (or mixed oxides[34] readily convertible to it).

Of course it is the last of these that the US found most unpalatable. The separated plutonium is "a lot more like a bomb than it is

[32]These difficulties include the accumulation of insoluble, intensely radioactive granules alloyed of various refractory-metal fission products. About a hundred thousand curies of these granules were the cause of an accident that contaminated the Windscale oxide plant and 35 workers (one of whom reportedly received a lung dose ~ 1000 rem) in 1973 (it has not operated since). Their main constituent, ruthenium-106, would be more than ten times as abundant in plutonium- as in uranium-based fuel, since the fission yield of ^{106}Ru is 0.38% for ^{235}U but 4.5% for ^{239}Pu.

[33]J.-C. Derian and I. C. Bupp, "Running Water: Nuclear Power on the Move in France," 6 September 1979 typescript available from Prof. Bupp (Harvard Business School). France claims to have "solved" the waste problem by developing a process for converting high-level reprocessing wastes to glass. The long-term stability of the glass, whether it can be stably made from LWR wastes or only from the much less radioactive wastes from gas-cooled reactors[31], where it can be put, and what is to be done with other reprocessing wastes (notably the low-level transuranic wastes,[131] which may present an even greater long-term hazard) are questions that cannot be answered from published, verifiable information in France.

[34]Of uranium and plutonium; the latter can be readily re-concentrated from this dilute form by chemical (or perhaps by physical) means using common, unshielded equipment. This task is far easier than reprocessing spent fuel.[36]According to NASAP,[9] it would be theoretically possible, though unwieldy, to make a bomb directly from fresh mixed-oxide fast breeder fuel (15–25% plutonium) without further separation.

like a reactor"[35], and presumably the UK and France would not dream of exporting bombs labelled "For Peaceful Use Only." Their own lack of faith in "strengthened international safeguards" is demonstrated by their policy of discouraging non-weapons states from getting their own reprocessing plants because military use of the extracted plutonium could not then be prevented. But their alternative proposal—to supply the plutonium themselves from abroad—can hardly allay this concern. The UK and France argue, further, that siting the reprocessing plant itself in a weapons state, or internationally managing it, solves the problem; but of course bombs are made of plutonium, not of concrete: the product and its disposition are the worry, not the plant itself. And their proposed technical measures to inhibit the use of the extracted and re-exported plutonium in bombs— chiefly by diluting or radioactively contaminating it so that further treatment would be needed—have all been shown to be impracticable or ineffectual, especially against governments.[36]

It is because plutonium commerce therefore poses grave risks to peace, and because neither it nor the reprocessing plants supplying it can be safeguarded even in principle, that the United States in 1976-78 sought by its own example, and for a time by mild persuasion (but not by exercising its legal veto over reprocessing US-enriched fuel), to discourage Britain and France from

[35]V. Gilinsky, "Nuclear Energy and Nuclear Proliferation," 3 November 1977 speech (USNRC S-11-77) reprinted at 83-91 in A. Wohlstetter *et al.*, *Nuclear Policies: Fuel Without the Bomb*, Ballinger (Cambridge, MA), 1978. See also Commissioner Gilinsky's equally incisive 1 November 1976 speech, "Plutonium, Proliferation, and Policy" (USNRC S-14-76) and his 27 September 1978 "Plutonium, Proliferation, and the Price of Money" (S-78-8) reprinted in *Foreign Affairs* 374, Winter 1978/79.

[36]Such measures include premixing mixed oxides,[34] or leaving the fuel radioactive via coprocessing or "CIVEX" cycles, or making it radioactive by light irradiation or by "spiking" with gamma-emitting isotopes. All these methods, and several others, have been exhaustively reviewed and found to be awkward, very costly, hazardous to workers and the public, a serious obstacle to materials accountancy, not fully effective against subnational diverters, and "not useful at all in restraint of national proliferation." US Congress, Office of Technology Assessment, *Nuclear Proliferatiion and Safeguards*, Praeger (NY/London), 1977. See also American Physical Society, Study Group on Nuclear Fuel Cycles and Waste Management, *Reviews of Modern Physics 50* (1), Part II, 1978; T. B. Taylor *et al.*, Report IRT-378-R to USNRC Special Safeguards Study, International Research & Technology Corp. (Arlington, VA), 1975; Snyder[26]; and GIR.[29] Most of these proposed methods also entail fuel fabrication by the supplier country, which is logistically difficult and likely to be unacceptable to countries which sought plutonium to enhance their energy independence. Few knowledgeable analysts take any of these options seriously today. Curiously, W. Marshall of the UKAEA[27] persists in arguing that they would make plutonium recovery very difficult, while recovery from the original spent fuel is relatively easy!

breaching the formidable barrier offered by the difficulties of re-processing. This policy threatened the nuclear industry's plans that a few decades hence, some tens of thousands of bombs' worth of plutonium per year will be running around as an item of commerce—within the same international community that has never been able to stop the heroin traffic.

Power reactors as bomb factories

Advocates of reprocessing and plutonium commerce in-stantly assaulted the 1976-77 US policy initiatives on two con-tradictory grounds: that the plutonium made in power reactors would not be attractive to bomb-makers, and that if it were, commercial reprocessing was not the only way to extract it.

The first limb of this argument claimed that the "reactor-grade" plutonium made by normal operation of power reactors—currently some thirty tons (about ten thousand bombs' worth) per year, a third of it in nonweapons states—could pro-duce only weak and unreliable explosions, and posed exceptional hazards to persons working with it. Countries seeking bombs would therefore pass up this inferior material in favor of "weapons-grade" plutonium whose greater isotopic purity of-fered optimal performance. Weapons-grade plutonium could be made in existing research reactors (now operating in about thirty countries) or in "production reactors" specially built for the pur-pose from published designs. This route was claimed to be easier, cheaper, more effective, hence more plausible than using power reactors. Concern over power reactors was thus deemed to be far-fetched.

The technical premise behind this reasoning, however, is false. A detailed analysis of weapons physics has now shown[37] that any practical composition of plutonium—including both "reactor-grade" plutonium and plutonium to which inseparable interfering ("denaturing") isotopes have been deliberately added—can be made by governments or by some subnational groups into bombs equivalent in power and predictability to those made from "weapons-grade" plutonium. Alternatively, power reactors can be so operated as to produce modest amounts of the latter without significantly increasing costs, decreasing effi-ciency, or risking detection.

More sophisticated bomb design is needed to achieve the same performance from reactor-grade as from weapons-grade plutonium, but this may be a small price to pay for the greater ease of obtaining the former in bulk. The power reactor has an

[37]A. B. Lovins, "Nuclear weapons and power-reactor plutonium," *Nature* 283:817–23 (1980) and typographical corrections, *id.* 284:190 (1980).

innocent civilian "cover" rather than being obviously military like a special production reactor. It is available to developing countries at zero or negative real cost with many supporting services. Its fuel requirements—LEU or natural uranium—are unspecialized and can be met by many suppliers without arousing suspicions. It bears no *extra* cost in money or time if one were going to build a power reactor anyhow. And unlike a research reactor[38], or a production reactor of convenient design and cost, it produces *extremely large amounts* of plutonium: so large that theft of a few bombs' worth per year is within the statistical "noise" and can be made undetectable in principle, while nearly a hundred bombs' worth per reactor per year—more than from any other option—is available if overtly diverted. The more power reactors a country has, the more useful both covert and overt diversion become and the more ways there are to deceive inspectors. In 1976, the International Atomic Energy Agency (IAEA) was unable to verify spent-fuel inventories in eight of thirty-four LWRs and in five of eleven on-load-refuelling reactors[39,40].

Power reactors, then, can be considered large-scale military production reactors with an electricity byproduct rather than benign electricity-producers with a militarily unattractive plutonium byproduct. They are not, as INFCE held, an implausible but rather potentially a peculiarly convenient type of large-scale factory for bomb material.

Of course plutonium in spent fuel from any kind of reactor is unusable in bombs until extracted by reprocessing, and it is here that plutonium advocates mounted their second line of attack. The official US view was that reprocessing is very hard, whereas making bombs is relatively easy, so reprocessing should be inhibited. Plutonium advocates retorted that, on the contrary, making

[38]As noted below under "Research reactors," even the research-reactor production that is the basis of India's bomb program is twenty times less than the production of a single thousand-megawatt LWR. Covert diversion from research-reactor output is thus normally far too little for a bomb program without risking detection.

[39]Such reactors—gas-cooled designs and the Canadian CANDU—lend themselves to illicit fuel manipulations because the fuel is shuffled continuously among a large number of channels during normal operation. In contrast, fuel cannot be moved within, into, or out of a LWR unless it is completely shut down, normally an annual event that is more easily monitored.

[40]IAEA, "Special Safeguards Implementation Report," GOV/1842, 8 June 1977 report to the Governing Board (IAEA, Vienna). This "official use only" document was widely leaked. Its 5 June 1978 followup, GOV/1897, is less explicit and no more encouraging. Both are generally available within the nonproliferation community.

bombs is very hard but reprocessing relatively easy[40a]. To support this latter claim, Oak Ridge scientists developed a conceptual design for a "quick-and-dirty" reprocessing plant which could allegedly separate a bomb's worth of plutonium per week, with only a modest risk of detection during the relatively short construction time (of the order of a year).[41] Restraints on commercial reprocessing (its advocates then argued), and indeed the timely-warning concept itself, were futile because any country seeking bombs could build its own crude reprocessing plant and get plutonium from its domestic spent fuel anyhow—an oblique way of admitting that reactors have a great deal to do with bombs.

This double-edged argument was inconsistent, however, with the same advocates' reassurances—made under oath in support of the Windscale expansion[42]—

• that providing commercial reprocessing services would dissuade customer countries from building their own plants (as Japan, the main customer for and financier of the Windscale expansion, was actually doing at the time);
• that international safeguards could be relied upon; and
• that bomb-making could be prevented by returning the plutonium "spiked" with unapproachably radioactive contaminants. (The recipient country could use its crude reprocessing plant to winnow out the plutonium from the spikants even more easily than from the original spent fuel.)

Thus the measures supposed to make reprocessing "safe" do not work. An argument meant to show there was no point discriminating against plutonium technologies showed only the

[40a] See, e.g., H. H. Hennies *et al., Nuclear News* 69–75, June 1979.

[41] The detailed claims made for the Oak Ridge design have been criticized by other experts: Comptroller General of the US, Rep. EMD-78-104, US General Accounting Office, 6 October 1978; W. H. Donnelly, "A Preliminary Analysis of the ORNL Memorandum on a Crude Nuclear Fuel Reprocessing Plant," US Library of Congress, Congressional Research Service, 4 November 1977; A. Wohlstetter, 23 December 1977 letter to R. V. Carlone, USGAO. But the broad feasibility of the approach was officially confirmed by NASAP,[9] which found that a plant separating tens of bombs' worth per year could be built in 1–2 years for tens of millions of dollars, a smaller one for less.

[42] The hundred-day public planning inquiry into the Windscale expansion was summarized by the report of the Inspector (Mr. Justice Parker). Many observers who did not attend and did not read the transcript are unaware that the Inspector's report omits or distorts beyond recognition many of the critics' arguments, in a way and to an extent they could not possibly have anticipated. For an antidote, see W. C. Patterson and C. Conroy, "The Parker Inquiry," FOE Ltd[29], 1978.

wider dangers of all fission technologies. Far from showing plutonium cycles were safe, it showed only that the rival once-through cycles were also very dangerous. For the real implication of the Oak Ridge design was that the reprocessing barrier is not so substantial after all: that both bomb-making *and* reprocessing are relatively easy (if normal requirements of profitability, environmental control, and worker safety are greatly relaxed).

This conclusion has been reinforced by the recent invention in several countries of unconventional medium- and small-scale methods of plutonium recovery, as yet untested, that are alleged to be substantially cheaper, simpler, and less conspicuous than normal reprocessing plants. If, as appears likely, at least one of these new methods or the Oak Ridge concept proves valid, then it does not mean the timely warning concept is invalid in principle; but it does mean that, under the erosion of technological progress, the number of nuclear fuel cycles to which it applies has dwindled to zero: that timely warning can be provided neither for separated plutonium *nor* for spent fuel, so that *all* nuclear fission is unsafeguardable in principle. (That is an even stronger conclusion than the finding that spent fuel becomes unsafeguardable once it enters a known reprocessing plant.) The obvious implication—that *all* forms of nuclear power are seriously proliferative—reveals a striking convergence between the views of plutonium advocates and of nuclear critics, arising from the former group's arguments

...that the relationship between the commercial nuclear fuel cycle and nuclear explosives is so remote that further controls are unnecessary—or, alternatively, if not remote, then so far gone that it is too late to reverse.[43]

The Ford-Carter policy that reprocessing is very dangerous, therefore, was correct, but did not go nearly far enough. By emphasizing—rightly—that plutonium fuel cycles are *more* dangerous than once-through cycles, it glossed over the risks of the latter. It lost sight of absolute risks by stressing relative risks. The INFCE findings that there is no technical solution to the plutonium problem, and even that once-through fuel cycles are not necessarily far less proliferative than plutonium cycles, are also broadly correct; for they show, however unintentionally, that reactors of *any* kind are perilously proliferative, and that matters are much worse than the Ford-MITRE analysis and the Ford-Carter policy supposed.

[43]Gilinsky[35], first reference.

New dangers at the "front end"

To make matters worse still, more careful scrutiny of the supposedly innocuous "front end" of the fuel cycle—the use of natural uranium or LEU as fresh reactor fuel—has lately suggested a similar conclusion on independent grounds. Traditionally, the front end has been considered highly proliferation-resistant because classical and emerging *commercial* methods of uranium enrichment to bomb-usable levels are very costly, energy-intensive, and conspicuous.[44] Experimental laser techniques that are highly efficient, relatively cheap, and probably concealable are also very high technologies[45], though the possibility of simplified designs cannot be ruled out. Uranium-enriching gas centrifuges now entering commercial service (US, UK, FR Germany, Netherlands, Japan) are relatively large, very high-technology devices which use exotic materials to achieve the high efficiency, high output, and long lifetime that led Pakistan to steal their design (presumably reproducible on paper as well as in metal, and hence valuable for re-export).

But these exacting commercial criteria are not the only imaginable ones. Natural uranium can also be gradually enriched to bomb-usable concentrations using low-technology centrifuges; the task is three-fifths easier if the starting material is LEU, and nearly a hundred times easier still if it is a mixture of uranium-233 and -238 from the front end of a proposed "denatured" thorium cycle[46]. An effective centrifuge design was published twenty years ago. Better versions—much less efficient than the high-technology cmmercial versions, but still adequate—have been made by a good machinist in a few weeks. Non-nuclear commercial centrifuges may also be adaptable to uranium enrichment; and it is apparently possible to evade some countries' export controls on key components for making quite respectable gas centrifuges, if not on the completed commercial machines themselves. Though tens or hundreds of crude centrifuges and tons of uranium would be needed for patient accumulation—perhaps, with inefficient designs, requiring years—of even one bomb's worth of HEU, the centrifuges are simple, modular, concealable, relatively cheap, and highly accessible. Uranium itself is even

[44]The gas-diffusion plants which fuel today's LWRs are among the world's largest installations of any kind. At times during the 1940s, the Oak Ridge plant consumed about a sixth of all US electricity. The Eurodif plant now being completed at Tricastin (France) is to be powered by four nearby 930-MWe reactors and to use roughly as much electricity as all France did in 1950.

[45]A. Krass, *Science 196*:721–31 (1977); *cf* G. Rathjens, *Hearings*[67] 106.

[46]A. B. Lovins, *op. cit.*[24]

easier to get: tens of thousands of tons per year are recovered
worldwide from ore or as a phosphate byproduct, subject to only
sketchy controls. Thus even without assuming any breakthroughs
in fast-moving new enrichment technologies—simplified laser
methods, or perhaps the newly discovered magnetochemical
methods—old, straightforward centrifuge designs suffice to make
even natural uranium, as Bernard Baruch noted in 1946, a
"dangerous" material.

There are also disquieting indications that without using any
conventional facilities such as LWRs or reprocessing plants, and
without serious risk of detection, one unirradiated LWR fuel
bundle could be made into one bomb's worth of separated
plutonium in one year by one technician with about one or two
million dollars' worth of other materials which, in at least one
European country, are available over the counter and apparently
subject to no controls. So far as is publicly known, this novel
basement-scale method has not yet been used, but the calculations suggesting its feasibility—unpublished for discretion—
appear valid. US authorities were apprised of this method during
1978-79, but no published assessment mentions it, and apparently
it was not seriously examined until we pointed it out in *Foreign
Affairs* in June 1980. LEU is not carefully guarded. In 1976,
IAEA inspections of LWRs were not able to verify by technical
means the fresh-fuel inventories in ten of twenty-six cases, nor
the core inventories in sixteen of thirty-four cases.[47] A large
LWR requires of the order of a hundred fresh fuel bundles per
year, and normally keeps several years' stock on hand.

A vivid, if indirect, confirmation that no nuclear fuel-cycle
material is officially considered "safe" comes from the new US-
sponsored Convention on the Physical Protection of Nuclear Material, recently opened for signature amidst an almost complete
lack of publicity about its civil-liberties implications. This instrument, if it comes into force, will make it an extraditable international crime (like genocide or piracy) for unauthorized persons to
meddle with any fissionable material other than uranium ore or
tailings, and explicitly *including* both LEU (such as LWR fresh
fuel) and purified natural uranium. States ratifying the Convention appear to be in the unpalatable position of having to support
one of two inferences: either that they are seeking, by means
largely insulated from normal legislative debate, a draconian instrument to suppress domestic interference (actual or threatened)
with shipments of nuclear materials and domestic protests about
nuclear operations, or that they consider real the threat—which

[47]IAEA, *op. cit*[40]

they have long denied—that the front end of once-through fuel cycles can place bombs in the hands of non-state adversaries.

Other routes to bombs

Proliferation pathways via the front and back ends of power-reactor fuel cycles are only the latest additions to an already long list:

• Conventional enrichment technologies: gas diffusion (US, USSR, UK, France, China), electromagnetic, aerodynamic (FR Germany, South Africa), chemical (experimental in France and US), laser (experimental in Israel, US, and elsewhere), centrifuge, and perhaps other methods.

• Production reactors. Normally these are cooled by gas and moderated by graphite. They produce military plutonium and, in some cases, electricity, and are operating in the US, UK, France, USSR, and probably elsewhere. A small graphite-moderated production reactor supplying several bombs' worth of separable plutonium per year could be built in a few years for perhaps $15-30 million using readily available plans and materials (plus the natural uranium fuel). Also fueled with natural uranium are heavy-water-moderated reactors—ideal as plutonium and tritium factories, especially on a modest scale. Several countries, including the US and Canada, have exported large amounts of heavy water (deuterium oxide, a near-perfect moderator), and deuterium is reportedly available in unlimited quantities in at least one trading nation. Useful amounts of deuterium (and of tritium and lithium-6—ingredients of hydrogen bombs) appear to be commercially available in the US.

• Research reactors, with which India makes twelve kilograms per year of extractable plutonium (some of which was exploded), Taiwan twelve, Switzerland nine, Israel eight, FR Germany four, Belgium two, Canada seventy-two, and Italy, Japan, and Norway three each.[48] Over one hundred fifty research and test reactors with thermal output over ten kilowatts are now operating in about thirty countries. In 1976 the IAEA inspected research facilities in forty-one countries, of which seven had at least five kilograms of plutonium (enough for one rather crude or several sophisticated bombs) already separated and thirteen had that much unseparated. Thirty-four states had unspecified lesser amounts separated for "peaceful" research. In six of fifty-nine

[48]Wohlstetter *et al., op. cit.,*[13] pp. 167–69 and 202–10.

research facilities, including five with strategic inventories, the
inventories could not be technically verified.[49]
• Highly enriched uranium supplied directly. HEU, like the
relatively uncommon medium-enriched uranium, is directly usable in bombs regardless of chemical form. HEU by the ton is the
main fuel of both naval reactors and the proposed HTGR (commercially abandoned in the US but still on the German research
agenda; the US may also revive prospects for similar breeder
designs). Both these programs have relatively lax physical security precautions. The cumulative imprecision of measurement of
HEU in US plants is several tons. HEU appears in kilogram
quantities in "booster rods" for many CANDU reactors; US exports to Canada for this purpose were apparently suspended a few
years ago owing to concern over the physical security measures
applied by both Canada and its export customers. About five tons
of HEU—hundreds of bombs' worth—were exported for research reactor fuel and critical assemblies[50], mainly by the US
starting in the mid-1950s, under agreements written loosely to
"prove America's good intentions"[51]. The US gave away at least
26 HEU-fueled research reactors to, among others, Argentina,
Brazil, Iran, Israel, South Korea, Pakistan, Spain, and Taiwan
(and supplied many bombs' worth of HEU to FR Germany, Italy,
Japan, and South Africa). Many other HEU-fueled research reactors have been sold, e.g. by France to Chile in 1977. A transfer of
70 kg of HEU from France to Iraq (which has refused to accept a
non-bomb-usable substitute) is planned for 1980–81. Some fast-
neutron research reactors in countries now racked by terrorism
are loaded with enough HEU for more than one bomb—Tapiro in
Italy (23 kg 93.5%) and Coral-1 in Spain (22 kg 90%)—but most
need only a sub-strategic 3-7 kg per loading.[52] It is necessary,
however, to keep a number of these relatively small fresh cores
on hand for high-power HEU reactors (Argentina, Australia,
Austria, Belgium, Canada, Denmark, FR Germany, Israel, Italy,
Japan, Netherlands, Pakistan, Rumania, South Africa, Sweden),
and it was until recently a common practice to do so unnecessarily for low-power ones too. One Prime Minister was upset to find
in 1973 that several bombs' worth of HEU were stored in his

[49]IAEA, *op. cit.*[40]

[50]The possibility of doing the critical experiments in weapons states was apparently not examined before the transfers.

[51]Iklé, *op. cit.*[13]

[52]Wohlstetter *et al., loc. cit.*[48]

capital in an unguarded and effectively unlocked warehouse. A few years ago, one sensitive country was accidentally found (just in time) to be shopping for fresh HEU cores among the four supplier countries, like a registered drug addict collecting a sheaf of prescriptions from different doctors. Though research reactors are being redesigned so they will not need HEU, and HEU exports have been restricted, large shipments are still leaving the US, the list of recipients has reportedly expanded (e.g. to include Rumania), and a great deal is still in circulation: the IAEA in 1976 inspected twelve states each holding over twenty kilograms.[53]

• Other directly exported bomb materials. Tons of plutonium and uranium-233 have been exported by the US, and separated and returned (or sold to third countries) by Britain and France, for fast breeder research and critical assemblies. In 1975, for example, Japan, like FR Germany and Italy, held approximately six hundred kilograms of separated plutonium—"an amount about thirty times as large as was used by the United States to accelerate the end of World War II."[54]

• Plutonium or uranium-233 bred with neutron sources other than reactors.[55]

• Stolen military bombs and their components. Tampering with modern US bombs scrambles their electronics so they cannot be set off, but if, as claimed, unauthorized persons (even with recent military training: there are said to be some 50,000 persons now guarding US bombs, not counting those in the bomb-making facilities) cannot defeat the protective devices, they can still dismantle the bomb and recover its core. For safety reasons, US bombs apparently do not explosively disperse their cores if tampered with. Some thefts of US nuclear weapons in Europe may have been attempted. Despite the most modern barriers and alarms, US army blackhat teams have been reported to have entered and left nuclear weapons storage bays without detection. The US has about 7000 tactical nuclear weapons, many easily portable, stored in Europe alone. Similar Soviet arrangements are unpublished. Most other weapons states, especially emerging ones, are unlikely to have developed the elaborate and very

[53]IAEA, *op. cit.*[40]

[54]H. York, *loc. cit.*[22] Hundreds of kg of plutonium remain in Japan today.

[55]See note 25 above.

costly mechanisms used in modern US and British bombs for command, control, and operational safety.[56]

Collectively, both familiar and newly emerging routes to bombs imply that *every* form of *every* fissionable material in *every* nuclear fuel cycle can be used to make military bombs, either on its own or in combination with other ingredients made widely and innocently available by nuclear power. Not all these ancillary operations needed are of equal difficulty, but none is beyond the reach of any government or of some technically informed amateurs. Hence not only in spreading knowledge, equipment, organizational structures, expectations, and threats, but also in the direct provision of nuclear explosive materials themselves, nuclear power in all its forms is directly proliferative—at the very center of the nexus of activities and relationships now spawning bombs worldwide.

---

[56]This is dangerous to everyone. When the US Air Force accidentally dropped a 24-megaton bomb near Goldsboro, North Carolina in 1961, only one of its six safety devices worked, so preventing an explosion larger than the cumulative total released in all wars in human history—twelve World War IIs or three Vietnams. D. Ellsberg remarks (*Not Man Apart* 20, February 1980) that such accidents dropped more thermonuclear weapons on the US "than the Russians had on ICBMs in 1961. We were then the only threat to our national security." For critical comments on the security of US military bombs in storage, see Senators Pastore and Baker, *Compendium*[73] 499–503; F. Barnaby, *New Scientist 66:*494 (29 May 1975); and US General Accounting Office, B-197458 (EMD-80-48), 19 February 1980.

Chapter Three

Disguises and "Safeguards"

Can the stark conclusion of the preceding chapter be weakened, and the unexpectedly intimate link between reactors and bombs be severed, by conceivable "safeguards" on nuclear materials?

Great ingenuity and care have been devoted to developing ways to measure fissionable material so as to detect (preferably with timely warning) illicit removal or, in the absence of such an alarm signal, to confirm continued presence. Unfortunately, physically conceivable ways of measuring plutonium[57] must be after-the-fact and statistically imprecise: so imprecise that they cannot, even in principle, provide reasonable assurance that many bombs' worth of plutonium per year are not being removed from, say, a good-sized reprocessing plant. (Broadly similar problems arise with other kinds of facilities.) In practice, materials accounting methods are readily deceivable in many subtle ways which defy detection[58]. Presently available methods are much worse than the ideal, and historically used methods worse still: the statistical "noise" of US measurements alone has already accumulated to tons of strategic material, including some strategic quantities officially suspected of being physically missing. (As is the way of statistical measurements, however, it is impossible to say for sure whether they are missing or not.) World nuclear power over the next two decades could produce over two thousand tons of plutonium. A mere half of one percent of this figure—about half of the ideal or a quarter of the currently typical

---

[57]Though broadly similar problems arise with all fissionable materials, plutonium is particularly hard to measure precisely because it is generally in an impure form, subject to both loss and gain by radioactive decay, highly toxic, very complex and fickle in chemistry, self-heating, and prone to stick to or to migrate out of containers. The nuclear properties normally used for assay are highly sensitive to isotopic composition, impurities, and interfering materials.

[58]D. M. Rosenbaum *et al.,* "A Special Safeguards Study," *Congressional Record 120*:S6621-30 (30 April 1974); GIR[29], Chapter 4. The more complex the plant and its accountancy methods, the more subtly the inspectors can be deceived: the plant, for example, may not be built according to the blueprints, standard samples can be biased, interfering materials added, instruments doctored, computers reprogrammed, etc. Such vulnerabilities are surveyed by Lawrence Berkeley Laboratory, *A Study of Nuclear Material Accounting,* NUREG-0290, 3 vols., USNRC, 1977. See also R. J. Smith, *Science 209*:250–52 (1980).

imprecision of inventory in spent fuel entering a reprocessing plant—would suffice to make thousands of bombs.

Because materials accounting is so fuzzy and *post hoc,* political arrangements for safeguards must rely primarily on physical security measures to limit access to materials and to deter or prevent their removal (or, if they are removed anyhow, to recover them). These measures must forestall well-equipped groups, perhaps including senior insiders acting in concert with the host government or a faction of it. History shows that any physical security measures can be overcome by sufficiently determined thieves or embezzlers, and careful analyses confirm that even modestly effective measures covering key plants and transport networks would be costly, fallible, and personally and socially intrusive.[59] In the Federal Republic of Germany, for example, they would exceed the authority of the Atomic Energy Act; amending it to permit them would be unconstitutional; and amending the Constitution to permit them would conflict with human-rights instruments to which the Federal Republic is a party.[60]

The institutional arrangements which rely on these inherently inadequate accounting and security measures—the latter being administered entirely by national governments—are woven around the International Atomic Energy Agency (IAEA), the Non-Proliferation Treaty (NPT), the EURATOM and Tlatelolco Treaties, and bilateral agreements. Though these instruments are a considerable achievement, they have well-known and collectively fatal flaws, reflected in many supplier governments' insistence on stricter (though still wholly inadequate) supplementary constraints through new bilateral arrangements or the London Suppliers' Group. These flaws include:

• Non-adherence of about fifty countries including half the world's population, including two of the five acknowledged weapons states (France, China), all three suspected ones (India, Israel, South Africa), and all major developing countries except Iran and Mexico (in particular, Argentina, Brazil, Egypt, Pakistan, and Spain).

[59]See for example Justice (UK Section, International Commission of Jurists), "Plutonium and Liberty," London, 1978 (fully accepted by the Parker report[42]); J. H. Barton, "Intensified Nuclear Safeguards and Civil Liberties," report to USNRC, Stanford Law School, 21 October 1975; R. Ayres, *Harvard Civil Rights–Civil Liberties Law Review 10*:369 (1975); R. Grove-White and M. Flood, "Nuclear Prospects," FOE[29]/CPRE/NCCC, London, 1976; Royal Commission on Environmental Pollution (London), *Sixth Report,* Cmnd. 6618, HMSO, 1976 (e.g., ¶¶185–6, 321, 325, 331–3, 505–7).

[60]P. Sieghart, Chapter 4.4 in GIR, *op. cit.*[29]

- Freedom to renounce.
- No prohibition on designing bombs or building and testing their non-nuclear components[61].
- Unsafeguarded duplicate facilities.
- Inadequate inspection staff, facilities, and morale.
- Virtual absence of developing-country nationals in key IAEA safeguards posts.
- High detection thresholds[62].
- Freedom of host governments to deceive, reject, hinder, or intimidate inspectors or to restrict their access (especially their unannounced access), often by such simple means as saying that a certain area cannot be visited because of a minor spill of radioactive material.
- Unknown effectiveness owing to confidentiality[63].
- Ambiguous agreements[64].
- Unsupported presumption of innocent explanations.

This last point deserves special emphasis. IAEA findings that no significant diversions have occurred are judgmental, not objectively supportable even according to the Agency's generous technical criteria. Inspections must rely on the good faith of precisely the countries that have the least incentive to exhibit it, and

[61]The non-nuclear components are in general the most difficult to develop and their designs the most secret aspect of weapons technology. Further, all agreements appear to leave the term "nuclear explosive device" and allied terms undefined. Can it mean a finished bomb lacking only a rapidly insertible key component or data—in which case Permissive Action Link-equipped US bombs are arguably not bombs? Nobody knows (though by this semantic ruse the US claims today not to be manufacturing neutron bombs—only their readily assembliable components). The US has insisted that laser-fusion target pellets, including those using fissionable materials, are not bombs.

[62]As noted in ref. 37, the IAEA's 8-kg design basis for detecting plutonium diversions[40] is several times the quantity needed to make a bomb.

[63]The IAEA Statute contains secrecy provisions which the Agency construes as broadly as possible—even to refusing to reveal which countries have how much of what kind of accounted-for nuclear materials. Acknowledged inadequacies[40] of accounting occurred in twelve of forty-one states inspected in 1976, but the IAEA declines to say which states. As a result, the USNRC Division of Nuclear Materials and Security and the US General Accounting Office (ID-75-65, 3 July 1975, based on earlier problems) have found that the adequacy of IAEA safeguards cannot be independently judged. Confidentiality rules are also "being used as an alibi for remaining ignorant about the inadequacies" of IAEA safeguards.[13]

[64]Iklé (*op. cit.*,[13] xiv) remarks that "some Washington bureaucrats would bend over backwards to interpret ambiguities (which they themselves may have written into the agreements) so as to exonerate the foreign government that had defied the intent of Congress."

conversely, restrictions and provisions for strict compliance are
"most likely to be accepted where they are least needed."[65] The
IAEA is a UN bureaucracy anxious to make no waves, give no
false alarms, and promote nuclear power[66]. If an alert, incorrup-
tible, omnipresent inspector instantly detected a big, blatant diversion and succeeded in getting the news instantly from his field
post to the Inspector-General, thence to the Director-General and
the Board of Governors, thence to the Security Council (subject
to veto)—would the exhaustive re-examinations on which they
would all doubtless insist even have been officially notified in all
the UN languages before a bomb went off?

In fact, the record so far suggests matters would probably
never get that far. The IAEA has *already* detected diversions of
quantities too small for bombs and has privately decided that
these did not justify even notifying the supplier states concerned.[67] IAEA inspectors "have found many [suspicious] indications and acts . . . , but the IAEA has never taken action on
any of them. This will probably continue to be true."[68]

Nor should this come as a surprise. All the resources of the
US Government, in more than a decade of repeated investiga-
tions, were unable to determine whether suspected plutonium
thefts at the Numec plant in Apollo, Pennsylvania had in fact
occurred. Large HEU losses over many years at an Erwin, Tennessee plant crucial to US naval reactor fuel supply led in 1979 to
relaxed accounting standards that would make the losses look
"acceptable".[69] How, then, could an intergovernmental bureaucracy, with all its tensions and constraints, be expected to inves-

[65]R. W. Fox and M. Willrich, "International Custody of Plutonium Stocks,"
International Consultative Group on Nuclear Energy (Rockefeller Foundation,
NY, and Royal Institute of International Affairs, London), November 1978.

[66]The IAEA Statute mandates the promotion of nuclear power, which the current
Director-General, a plutonium enthusiast, does not even believe is linked to
proliferation—a "risk which may never materialize" and which he ranks as less
important than propagating fast breeder reactors (see his 8 December 1977 address, reprinted in *Reader*[20] 127–29).

[67]R. Rometsch, remarks in panel discussion before the Institute of Nuclear Mate-
rials Management, 20 June 1975, reprinted at 1214–17, US Senate Committee on
Government Operations, *Hearings on the Export Reorganization Act of 1976*,
USGPO 71-259, 1976.

[68]D. M. Rosenbaum, *International Security 1*(3):140 (Winter 1977).

[69]This "solution," accompanied by improved physical security measures, succeeded an earlier policy, where losses were outside acceptable statistical limits, of
repeating and averaging the measurements until losses came within those limits—
like losing a game and then deciding on best two out of three.

tigate suspected thefts in and perhaps by a recalcitrant foreign country?

Finally, the momentum and bureaucratic entrenchment of nuclear programs generally prevent effective sanctions against even an obvious, sharp violation, let alone a dimly suspected, creeping one. Such action as is rarely taken—as in the skilled demolition of an Iraq-bound French reactor by unknown saboteurs in 1979—is in default of official responses but can hardly substitute for them. The international community has never been adept at sanctions generally (Rhodesia, Chile, Namibia, Afghanistan), and the nuclear record is even worse. The US failure to take effective measures against India, Israel, or Pakistan illustrates the low priority that is likely to be mustered in practice, and may even increase the value of a putative bomb program as a bargaining chip. The breach of EURATOM safeguards by the theft of an entire 200-ton shipload of natural uranium in 1968—presumably bound for Israel's unsafeguarded Dimona reactor, which France had supplied in return for heavy-water technology—was detected within three months but kept secret by the governments concerned for nearly ten years. All the relevant governments knew about India's bomb program a decade before the 1974 test: Canadian scientists, for example, had warned their government that Indian trainees in plutonium metallurgy around 1963-65 were displaying untoward interest in purely military subjects. But this foreknowledge evoked only diplomatic murmurs, and the actual test, as Albert Wohlstetter remarks, "inspired only ingenious apologies" from the US State Department—anxious to conceal the US contribution of heavy water—and a congratulatory telegram from the Chairman of the French Atomic Energy Commission. As front pages in 1979 heralded the Pakistani bomb program, Pakistan was being unanimously elected to the IAEA's Board of Governors. As suspicions grew that Iraq (a party to the NPT) was pressing France for a promised HEU shipment partly out of military motivations, an Iraqi was chairing the 1980 NPT Review Conference.

In sum, present safeguards—consisting in essence of infrequent (quarterly or less) inventories that may belatedly detect statistical indications of large, incompetent diversions from safeguarded facilities in cooperative countries—may be better than nothing if their limitations are clearly understood. But this appears not to be the case among many credulous people for whom an "insouciant lack of realism"[70] and soothing repetition of the word "safeguards" have lulled a sense of danger and

[70]Iklé, *op. cit.*[13]

cloaked dangerous activities in benignity. Indeed, this sense of complacency about transferring larval bombs "under international safeguards"—as if bomb-making had thereby somehow been prevented—may arguably be worse than not having either safeguards or their false sense of security. At first the world was told there was no problem—the IAEA would fix it—and then that there is no solution. Some analysts seem to hold both these views, rationalizing that perhaps proliferation is not so bad anyway. The IAEA's Director-General advocates faith healing:

After all the ingenuity displayed in the development of nuclear power, we would demonstrate unbelievable incompetence if we were suddenly to lose confidence in our ability to cope with the problem of proliferation.[71].

But if there is a solution, it does not lie in the realm either of a sanguine state of mind or of a strengthened IAEA in a world of sovereign nation-states. We need something more fundamental, built on first principles.

"There is a melancholy lesson," remarked Victor Gilinsky, "in the fact that today we have come almost full circle in our thinking"[72] and returned to the central finding of the percipient Acheson-Lilienthal report of 1946:

[T]here is no prospect of security against atomic warfare in a system of international agreements to outlaw such weapons controlled *only* by a system which relies on inspection and similar police-like methods. . . . So long as intrinsically dangerous activities may be carried on by nations, rivalries are inevitable and fears are engendered that place so great a pressure upon a system of international enforcement by police methods that no degree of ingenuity or technical competence could possibly hope to cope with them. . . . In short, any system based on outlawing the purely military development of atomic energy and relying solely on inspection for enforcement would at the outset be surrounded by conditions which would destroy the system.[73]

Realistically, during the geological, or rather theological, periods in which bomb materials remain potent, national rivalries, subna-

[71]S. Eklund, *loc. cit.*[66]

[72]V. Gilinsky, S-14-76,[35] among the best short histories of the problem.

[73]*Op. cit.*[11] The Report is reprinted in US Senate Committee on Government Operations, *Peaceful Nuclear Exports and Weapons Proliferation: A Compendium*, USGPO, 1975.

tional instabilities, and human imperfections[74] will remain stronger than treaties and inspections. Despite thirty-five years of sincere and devoted efforts, the basic contradictions identified by Acheson-Lilienthal ensure that no credible technical or political arrangements can, even in principle, reserve infallibly and perpetually to peaceful uses the enormous amounts of bomb materials that nuclear fuel cycles create.

The crucial role of ambiguity

The logical consequence of the unworkability of safeguards, in principle and in practice, is that we cannot have nuclear power without proliferation. As was shown earlier, we *can* have proliferation *with* nuclear power, via either end of any fuel cycle. Can we, then, have proliferation *without* nuclear power?

It is true that naval reactor fuel and military bombs provide non-civilian routes to more bombs; but that means only that nuclear armaments encourage their own refinement, multiplication, and spread: that vertical proliferation encourages both vertical and horizontal proliferation and provides additional routes for the latter (which, as we have noted, symbiotically returns the favor). But it does not mean that there are significant civilian routes to bombs that are unrelated to nuclear power. With trivial exceptions unimportant to this argument—large particle accelerators, proposed fusion reactors, radioisotope production reactors[75]— *every* known civilian route to bombs involves *either* nuclear power *or* materials and technologies whose possession, indeed whose existence in commerce, is a *direct and essential consequence* of nuclear fission power. Apologists, apparently intending to be reassuring, often state nonetheless that since power reactors themselves are only one of (say) eight ways to make bombs, restraining power reactors is like sticking a thumb in one of eight holes in a dike.[76] But the other holes were made by the same drill. Arguing that reactors have little to do with bombs is like arguing that fishhooks do not cause the catching of fish, since this can also involve rods, reels, and anglers.

[74]A striking short list of examples to spring 1977 appears in the precursor of this book, Chapter 11 of A. B. Lovins, *Soft Energy Paths: Toward a Durable Peace,* Ballinger (Cambridge, MA), 1977, and Harper Colophon (NY), 1979, at 191–92. (See also J. Emschwiller, *Wall Street Journal* 1, 3 September 1980.)

[75]There is probably a good case, even after the elimination of nuclear power, for retaining a handful of small research reactors to make medical and allied radio-isotopes. This is such a specialized, small-scale operation that effective international controls could be realistically contemplated.

[76]See e.g. C. Starr, 19 April 1977 speech reprinted in *Reader*[20], 416.

The foregoing reasoning implies that eliminating nuclear power is a *necessary* condition for nonproliferation. But how far is it a *sufficient* condition? Suppose that nuclear power no longer existed. Again, with trivial exceptions[77], there would no longer be any innocent justification for uranium mining[78], nor for possession of ancillary equipment such as research reactors and critical assemblies, nor for commerce in nuclear-grade graphite and beryllium and zirconium, tritium, lithium-6, more than gram quantities of deuterium, most nuclear instrumentation—in short, the whole panoply of goods and services that provides such diverse technological routes to bombs. If these exotic items were no longer commercially available, then

- they would be much harder to obtain;
- efforts to obtain them would be far more conspicuous; and
- such efforts, if detected, would carry a high political cost

for both supplier and recipient because for the first time they would be *unambiguously military* in intent.

This ambiguity—the ability of countries, willfully or by mere drift, to conduct operations "indistinguishable from preparations for a nuclear arsenal"[79]—has gone very far. An NPT signatory subject to the strictest safeguards can quite legally be closer to having working bombs than the United States was in 1947.[80] For example, precisely machined HEU spheres have recently been seen in Japan, doubtless for purely peaceful criticality experiments. But such spheres are also—if other, perfectly legal, preparations outside any inspectors' purview have been secretly made—only hours away from working bombs.[81]

---

[77]The only obvious ones are fusion reactors and large particle accelerators[25] and radioisotope production reactors,[75] none of which affects the argument.

[78]Except for a few percent used in glass, ceramic glazes, catalysts, weights, and armor-piercing projectiles—all applications in which it is effectively substitutable—all the uranium mined is used in naval reactors, power reactors, bombs, and the like.

[79]Iklé, *op. cit.*[13]

[80]A. Wohlstetter, "Spreading the Bomb Without Quite Breaking the Rules," *Foreign Policy* 88–96&ff., Winter 1976/77.

[81]This is itself dangerous because this capacity and the unknowability of Japanese intentions may lead other countries to suspect a threat where it may not in fact exist. To avoid "international tensions, if not worse," Japan should "take steps to ensure that confidence is engendered in other nations that a nuclear weapons capacity, or intention, or both, are absent."[65] But it is hard to see how even the

Bernard Baruch warned in 1946 that the line dividing "safe" from "dangerous" (proliferative) nuclear activities would change and need constant reexamination. No mechanism to do this was ever set up. The variety and ease of proliferative paths expanded unnoticed to embrace virtually all activities once presumed "safe", while most of those activities were broadcast worldwide with generous enthusiasm. Yet their direct facilitation of bomb-making was probably a less grave threat than the innocent disguise which their pursuit lent, and lends today, to bomb-making. Baruch, noting the importance of adequate "advance warning . . . between violation and preventive action or punishment",[82] had sought a technological monopoly so that visible operation or possession of "dangerous" steps other than by a special International Atomic Development Authority, regardless of purpose, "will constitute an unambiguous danger signal." Today, with dozens of countries on the brink of a bomb capacity, such a neat solution cannot immediately be realized. But the principle remains sound: detection and deterrence of bomb-making require that it be unambiguously identifiable; and for that, phasing out nuclear power and the supporting services and "research programs" it justifies would be *both* a necessary *and* a sufficient condition.

Removing the present ambiguity will not make proliferation impossible. Pakistan, already operating and planning power reactors, sought an obviously uneconomic French reprocessing plant transparently rationalized as an aid to energy independence, then, when thwarted, decided to pursue bombs more directly with clandestine centrifuges. Pakistan probably did not expect that effort to be accidentally unmasked at an early stage, but was presumably willing to bear the political cost of eventual detection (if there was one: India has not yet, at this writing, been made to bear such a cost[83]). Yet the key point is that the reactors, the

most stable nation possessing HEU spheres could do this. Further, since the longevity of bomb materials is the same as that of long-lived nuclear wastes—they are often the same materials—present intentions are an inadequate assurance for the future. Plutonium-239 lasts over a hundred times as long as our oldest governments (such as Iceland) or uninvaded countries (such as Nepal).

[82]B. Baruch, statement to the UNAEC, 14 June 1946, reprinted in *Compendium*[73] 203–13, which also reprints the 8 December 1953 Eisenhower UN speech. They are also in *Reader*[20] starting at 1 and 12 respectively.

[83]In September 1980, by two Senate votes, the Carter Administration overrode the USNRC (and the House) and continued shipping fuel for the Tarapur reactors, which already have 50 tons of fresh fuel stockpiled (enough to last until about early 1983): the stockpile actually increased after the 1974 explosion. Commissioner Gilinsky, in his 5 February 1980 speech S-2-80, describes the tangled his-

uranium supply allegedly needed for them, the hoped-for reprocessing plant, the participation of the Pakistani spy in the Dutch
project, the very existence of that project and of the uranium-
mining industry itself—*all* were justified and swathed in innocent
guise by nuclear power.

For bomb-making by any route, denuclearization would
greatly increase the technical difficulty of obtaining the ingredients, and would automatically stigmatize suppliers as knowing
accessories before the fact, hence clear violators of NPT Article I
in letter or spirit. By providing unambiguous danger signals, denuclearization would make the political costs and risks to all concerned very high—perhaps prohibitively high.[84] This does not
mean that a determined and resourceful nation bent on bombs can
by non-military means be absolutely prevented from getting
them: much is already out of the barn. But denuclearization
would brand as military the use of those escaped resources and
inhibit their augmentation and spread. It would narrow the proliferative field to exclude the vast majority of states—the latent
proliferators who sidle up to the nuclear threshold by degrees,
and those easily tempted.

Yet is not the complete civil (and, in due course, military)
denuclearization required to remove every last shred of ambiguity
a fantastic, unrealistic, unachievable goal? On the contrary, as
the following Chapters show, that goal—and more straightforward interim steps on the way to it—would follow logically
and practically from obeying the economic principles to which
most governments claim to adhere.

---

tory of the unique US-India Agreement for Cooperation. Advocates of the ship-
ment argue that failure to ship would breach the Agreement; critics, including
Gilinsky, maintain that shipping the fuel would breach US law and hence the
Agreement. Advocates say that India would use such a breach as an excuse to
recover the plutonium (over a ton) now in Tarapur spent fuel; critics point out that
India can do so anyhow if it is willing to breach the Agreement. Advocates fear
India might shift to buying Tarapur fuel from the Soviet Union; critics suggest this
shift (which would itself breach the Agreement) might be helpful, since the USSR,
always fearful of bombs on its borders, requires return of any plutonium arising.
Advocates generally ignore critics' point that Pakistan's bomb program cannot be
deterred if India's bears no penalty. Typically, the Tarapur reactors (the sole
subject of the Agreement) were financed at 0.75% annual interest, with repayment
over 40 years and a 10-year initial deferment, under the rationale of promoting
nuclear safeguards generally and within India in particular. In practice, the Indian
explosion relied upon US heavy water (shipments totalled about 166 tons), British
reprocessing equipment, and other contributions from Canada, France, and FR
Germany.

[84]Possible failure to work perfectly in all cases is no reason for rejection. As then
British Foreign Secretary Owen remarked (*Atom* 249:132–5 (1977), *Reader*[20]
362–66), to argue from the impossibility of absolute effectiveness "that we should
not make a maximum effort to prevent the spread of nuclear weapons . . . is an
argument not only of despair, but of folly, which I totally reject."

Chapter Four

The Irrelevance of Nuclear Power

Nuclear power has been promoted worldwide as both economically advantageous and necessary to replace oil. Potential proliferation, in this view, is either a small price to pay for vast economic advantages or an unavoidable side effect which we must learn to tolerate out of brutal necessity. But rational analysis of energy needs and economics strongly favors stopping and even reversing nuclear power programs. The risks of nuclear power, including proliferation, are therefore not a minor counterweight to enormous advantages but rather a gratuitous supplement to enormous disadvantages.

Replacing oil is undeniably urgent. But nuclear power cannot provide timely and significant substitution for oil, for it is the wrong kind of energy, too slow, and too expensive.

Limited oil displacement

Only about a tenth of the world's oil is used for making electricity[85]. Electricity is the only form of energy that nuclear power can yield on a significant scale in the foreseeable future[86]. The other nine-tenths of the oil runs vehicles, makes direct heat in buildings and industry, and provides petrochemical feedstocks. If, in 1975, *every* oil-fired power station, whether thermal or combustion turbine, in the industrialized countries represented by the Organization for Economic Cooperation and Development (OECD) had been replaced *overnight* by nuclear reactors, OECD oil consumption would have fallen by only twelve percent[87]. The

[85] In the first quarter of 1980, US electrical generation was 52% coal, 14% gas, 12% oil, 12% hydro, and 10% nuclear—down from 15% oil in 1979, when electric utilities burned 8% of all US oil (EIA[92]).

[86] Though some enthusiasts for high-temperature gas-cooled reactors envisage their eventual use for direct process heat, e.g. in steelmaking, the engineering difficulties are formidable and the nuclear heat source is seldom as reliable as industry requires. The nuclear process steam project of the Dow Corporation and the Midland reactor has been a costly debacle. Nuclear district heating (perhaps, as conceived by some Swedish promoters, using urban-sited small reactors designed especially for the purpose) appears to have similar problems of reliability as well as of politics and economics. If these problems were overcome somehow, the constraints on deployment rates would be similar to those of nuclear-electric plants, and would prevent a significant contribution for the next half-century or so.

[87] This calculation (extending through the following paragraph) is by Vince Taylor. Details are in his "Energy: The Easy Path," 1979, available from Union of Concerned Scientists (1384 Massachusetts Ave., Cambridge MA 02138).

fraction of that oil consumption that was imported would have fallen from about sixty-five to about sixty percent (compensated by greatly increased dependence on imported capital and uranium, which is apparently an almost equally cartelized, politicized, and ultimately scare commodity). In the most favorable case, Japan, this substitution would have required forty-five gigawatts[88] of nuclear capacity—three times as much as the government has with great difficulty been able to build so far. This capacity would have reduced oil consumption (ignoring refinery blending requirements and inflexibilities) by twenty-seven percent and oil imports by twenty-nine percent; yet over ninety percent of all oil consumed in Japan would still have been imported, and the oil saved would quickly have been swallowed up by projected growth in demand.

In the European countries whose rhetoric most reflects a faith in nuclear displacement of oil, the overnight nuclear substitution would have reduced 1975 French oil consumption by ten percent, FR German by four, and British by fourteen. (These changes are so small because one-third of French electricity was from hydropower and nearly two-thirds of German and British electricity was from coal.) The imported fraction of national oil consumption would have dropped by much *more* for the United States (7.3 percentage points) than for Japan (2.6), France (0.5), Germany (0.3), or Britain (0.8)—contrary to the all but universal belief that Europe and Japan, lacking most indigenous fuels, can benefit more from nuclear power than can the US. That belief is false because the scope for replacing imported oil with nuclear power does not depend only on how much of the oil used is imported; it depends also on how much of that oil is used in power stations.

In practice, US nuclear expansion has served mainly to displace *coal,* not oil, by running coal-fired power stations less of the time: the utilization of their full theoretical capacity dropped from sixty-two to fifty-five percent during 1973–78. In overall quantitative terms, the entire 1978 US nuclear output could have been replaced simply by raising the output of partly idle coal plants most of the way to the level of which they are practically capable. And, contrary to the widespread assumption that a nuclear shutdown would cause serious regional shortages, an analysis of the balance within each regional power pool[89] found

[88] A gigawatt (GW) is a thousand megawatts (MW) or a million kilowatts (kW) or a billion (10^9) watts. The largest nuclear reactors sold today have electrical net output capacities around 1.2–1.3 GW—sometimes specified as GWe (electric), to distinguish from the heat output, GWt (thermal), which is three times as great.

[89] This is the correct basis for such calculations, since available power is shared and dispatched within each pool (and, increasingly, between pools where transmission capacity permits). Statements that particular localities, such as Chicago,

that in 1978 all but thirteen US reactors, or all but two if surplus power were interchanged between regions using existing transmission capacity, could have been shut down forthwith without reducing any region's "reserve margin" (spare capacity in excess of peak demand) below a prudent fifteen percent of peak demand.[90] Further confirming the loose coupling between nuclear output and oil saving, between 1978 and 1979 the United States reduced by sixteen percent the amount of oil used to make electricity, while US nuclear output simultaneously *fell* by eight percent: the oil saving came instead from conservation and from coal and gas substitution. Between the first two months of 1979 and of 1980, total US oil-fired generation fell by a startling thirty-two percent while nuclear output simultaneously fell by twenty-nine percent—hardly a substitution.[91]

Too little, too late

The OECD calculation above for 1975 exaggerates potential oil displacement by nuclear power. Reactors take not one night

---

get (say) half their electricity from nuclear power incorrectly imply that without nuclear power they would lose half their electricity. (This inference is especially false in the case of Chicago, since Commonwealth Edison Co. has so much excess nuclear capacity that it is having to idle its coal plants and even throttle back some of its nuclear plants much of the time—so-called "cycling" operation which is neither technically nor economically desirable for nuclear plants.) Arrangements made temporarily a few years ago to "wheel" (transmit) surplus power from mainly coal- to mainly oil-fired regions of the US are tending to become permanent because they save everyone money.

[90]S. Nadis, "Time for a reassessment," *Bulletin of the Atomic Scientists* 37–44, February 1980. The US did, of course, have 153 GWe of oil- and gas-fired capacity in 1978 (including combustion turbines and other peaking plants for which nuclear power could not substitute in any case). This capacity should also be displaced, and will have to be anyhow on account of its age: of the 228 GWe of US generating capacity commissioned in 1955-70 and therefore presumably requiring replacement over the next two decades, 137 GWe was oil- or gas-fired. But we shall suggest[116] that considerably more than the total oil, gas, *and* nuclear capacity— probably even essentially all the coal plants as well—can be displaced by efficiency improvements supplemented by readily available microhydro and wind and by filling empty turbine bays at existing large dams (whose continued operation is assumed too).

[91]Between the first quarters of 1979 and of 1980 (likewise correcting for Leap Year) the respective drops were 26% and 25%; coal generation meanwhile increased 11%, gas generation increased 12%, and total generation fell 2%, while hydro generation (which fluctuates seasonally and annually) fell 3%. During the first five months of 1980, US utilities' oil burn fell 25.5%, or 396,000 bbl/d, while total generation fell only 0.7%: DOE/EIA/AR-0238, August 1980. Other sources, such as pulp-mill cogeneration, are not included in the statistics, but are increasing rapidly. It is also interesting that in March 1979, 35 of the 72 "operating" US reactors were shut down for refueling, maintenance, or safety problems, about 15 more, in effect, were operating enrichment plants, leaving about 22 to help run the national economy.

but about ten years to build, and this time is lengthening in essentially all countries, regardless of their economic or political system.[92] Reactors ordered today can replace no oil in the 1980s—and surprisingly little, compared to total oil demands, even in the long term. The relatively small and late contribution of even a large nuclear program can be illustrated by some simple "rate and magnitude" calculations:

• To meet via nuclear power a quarter of the officially projected (in September 1978) US primary energy demand in the year 2000, if each unit of nuclear electricity displaced a generous two units of primary fossil fuel throughout the economy, would entail ordering a large new nuclear plant every five days—and would cost at least three-quarters of all discretionary investment in the entire US economy.[93]

• France projected in 1976 a nuclear capacity of one hundred four gigawatts in the year 2000—sufficient nearly to quadruple the 1975 level of total French electricity generation. Nevertheless, even if total energy growth slowed as projected by the Workshop on Alternative Energy Strategies, projected oil and gas needs in 2000 would still be seventy percent greater than in 1975—to which must be added uranium imports equivalent to anywhere from half to all of the oil import requirements.[94]

[92]R. K. Lester, "Nuclear Power Plant Lead-Times," ICGNE[65],[1978] In Japan, often cited for fast construction (6 years and lengthening), the *total* time, starting with initial siting discussions, is now about 15–16 years (Interdevelopment Inc., *op. cit.*[142]). See also note 215.

[93]Assuming USDOE 1978 Solar Domestic Policy Review median forecast (oil price \$25/bbl in 1977 dollars) of primary demand (114×10^{15} BTU/y), 12-year lead time and 62% capacity factor (both better than recent experience), inclusion of plants already built or being built, whole-system marginal capital cost of \$1717/kWe installed[103] (1976 \$), and net private domestic investment equal to 7% of GNP with real GNP growth of 3.5%/y. NPDI is integrated over 1979–2000, but costs of plants not yet commissioned by 2000 are excluded—a double conservatism.

[94]Assuming primary demand growth during 1976–2000 by 3.8%/y, compared to 5.3%/y during 1963–73: WAES, *Energy Supply-Demand Integration for the Year 2000* (MIT Press, 1977), Case C-2, p 347. This example was kindly pointed out by Vince Taylor, who further calculated[87] that even with ambitious and highly successful programs to breed and use as much plutonium as possible, and even with extensive domestic uranium mining, France in 2000 would import nearly half its large uranium requirements. To imports in that year of about 130 million metric tons of oil, 65 MTOE (million metric tons oil equivalent) of gas, and 7 of coal, France would have to add 70 of uranium (or 127 without plutonium thermal recycle)—about 8600–15,600 short tons of U_3O_8 per year. More recent French projections place, necessarily, more emphasis on improved end-use efficiency.

• If Japanese energy demand were consistent with official 1978 projections, then even if an implausibly large nuclear program (two hundred seventy-four gigawatts, costing about a hundred trillion of today's yen and requiring a large reactor to be ordered every twenty days) met half of all delivered energy needs in the year 2000 (displacing two delivered energy units with each unit of nuclear electricity), fossil-fuel imports would still rise by seventy-three percent.[95] Alternatively, Japan's 1990 nuclear target—an ambitious sixty gigawatts, or four times present capacity—would only reduce projected oil import dependence by about ten percent[96], and energy import dependence by zero.

Such calculations, or equally discouraging versions for other countries[97], are not setting up a strawman of trying to meet *all* oil or energy needs with nuclear power[98]; nor is their point

[95]MITI's 1978 interim forecasts—later reduced—assumed 6%/y real GNP growth to 1985 and a "maximum possible" conservation savings of 13.5% by 1990. We assume here real GNP growth at 6%/y to 1990, 4%/y 1990–2000, and a 1975–2000 average conservation savings of 18%, resulting in primary demand of about 1.13 trillion (10^{12}) liters of oil equivalent, or about 41 EJ, in the year 2000. We also count plants built or being built, assume 6-year lead time (probably too short in view of recent Japanese experience[92]), and assume a 62% capacity factor, markedly higher than the Japanese average so far.[128]

[96]J. S. Nye, 12 July 1978 speech to Uranium Institute (London), in *Reader*[20], 339.

[97]See e.g. Taylor[87]; A. B. Lovins, "Re-examining the Nature of the ECE Energy Problem," *Energy Policy* 178–98, September 1979 (a revision of the 9 February 1978 UN Economic Commission for Europe paper ECE (XXXIII)/2/Add.3), at 196; ——, "Is Nuclear Power Necessary?" FOE Ltd,[29] 1979, at 9–10; and, for a summary table, ——, "Economically Efficient Energy Futures," in W. Bach *et al.*, eds., *Energy/Climate Interactions*, Reidel (Dordrecht, Netherlands), 1980, at 21. For related arguments on the futility and internal inconsistency of high-electric-growth forecasts, see e.g. F. von Hippel & R. H. Williams, "Energy waste and nuclear power growth," *Bulletin of the Atomic Scientists* 18–21&ff, December 1976, and D. A. Casper, "A less-electric future?", *Energy Policy* 191–211, September 1976.

[98]Though that is apparently what the drafters of the Resolution at the Persepolis Conference on Transfer of Nuclear Technology had in mind with their opening declaration:
> The essential point is that most countries look upon nuclear power as the only route to energy independence. * * * In the interim until independence is achieved through the breeder, most countries are likely to take the view that Uranium offers no more security than oil. . . . .

The implied substitution hardly seems achievable in principle: Vince Taylor has calculated that even if fast reactors supplied all electricity in 2025, and if electricity grew several percentage points per year faster than total energy supply until then, about two-thirds of delivered energy would still have to come from nonnuclear sources. What if we calculate from a different basis—trying to save oil?

much altered by assuming lower energy demand forecasts[99]. They do show—in its proper context—an energy contribution from nuclear power, and it may be said that without that contribution, the examples would look even worse. But their point is that even prohibitively large nuclear programs cannot go far to meet officially projected[100] energy needs. The official projections reflect an inability to face the fact that nuclear power is *physically incapable* of playing a dominant role in any country's energy supply for the foreseeable future, and hence cannot merit a dominant priority. Solving the oil problem will clearly require, not a nuclear panacea, but a wide *array* of complementary measures, most importantly major improvements in energy efficiency (Chapter Seven).

It is therefore necessary to *compare* the elements of this array in costs, rates, difficulties, and risks, to ensure that one is displacing oil with the cheapest, fastest, surest package of measures. Just as a person shopping for the most food on a limited budget does not buy caviar simply for the sake of having some-

---

To replace only half the world's 1970 use of oil and gas with nuclear power, displacing two units of primary fossil fuel with each unit of nuclear electricity, would require over 1600 GWe (at 62% capacity factor)—more than the 1970 *total* generating capacity of the US, USSR, EEC, and Japan. To do that by the year 2000 (assuming 8-year lead time) would mean ordering a plant every 3.4 days starting now, and at 1976 prices it would cost[103] around 2.7×10^{12}. Trying to replace only half the oil and none of the gas would reduce these daunting figures by only 32%. Clearly, even the most ambitious nuclear programs cannot provide substantial oil displacement before the oil runs out.

[99]Paradoxically, lower *primary* demand forecasts (the kind considered here) may *reduce* the fractional nuclear contribution, because nuclear power cannot capture more than 100% of the market for new power stations, and electrical growth (with its trebling of electrical output to reflect conversion losses) dominates primary energy growth. This is nicely illustrated, as Taylor[87] points out, by the forecasts in the OECD/NEA and IAEA joint report *Uranium Resources, Production, and Demand* (OECD, Paris, 1977), p 27. In the base case, the non-Communist world's primary energy demand increases 3%/y to 2000 and 1.6%/y thence to 2025, while nuclear capacity (with bizarre disregard of logistical arithmetic[142]) is forecast to reach 1000 GWe in 2000 and 2100 GWe in 2025. Non-nuclear energy requirements nonetheless increase by 89% during 1975–2000 and increase by 150% (more than doubling) during 1975–2025. An "accelerated growth" case assumes three times as much nuclear capacity—but also, for self-consistency in primary demand, requires more than a fourfold increase in *non*-nuclear energy requirements.

[100]Such projections are still widely derived by projecting past exponential trends for gross primary energy (fitting exponentials even where actual trends are linear or less—see Casper[97]), subtracting a small percentage for unspecified "conservation," subtracting hoped-for supplies of fossil fuel, subtracting another percent or so for solar, and labelling the difference—the dreaded "energy gap"—"nuclear." This is in essence the method still used by the EEC and OECD. No nation today appears to base its demand forecasts on a detailed, physically concrete analysis of end-use needs and efficiencies.

thing from each shelf, but seeks the best bargain in a balanced diet, so every dollar devoted to relatively slow and costly energy supplies actually *retards* oil displacement by not being spent on more effective measures. Nuclear power programs have so far been justified not by this rational test but by intoning the conventional wisdom stated by Sir Brian (now Lord) Flowers of the UK Atomic Energy Authority:

Alternative sources will take a long time to develop on any substantial scale. . . . Energy conservation requires massive investment . . . , and can at best reduce somewhat the estimated growth rate. Nuclear power is the only energy source we can rely upon at present with any certainty for massive contributions to our energy needs up to the end of the century, and if necessary, beyond.[101]

Failure to assess *comparative* rates of oil displacement, as we shall do in Chapter Seven, runs the risk that, having like Lord Flowers dismissed alternatives as slow, conservation as costly, and both as inadequate, one may choose a predominantly nuclear future that is simultaneously slow, costly, *and* inadequate.

What is the energy problem?

Nuclear power is not only too slow; it is the wrong kind of energy source to replace oil. Most governments have viewed the energy problem as simply how to supply more energy of any type, from any source, at any price, to replace oil—as if demand were homogeneous. For planners unaware of other possibilities, this boils down to which kind of new power station to build—which is why nuclear power is often loosely described as a source of "energy." But it is actually a source of electricity, which is only one form of energy. There are many different forms whose different prices and qualities suit them to different uses. It is the uses that matter: people want comfort and light, not raw kilowatt-hours. Assuming (as we do) equal convenience and reliability to the user, the objective should be to supply the amount and type of energy that will do *each task most cheaply*[102].

[101]B. Flowers, "Nuclear power: A Perspective of the Risks, Benefits and Options," *Bulletin of the Atomic Scientists* 21–26&ff, March 1978. Lord Flowers is here quoting the conventional view—apparently with approval, as one can infer from his personal statements later in the same article.

[102]This economic comparison should in principle take account of all social costs, including those now "external" to market prices. As a conservatism, however, we base our comparison in this book on internal costs only, and generally on private (rather than social) internal costs. Internalizing the externalities—counting, for example, effects on health and safety, environment, jobs, political freedoms, vulnerability, etc.—would only strengthen our case.

This common-sense redefinition of the problem—meeting particular, concrete needs for energy services with an economy of means, using the right tool for the job—profoundly alters conclusions about new energy supply. Electricity is a special, high-quality, extremely expensive form of energy. Electricity delivered from a newly ordered nuclear plant will probably cost (in 1980 dollars) about as much per unit of heat content as oil at $130 per barrel, or roughly four times the 1980 OPEC crude oil price.[103] This costly energy may be economically worthwhile in such premium uses as motors, lights, smelters, railways, and electronics; but no matter how efficiently it is used, it cannot come close to competing with presently available efficiency improvements, or with present direct fuels, or with presently commercial renewable sources, for supplying heat or for operating road vehicles. These uses plus feedstocks account for about ninety percent of world oil use and for a similar or larger fraction of delivered energy needs. The special, "electricity-specific" applications represent typically only seven or eight percent of all delivered energy needs—much less than is now supplied in the form of electricity.[104]

In most industrial countries, therefore, a third to a half of all electricity generated is already being used, uneconomically[105],

[103]This is in terms of the heat content of electricity or oil without regard to the end-use efficiency of either: that is, 1 kW-h of electricity is considered to contain 3.6 MJ or 3413 BTU, so that 8¢/kW-h corresponds on a heat basis to $129/bbl. This is a typical US utility estimate of short-run marginal price to residential or commercial customers; typical European values are comparable or higher. Our calculations lead to a similar US result—about 3.7¢/kW-h busbar or 6.3¢/kW-h delivered (1976 $) from a 1.1-GWe PWR ordered in 1976. The details are set out at 105–113 in A. B. Lovins, *Soft Energy Paths*,[74] and schematically summarized at 42 in "Is Nuclear Power Necessary?"[97] The nuclear costs are debated in letters in *Science*—*200*:381–82 (28 April 1978), *201*:1077–78 (22 September 1978), *202*:1242–43 (22 December 1978), and *204*:124–29 (13 April 1979), of which the last is the most detailed. (Its note 18 cites a higher estimate by the Electric Power Research Institute.) For a comparison of capital costs and delivered energy prices with other options, see A. B. Lovins, "Soft Energy Technologies," *Annual Review of Energy 3*:477–517 (1978), updated in "Re-examining . . ."[97]

[104]See "Re-examining . . ."[97] and "Economically Efficient . . ."[97] for national data. Electrification, though appropriate for only about 7–8% of delivered energy needs (12% in Japan, the highest figure for any major industrial country), typically gets about three-quarters of all energy investment and research funding. A notable exception, at least in research, is Sweden, whose 1978–81 R&D budget is 32% conservation and nearly all the rest end-use-oriented renewables: see Energy Research & Development Commission (Sveavägen 9–11, 9 tr, 11157 Stockholm), *Energy Research and Development in Sweden 1978/81*, DFE-13, September 1978. The fission budget, 2% of the total, was to be phased out in 1979.

[105]That it is uneconomic may not be immediately obvious to a consumer from whom the high marginal cost of recently built or newly ordered plants is concealed by "rolling in" their price with that from older, cheaper plants; nor when electric

for low-temperature heating and cooling—space-conditioning buildings and heating water.[106] Additional electricity could *only* be so used. Arguing about what kind of new power station to build is thus like shopping for brandy to burn in the car or Chippendales to burn in the stove.

If one does not build a nuclear power station, the substitute for it is neither an oil-fired nor a coal-fired power station. It does not matter in the least which kind of new power station can send out the cheapest electricity, because *none* of them can even remotely compete in either cost or speed with the *real* competitors—the cheapest ways to do the same unsaturated end-use tasks—such as weatherstripping, insulation, heat exchangers[107], greenhouses[108], window overhangs and coatings,

---

heating is promoted by special tariffs cross-subsidized by other users. New nuclear plants are commonly justified by economic calculations based on perhaps 6000 hours of annual use, and their output then sold at a corresponding tariff, only to be used for "peaky" heating whose load factor is a quarter that much or even less. Further, many countries provide large direct and indirect tax subsidies to nuclear power or otherwise artificially depress its apparent price. EURATOM loans, for example, are now being expanded to help European reactor-building. Many US states allow consumers to be charged compulsorily for building plants which shareholders are unwilling to finance. Canada gives Federal grants for the first reactor in any Province. Other, more peculiar examples abound. In the US, a preliminary survey of Federal subsidies to nuclear power identified about twenty categories of subsidy, of which several had effectively infinite value (the industry could not exist without them), most were unquantifiable, and three which were quantifiable were together enough to reduce the apparent price of nuclear electricity by more than half. (A. B. Lovins, "Federal Subsidies to Nuclear Power," statement supplemental to testimony of 20–21 November 1979 before the District Court of Rogers County, Oklahoma, submitted 11 January 1980, and available from FOE Inc.[29]) At this writing, the Canadian Federal government is preparing an "off-oil" program of grants to help householders to switch to, among other options, cross-subsidized off-peak electric-resistance space heating—a way to provide a load for looming nuclear overcapacity.

[106]For example, between a third and a half of all electricity now purchased in the US, UK, France, FR Germany, Switzerland, and Sweden is now used for these purposes, which are also responsible for most of the projected growth in electrical demand.

[107]These simple devices can cut water-heating loads by about a third by preheating incoming domestic water with heat recovered from outgoing graywater. (See the September 1980 *Solar Age* survey on reducing water-heating loads.) They can have an even more dramatic effect on buildings' energy needs when used to recover heat (or coolth) from exhaust ventilation air. Provided the building is tight enough that most of the ventilation is controlled, rather than through cracks, increasing thermal insulation soon makes air exchange the dominant heat loss. For dry climates, an average of about 80% of the heat in the outgoing air can be recovered with a simple "recuperator" (technically, a counterflow heat exchanger) whose design is described by R. W. Besant, R. S. Dumont, and D. Van Ee, "An Air to Air Heat Exchanger for Residences," 1979 (Dept. of Mech. Eng., U. of Saskatchewan, Saskatoon S7N 0W0, Canada). A crossflow heat exchanger which also exchanges latent heat is commercially available (Mitsubishi Lossnay™)

pyrolysis of logging wastes, etc. Indeed, because these measures, intelligently done, generally cost less than the running cost *alone* for a nuclear plant, a nation that has just built such a plant would probably save money by writing it off and never operating it.[109]

at a similar price—about $200. Performance data are available from A. H. Rosenfeld (Lawrence Berkeley Lab., Berkeley, CA 94720), who reports that a residential Lossnay™ with a 45 W blower can typically save about 500 W of heating in a cold climate or 750 W of cooling in a hot, humid one.

[108]Greenhouses with a double shell of translucent material, good thermal insulation on sides not exposed to much solar input, and an adequate thermal mass (heat storage capacity in water, rocks, masonry walls, etc.) are a cheap and effective method of space heating; provide a pleasant "sunspace" and fresh fruits and vegetables most or all of the year; can be built by unskilled people using scrounged materials[249] or cheap plastics; and work especially well in cloudy climates. Solar water-heating panels put inside the upper part of such a greenhouse cannot freeze and hence can be built far more simply and cheaply than on a roof. Greenhouses can be designed into or retrofitted (added after construction) to most types of buildings, e.g. as an attached lean-to on the south side.[248]. Alternatively, other "passive solar" measures—those by which a building captures and stores solar energy in its own fabric rather than needing special collectors—can be designed in or retrofitted, e.g. by painting a south-facing brick wall black and glazing it as a conductive Trombe wall. See *Passive Solar Design Handbook*, DOE/CS-0127/1–2 (1980) and *Passive Solar Buildings,* SAND 79-0824 (1979), Sandia Laboratories (Albuquerque NM 87185).

[109]The extra electricity can be used only for low-temperature heating and cooling. All it is worth paying for those functions is what it costs to do them in the cheapest way: efficiency improvements and passive solar. Those generally cost considerably less than the total marginal running cost of a new reactor, which is in the vicinity of 2¢/kW-h (1980 $): about 1¢/kW-h for fuel-cycle costs including spent fuel management. 0.3¢ for operation and maintenance costs for the plant, 0.6–0.9¢ for operation and maintenance costs for the associated marginal transmission and distribution capacity, and perhaps 0.1¢ (probably a great underestimate) for decommissioning. In contrast, most utility conservation programs being implemented in 1979–80 are reporting a cost of electricity savings around 1–1.5¢/kW-h in residences (despite a general failure to pursue optimally cost-effective measures) and much less in the commercial sector. A detailed analysis of conservation costs by the staff of the California Energy Commission found that commercial-sector savings could provide more than half of the expected 6.7 GWe of peak savings by 1995 at an average cost of only 0.3¢/kW-h (compared to 3¢ for residential). (Conservation Division, Supporting Document # 16 to Staff Summary Report for AB1852 Proceeding, January 1978, Ca. Energy Commission, Sacramento.) Most of the conservative empirical studies of conservation costs for building retrofits or for all sectors—e.g. those by Ross and Williams[210] and by Sant[113]—find average costs around $12–14/bbl, equivalent to about 0.7–0.9¢/kW-h. The Santa Cruz Summer Study[210] estimated about $10/bbl for all buildings. Preliminary data from Lawrence Berkeley Laboratory's detailed supply curve for California energy conservation suggest that with a 5%/y real discount rate and 10-y time horizon, electricity equivalent to 1.1 GWe at 69% capacity factor can be saved by efficiency improvements costing less than 1.7¢/kWe-h in the residential sector alone; savings worthwhile against marginal cost are nearly twice as large, and if the commercial sector were included, the savings would be probably at least five times as large.

Under US tax law, the additional saving on future profits and tax subsidies would probably permit the recovery of the sunk capital cost too [110,111].

The importance of redefining the energy problem as "how to provide end-use services in the cheapest way" is vividly illustrated by a sad story from France. Energy planners there, as elsewhere, contemplated a chart of national energy flows, looking somewhat like a tangle of spaghetti (stylized in Fig. 1): primary fuels and electricity entering on the left-hand side, going through various conversion processes, and emerging on the right-hand side as various delivered energy forms that perform such services as heating buildings, making steel, and running cars. Several years ago, the energy conservation planners in the French government started on the right-hand end. Observing that their largest single use of energy was for heating buildings, they sought the best method, and decided that the worst, even with heat-pumps, was to use electricity. They won a highly publicized battle with Électricité de France, as a result of which electric heating in France is supposed to be discouraged or even phased out because

---

[110]The post-commissioning stream of utility profits and unpaid Federal tax subsidies adds up to the equivalent of two-thirds of the capital cost. (D. Chapman, "Nuclear Economics: Taxation, Fuel Cost and Decommissioning," Report A.E.Res. 79-26 to California Energy Commission from Dept. of Agricultural Economics, Cornell U. (Ithaca, NY), October 1979. An improved model is in preparation. Exact values depend on state and local conditions. We have not discounted the stream of future savings because, we would argue, it is hard to find long-term investments today that actually yield significantly positive real interest.) The other third of the sunk capital cost can also be recouped if the measures that replace the plant[109] are cheaper than its total running cost by$\gtrsim$ 0.3¢/kW-h. This means that the conservation and passive solar measures used must be cheaper than about $20–25/bbl—an easy target to beat.[210] Our comparison implicitly assumes that the capital cost has somehow been socialized; otherwise we would be comparing a social saving with a cost internal to the utility.

[111]The same argument applies *a fortiori* to partly built, partly amortized, or fossil-fueled plants, down to the capacity needed to meet electricity-specific end-use needs at a cost-effective level of end-use efficiency.[116] (Re partly built plants, see J. D. Peach, US General Accounting Office, letter B-198245 (4 April 1980) to Rep. J. H. Weaver, USHR.) A further subtlety must be noted: it may be argued that additional nuclear electricity displaces existing fossil generation. But to justify nuclear investment for mere displacement, its total cost must be less than the running cost of the fossil plant (which is implausible for coal and dubious even for very efficient oil-fired plants) *and* all the cheaper alternatives to central stations, as noted below, must have been exhausted first. The latter must be shown even to justify continuing to operate *existing* nuclear plants: all opportunities below about 2¢/kW-h (including at least the first three categories bulleted under "Economic priorities" below) must have been fully used before it is worthwhile to operate the nuclear plant even assuming its external social costs to be zero.

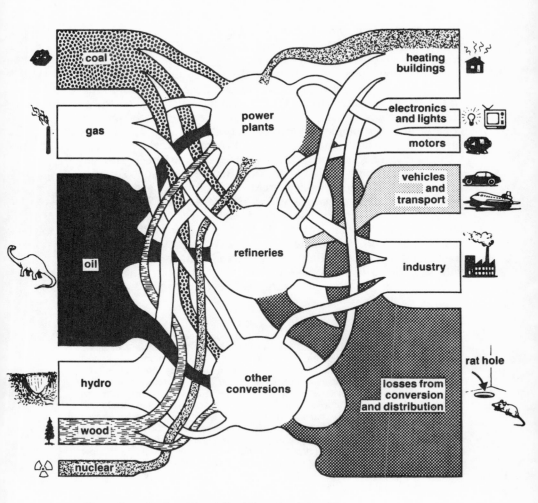

Figure One: A schematic, stylized "spaghetti chart."

it is so wasteful of money and fuels.[112] But meanwhile, down the street, the far more influential energy supply planners in the French government had started on the left-hand end of the chart. Obsessed with its large input of nasty imported oil, they asked: "How can we replace that oil? Oil is energy," they mused. "We must need some other source of energy. Voilà! Reactors give us

[112]In practice, ÉdF has been able largely to evade this mandate: upwards of 40% of new French housing starts are electric-resistance heated, keeping electrical demand growth on target—at a ruinous economic cost.

energy: we'll build reactors all over the place." Unfortunately, they paid little attention to where that energy would go. The two sides of the French energy policy establishment thus pursued their respective solutions to two different French energy problems, until in early 1979 their conflicting perceptions collided in the middle: the Ministry of Industry suddenly realized that the only way to sell most of the planned nuclear electricity would be for electric heating, which they had already agreed not to do. Many other countries, including essentially all industrial countries, are today in the same embarrassing position. Which side of the chart a nation starts on, what it thinks the *energy problem* is, is not an academic abstraction: it determines what energy supplies to buy. It is the single most pervasive dispute underlying the energy debate.

Economic priorities

The economic absurdity of new power stations is illustrated by an authoritative calculation[113] of how much energy Americans would have bought in 1978 if for the preceding decade or so they had simply met their end-use needs by making the cheapest incremental investments, whether in new energy supplies or in efficiency improvements. Had they done so, they would have reduced their 1978 purchases of oil by about twenty-eight percent (cutting imports by half to two-thirds), of coal by thirty-four percent (making the stripping of the American West unnecessary), and of electricity by forty-three percent (so that over a third of today's power stations, including the whole nuclear program, would never have been built in the first place). The total net cost of such a program: about seventeen percent less than Americans *did* pay in 1978 for the same energy services. Detailed studies of the scope for similar measures throughout the industrial world (and, where data are available, in developing countries) have given qualitatively similar or stronger results.[114]

[113]R. Sant, "The Least-Cost Energy Strategy," report and technical appendix, Energy Productivity Center, Mellon Institute, Suite 1200, 1925 N. Lynn St., Arlington, VA 22209, 1979; summarized in *Harvard Business Review*, 6 & ff, May–June, 1980.

[114]See e.g. G. Leach *et al.*, *A Low Energy Strategy for the United Kingdom*, International Institute for Environment and Development (10 Percy St., London W.1, UK), 1979; D. Olivier *et al.*, "Technical Fix" scenario reported to the Energy Technology Support Unit (Harwell) by Earth Resources Research Ltd. (40 James St., London W.1, UK), 1980; F. Krause, *Energiewende: Wachstum und Wohlstand ohne Öl und Uran*, ÖKO-Institut (Schönauerstr. 3, 7800 Freiburg i.Br., FRG), 1980; J. S. Nørgård, *Husholdninger og Energi*, Polyteknisk Forlag (København), 1979; CONAES Demand & Conservation Panel, *Science 200*:145–52 (1978); refs. 216; and other citations in Chapter Seven below and in Lovins, "Is Nuclear Power Necessary?"[97] and "Economically Efficient . . ."[97].

If we did want "more electricity", we should get it from the *cheapest sources* first. In virtually all countries, these are, in approximate order of increasing price:

* Eliminating waste of electricity (such as lighting empty offices at headache level).
* Replacing with efficiency improvements and cost-effective solar systems the electricity now used for low-temperature heating and cooling.[115]
* Making motors, lights, appliances, smelters, etc. cost-effectively efficient.[116]

[115]Some US utilities—e.g. Pacific Power & Light (Portland, OR)—now give zero-interest loans for this purpose which need never be repaid until you sell your house. Some will even insulate your electric water-heater free because it saves them so much money: they can resell the saved electricity without having to build a costly new plant to generate it. Peak-load savings, however, are often larger in the US for cooling than for heating, even though savings on air conditioning have attracted few utility investments so far. The techniques needed are often the same—roof insulation, heat exchangers, weatherstripping—plus devices to block direct solar gain (window overhangs and coatings and blinds), trees (just the transpiration cooling from a good-sized tree is the equivalent of about ten room air conditioners), and, if needed, passive solar cooling devices such as roof ponds and earth pipes. (See, for example, the July/August 1980 issue of the Rodale journal *New Shelter.*) Properly designed buildings do not require air conditioning for comfort, even in the tropics.

[116]Industrial electric motors, nominally about 90% efficient, are typically in practice only about 25–35% efficient, and this can be at least doubled by proper sizing, coupling, and power-factor controls, with a payback time of a few years. See W. Murgatroyd and B. C. Wilkins, *Energy 1:*337–46 (1976), a UK analysis, and extensive supporting data in the "Fichtner-Studie," *Technologien zur Einsparung von Energie,* Bundesministerium für Forschung und Technologie (Stuttgart/Essen), 1977. (Some US utilities privately estimate even higher savings.) For US assessments, see D. J. BenDaniel & E. E. David, Jr., *Science 206*:773–76 (1979) and "Classification and Evaluation of Electric Motors and Pumps", DOE/CS-0147, USDOE, 1980. In most industrial countries, industrial motors use over half of all non-thermal electricity consumption, so this *one* saving typically exceeds the entire output of the existing nuclear programs. The use of efficient lights and fixtures, task lighting, ample but not physiologically harmful lighting levels, and daylighting of peripheral offices typically saves half to two-thirds of lighting energy (paying back in a few years), and often saves even more on air conditioning. Cost-effective household appliance design roughly quadruples present North American efficiencies: J. S. Nørgård, *Energy Policy* 43–56, March 1979, and "Low-electricity future household," IEE conference paper, 29 April 1980, Physics Laboratory III, Technical University of Denmark (2800 Lyngby). At 5¢/kW-h (1978 $), the average payback time is six years. With payback times of up to ten years, about 40% of the energy needed for alumina reduction can be saved by using the best processes (9–11 kW-h/kg Al, as against the typical 16–18 today). (This payback is too long for many industrialists, but far better than a power station.) Such savings imply that the US, for example, could supply today's economic output, with no change in lifestyle, using about a *quarter* as much

• Industrial cogeneration[117], combined-heat-and-power stations, low-temperature heat engines operating from industrial waste heat ("bottoming cycles") or from solar ponds[118], modern wind machines[119], filling empty turbine bays in existing dams, and small-scale hydroelectricity[120].

• Central power stations—the slowest and costliest known source, which should not even be considered until cheaper opportunities have demonstrably been exhausted.

---

electricity as now—and hence requiring *no thermal power stations of any kind,* but only present hydro, microhydro, and wind—just by using electricity in an economically efficient way, compared to the cost of building new power stations.[139] Such countries as Canada, France, Switzerland, Norway, Sweden, and New Zealand would have a surplus of exportable electricity based only on their present hydro capacity. Similar formulas—no electricity made from oil, gas, coal, or uranium—could accommodate significant economic growth too. Studies in about fifteen countries have found no exception to these conclusions.[114] The most detailed study of long-term electricity demands (Oliver[114]) suggests that by cost-effective technical fixes, the UK could support a real GDP 2.9× today's and an industrial production 2.3× today's with a total per-capita electrical demand under 200 W, or about a sixth of the present US level. This represents an efficiency improvement of nearly seven-fold in average UK electricity use.

[117]The US has about two hundred reactors' worth of untapped opportunities for making electricity in factories as a byproduct of process heat: R. H. Williams, *Annual Review of Energy 3*:313–56 (1978). FR Germany has about sixteen: H.-J. Budde, *Die Zeit* 24, 25 March 1979. Capital and fuel costs are about half those of new central stations. Construction times are a year or two. Clean coal-burning is among the options, using fluidized-bed or conventional boilers.

[118]Shallow brine ponds insulated by a shallow surface layer of fresh water are cheap, low-technology sources of continuous heat near the boiling point in at least temperate latitudes; with commercial Rankine or Ericsson engines they appear to be the cheapest known source of baseload electricity. The technology has been demonstrated in Israel and, to a lesser extent, in the US, with typical heat prices around \$3.3–5.3/GJ in excavated US ponds. See M. Edesess *et al.,* "A Simple Design Tool for Sizing Solar Ponds," SERI/RR-351-347, Solar Energy Research Institute (Golden CO 80401), December 1979.

[119]The best modern wind machines now commercially sold in the US and Denmark can, in decent sites, offer a large cost saving over any new central station. Elegantly simple designs requiring virtually no maintenance are now entering the market (e.g. from Bergey Windpower Co., 2001 Priestley Ave., Norman, OK 73069).

[120]The US alone has nearly as much unused (but often formerly used and abandoned) small-scale hydro potential as its present large-scale hydro capacity. Tens of thousands of existing small dams lie unused. Many can be used without serious environmental problems. Typical New England sites have median costs around \$700/kW (but highly site-dependent) and capacity factors around 0.6–0.7. Microhydro is surprisingly widely distributed: the state with the most small dams is said to be Kansas. See the papers of the Energy Law Institute (2 White St., Concord, NH 03301).

The notion that despite all constraints—time, money, politics, technical uncertainties—nuclear power stations are at least a source of energy, and as such can be substituted for significant amounts of the dwindling oil supply, has long exerted a powerful influence on otherwise balanced imaginations. But it does not withstand critical scrutiny. It is both logistically and economically fallacious. A kilowatt-hour of electricity is *not* simply substitutable for 0.3 liters of oil (the amount that would have to be burned in a rather inefficient power station to generate one kilowatt-hour of electricity). The high cost of nuclear power *today* limits its conceivably economic role to the baseload fraction[121] of electricity-specific end-uses: typically about four percent of all delivered energy needs and an even smaller fraction of total oil consumption. In purely pragmatic and economic terms, therefore, nuclear power falls of its own demerits.

This economic failure, despite desperate efforts to shore it up, is already being perceived and acted upon in the marketplace, where for predominantly *economic* reasons, denuclearization (at least at the margin) has been taking place for several years. The greatest collapse of any enterprise in industrial history is already underway.

---

[121]That is, the fraction—typically around half—of total demand that is steady rather than fluctuating by the day, week, or season. Nuclear plants cannot economically tolerate a more than slightly varying demand and cannot technically tolerate on-off operation (a "peaking" role), owing to instabilities in neutron flux and thermal stress on major components such as the pressure vessel.

Chapter Five

The Collapse of Nuclear Power

A few years ago, the foregoing arguments that nuclear power is largely irrelevant to the energy problem might have seemed remote and abstract. The technology was, after all, being bought, and although dissatisfaction lurked in village square and boardroom alike, official confidence was unbounded: projections of tenfold or greater increases in nuclear capacity in the next few decades were commonplace. But by now it is unbearably obvious that the sales pitch has not convinced the marketplace. Rising costs, falling political acceptance, and dramatically decreased prospects for electricity demand and utility finance have brought the world nuclear power enterprise to a virtual standstill.

Costs

Universally—in the United States and in the Soviet Union[122], in France and in Brazil, under the most diverse conditions of regulation and economic policy—the direct economic costs of nuclear power in real terms (corrected for general inflation) have risen unrelentingly since reactors went "commercial". Full, up-to-date cost data are secret in most countries and available in sufficient detail for proper analysis only in the United States, which has historically accounted for about half of the world nuclear market. But such data as are available strongly suggest that US trends and conclusions are generally valid elsewhere. An exhaustive statistical analysis of all the US historic data, explaining ninety-two percent of their variation, has revealed that during 1971–78, real capital cost per installed kilowatt (after correcting for inflation in the prices of the ingredients needed to build steam power plants generally) increased more than twice as fast for nuclear as for coal plants and already exceeds the latter by fifty percent, despite investments that decreased coal plants' air pollution by almost two-thirds (and will have done so by about nine-tenths from 1971 levels by the late 1980s)[123].

[122]N. Dollezhal and Y. Koryakin, *Bulletin of the Atomic Scientists* 33, January 1980.

[123]C. Komanoff, "Cost Escalation at Nuclear and Coal Power Plants," submitted to *Science,* February 1980, revised 15 August 1980: Komanoff Energy Associates, 475 Park Ave. S., 32d floor, New York NY 10016. As we note in our Autumn 1980 *Foreign Affairs* response to B. Wolfe, a statistical analysis of historic data by this technique (multiple regression) is only an objective tool for determining which factors were significant and by how much; it cannot *prove* causality, though Komanoff's cross-checks do, where possible, tie the statistical results to demon-

Based on the established relationship between nuclear sector size and costs [real cost doubles for each 3.3-fold increase in nuclear capacity built or being built], nuclear capital costs will exceed those of coal by 75 percent for plants now starting construction. New reactors' generating costs will then be 25 percent greater than for new coal plants, indicating that many of the 90 US [nuclear] units with construction permits could be converted to coal to provide cheaper electricity.

This projection excludes any possible impact—which most observers think will be heavy—of tighter safety standards in the wake of Three Mile Island. Indeed, even for all plants *operating* in 1978, US nuclear generating costs averaged about seven percent higher than coal generating costs[124]: not the right comparison, as we showed in Chapter Four, but still a matter of interest to utilities, their bankers and regulators, and the public.

The real costs of operating the nuclear fuel cycle, from uranium mining to spent fuel storage, have risen even faster, at least balancing the slight saving from a recent drop in the forward real price of uranium as demand forecasts collapse[125]. Unexpect-

strable engineering costs in a remarkably persuasive way. His results must be accepted as definitive until someone comes up with a better fit to the data.

[124]Widely quoted claims to the contrary, including those by government agencies, are derived from the Atomic Industrial Forum's May 1979 survey of power costs, which selectively omitted nearly all the costliest and least reliable nuclear plants and the cheapest coal plants: see C. Komanoff's "Power Propaganda: A Critique of the Atomic Industrial Forum's Nuclear and Coal Power Cost Data for 1978," Environmental Action Foundation (724 Dupont Circle Bldg., Washington, DC 20036), 1980. At this writing, data for 1979 are not yet available, but they will almost certainly show that the nuclear cost disadvantage has widened. Readers must be cautioned that there is a world of difference between hoped-for and empirical costs (both capital and total costs) and between those for old and for newly ordered plants. Essentially every official and vendor study of nuclear economics ignores the up-to-date empirical data in favor of the lower costs experienced with old plants or hoped for (in defiance of statistical trends)[123] from new plants. Nuclear economics depends on about fifty main variables of which all are disputed, few are known within a factor of two, and many are interactive; hence almost any power cost within a factor of ten can be calculated from assumptions which some analyst, however disingenuously, can be found to defend. But total busbar (i.e. sent-out) costs of nuclear electricity are dominated by assumed capital cost and capacity factor.[128] Remarkably, the widely cited energy study of the International Institute for Applied Systems Analysis (IIASA) in Laxenburg, Austria, among its egregious defects of structure and execution, assumed nuclear capital costs about half those empirically observed—on the curious basis that that is what reactors *would* cost if society did not foolishly require all those silly precautions and delays. (This might be called a "forgetting curve," but has the same effect as the "learning curve" more traditionally postulated to lower the future cost of currently uneconomic technologies.)

[125]As pointed out in Vince Taylor's *The Myth of Uranium Scarcity* and other papers of the past few years for Pan Heuristics,[8] the uranium price was artificially

edly high estimated costs for waste management, for decommissioning nuclear plants after at most a few decades, and for cleaning up past mistakes (for example, burying the hazardous tailings left over from uranium mining) add many billions of dollars in unbudgeted liabilities.[126] Erratic reactor performance—poor reliability, cracks in key components, maintenance problems seeming to go with scarcely a pause from the pediatric to the geriatric[127]—have afflicted most countries, further boosting nuclear generating costs[128] and raising serious problems of occupational safety. And as cumulative losses mount into the billions of

forced up by the US Government, presumably to make a better case for the breeder, and was further raised by cartel action and by utilities' scramble to cover themselves twice when caught short by Westinghouse's default on long-term supply contracts. Currently, however, as the import of Figure 2 sinks in, contract prices are falling back toward levels consonant with real production costs, and many Colorado and New Mexico mines are closing down. See G. Getschow, *Wall Street Journal* 1, 26 August 1980. (DOE even forecasts in DOE/RA-0038, August 1979, that net US uranium imports will be about 3200 ston/y in 1981–85, about 30% foreign fueling for 72 operating plants.) The resulting loss of confidence is in turn inhibiting new mining and milling investment (as is uncertainty over who will pay how much to control tailings and emissions), and this may further reduce confidence in nuclear power. Meanwhile, however, the price of enrichment—the other main front-end fuel-cycle cost for LWRs—is being strongly driven upwards by the rising price of electricity (derived in the US mainly from strip-mined Appalachian coal), and may be boosted still higher by fixed charges as a world capacity glut develops and as a possible billion-dollar shortfall from Iran's Eurodif withdrawal must be made up.

[126]Some were budgeted but in grossly inadequate amounts, and some were spent for other purposes. In at least seventeen US states, for example, ratepayers are paying for future reactor decommissioning costs, computed as a "negative salvage value" earning a rate of return, but the state regulatory commissions have permitted the proceeds to be spent for general purposes (i.e. new plant construction) rather than escrowed. When the time comes to decommission, the utilities will not have the money and will need to collect it all over again.

[127]That is, problems expected to dominate late in the plant's life—corrosion, wear, metal fatigue, accumulation of radioactive "crud"—turned out to dominate starting in the first few years.

[128]This is because lower "capacity factor" (the electricity actually sent out by a plant as a fraction of what it would send out operating full-time at full rated power) means that the same capital charges must be spread over less output. A reduction from 75% to 61% capacity factor increases capital costs per kilowatt-hour by 23%. In the US, nuclear capacity factors through 1979 averaged only 61% for all plants and about 55% for those over 800 MWe, compared with a hoped-for 70–80%. (These data are weighted by unit and would be about one percentage point lower if weighted by capacity.) Swiss plants were more reliable (about 75%); FR German, about the same (roughly 56%); Japanese and French disastrously worse (about 51% and 49% respectively). CANDU plants, which automatically gain more than ten percentage points on LWRs by not requiring shutdown for annual refueling, started well but have lately run into problems too, and have a cumulative average capacity factor around 71%.

dollars, no vendor in the world appears to have made a nickel on total reactor sales[129].

Politics

Added to these economic woes is an ever less receptive political climate. Both the new news (Browns Ferry, Three Mile Island, and a large supporting cast) and the old news (from Utah to the Urals) has seemed bad news. Each major incident, though a catalyst that crystallized inchoate concerns, was not the first and will not be the last explicit reminder of technical and institutional immaturity—neatly encapsulated in the February 1980 shutdown of the Tihange reactor in Belgium after the management lost control of it to a hundred workers who occupied the control room. The unmanageability of the technology, a dawning truth illustrated by the Three Mile Island accident as brilliantly recounted in the NRC's 1980 Rogovin Report, is becoming too obvious for even the most sanguine devotees to accept bland assurances. The resulting unease now reverberates around the world, spilling from one country to the next. The nuclear debate has irrevocably gone critical, like the Vietnam war in 1969–70, a delayed reaction to a technology imposed on a public that did not demand it by technocrats whose psychological needs did. Indeed, as Lewis Perelman of the CalTech Jet Propulsion Laboratory perceptively noted in 1979, a common litany of response by nuclear advocates after Three Mile Island—"nothing happened," it proves nuclear power is safe, and anyhow there can be no turning back— suggests "the psychological processes of denial, rationalization, and fatalism, a pattern characteristic of the pathology of addiction." Like an aircraft hijacking, the accident "terrorized and held hostage several million people . . . for twelve days" (and is not really over to this day), causing real psychological trauma intensified by official denials that anyone was hurt. When hijacking hostages were rescued, "no official proclaimed that 'nothing happened' simply because none of the passengers had been killed, or that the incident proved that airline security measures were effective."

In this new and more critical atmosphere, old assumptions have been reweighed and found wanting. Demolition by peer reviewers compelled the US Nuclear Regulatory Commission

[129]Despite extensive subsidies for both domestic[105] and export[145] orders. Some vendors' claims of profits turn out to rest on writing off past losses or balancing losses on reactor sales with profits on recent servicing (a flourishing trade) and supplies. Framatome in 1979 claimed an overall profit, but is hardly a free-market enterprise, and most observers doubt the French nuclear program produces profits for anyone.

(NRC) to declare that its 1975 Rasmussen Report, claiming that reactors are very safe, was no longer considered reliable, and the Canadian Atomic Energy Control Board to declare its Inhaber Report, claiming that renewable sources are very dangerous, officially out of print.[130] The classically assumed "solution" to the nuclear waste problem—reprocessing, turning the high-level wastes into glass, burying them in salt, and not talking about the low-level transuranic wastes[131]—turned out to be technically flawed[132]. The nuclear industry's credibility, heavily committed to these and similar premises, suffered a meltdown that seems irreversible: as Mark Twain remarked, a cat that sits on a hot stove lid will not do so again, but neither will it sit on a cold one.

[130]The main critic, J. P. Holdren ("Risk of Renewable Energy Sources: A Critique of the Inhaber Report," ERG 79-3, from 100 T-4, U. Ca., Berkeley, CA 94720, 1979), received the 1979 Public Service Award of the Federation of American Scientists for his persistence in exposing this scandal. For the out-of-print designation, see AECB (Ottawa), form letter 34-9-1-0 from H. J. M. Spence, 11 December 1979, and *Toronto Star* A18, 28 November 1979. Risk assessment is full of chicanery: for example, industry and government claims that nuclear plants kill only a tenth as many people as coal plants (ignoring the dominant risks on both sides[198]—proliferation and climatic change) turn out to ignore the long-term hazard of radon from tailings and of carbon-14 from reprocessing. Giving that hazard equal weight with shorter-term ones reverses the relative risk by a thousandfold: W. Ramsay and M. Russell, *Public Policy 26*:387–403 (1978) (Harvard University).

[131]These are generally tens of times more bulky than the processed high-level wastes and, though only weakly radioactive, contain a roughly equal amount of the plutonium and other long-lived isotopes that dominate the long-term hazard. The chemical and physical diversity, enormous surface area, and low chemical binding energy of these wastes makes them in principle more susceptible to leaching and weathering than the compact high-level wastes even if both are stored in equally impregnable places (which currently they are not: the low-level transuranic wastes are generally buried in shallow trenches which leak—e.g. A. B. Lovins, *Nature 265*:390 (1977)). It is therefore possible that the generally ignored low-level wastes are even more dangerous in the long run than the commonly considered high-level ones.

[132]Numerous 1978-9 publications by the President's Interagency Review Group on Nuclear Waste Management, the US Geological Survey, and independent researchers noted that salt domes are not dry, may not be stable, and offer the potential for hot brines which rapidly dissolve glassy wastes or almost anything else. Fundamental rethinking of wasteforms, geological environment, and their interactions is now beginning, but has a very long way to go before any type of "solution," let alone a particular scheme, can be approached with confidence. It is interesting that the waste problem, though probably far from the greatest risk of nuclear power, tends to dominate public perceptions of risk as expressed by groups as diverse as the National Council of Churches, United Auto Workers, and National Urban League. It even commands prominence—while proliferation gets no mention—in the plank adopted 130-2 on 23 June 1980 (over Administration opposition) by the Democratic National Platform Committee:

Efforts to repair the effects of past lack of candor or foresight have exacted a high cost in top-level managerial attention—also a scarce resource—out of all proportion to nuclear power's modest potential energy contribution. And as governments have tried to counter these problems, their usual reflex has been to increase central dictation at the expense of local autonomy, so reinforcing powerful centrifugal trends, reducing their own credibility, and strengthening local determination to resolve suspicions by substantive study. In the US, for example, this trend seems likely in the 1980s to produce a direct legislative confrontation between advocates of Federal preemption and states' rights in nuclear regulation[132a].

Demand

As nuclear costs rise and credibility falls, the market for more electricity from any source is quietly evaporating. With the inevitable response to higher prices beginning, forecasts of electricity demand growth in most countries have been falling steadily, often by a percentage point per year. Some are now nearing zero or negative values despite forecasts (at least for political consumption) of continued economic growth. US electricity demand has consistently been growing more slowly than real GNP of late, and all the trends are downward. Forecasters unfortunately responded more slowly than consumers: over the past six years, US private utilities forecast that peak demand for the following year would grow by an average of 7.8 percent, but the

We must make conservation and renewable energy our nation's energy priorities for the future. Through the Federal government's commitment to renewable energy sources and energy efficiency, and as alternative fuels become available in the future, we will retire nuclear power plants in an orderly manner.

We must give the highest priority to dealing with the nuclear waste disposal problem. Current efforts to develop a safe, environmentally sound nuclear waste disposal plan must be continued and intensified.

The NRC shall issue no licenses or permits for new nuclear plants until the Kemeny Commission recommendations are fully implemented.

Existing plants must be required to meet the safety recommendations of the Kemeny Commission. The Democratic Party supports prompt implementation of their recommendations. No plant unable to meet these standards can be allowed to operate.

[132a] For a remarkable example, see Brief of Appellants, Pacific Gas & Electric Co. & Southern California Edison Co. *vs* State Energy Resources Conservation & Development Commission & Natural Resources Defense Council, 9th Circuit Court of Appeals (Nos. 80-4265, 80-4273), 1980.

[133] *The Energy Daily* 3–4, 30 October 1978 and 20 December 1979. California utilities' forecast peak demand for 1985 fell from 68 GWe in 1971 forecasts to 39 GWe in 1979 forecasts and is still falling rapidly toward the actual trend line.

actual growth averaged only 2.9 pecent[133]. Overcapacity in the US will probably hit forty-three percent in 1980 and continue to rise (perhaps past the British level of about fifty percent), and the resulting fixed charges on idle capacity will reinforce the price spiral. US overcapacity in excess of a prudent fifteen percent reserve margin is already well over twice the present nuclear contribution. It is indeed so large that if *all* US power-plant construction were stopped immediately, growth in peak demand at an average rate of 1.2 percent—twice that experienced in the "normal" year 1979—would still leave a national reserve margin of fifteen percent in the year 2000 (neglecting regional differences). Growth by at least 2.2 percent per year could be accommodated if the economically advantageous industrial cogeneration potential were tapped. In fact, given the prices already in place or unavoidably on the way, it is plausible that US electricity demand will be constant or declining from now on, regardless of economic growth[134]: the main problem in any careful analysis of the US energy future is trying to figure out what to do with all the excess electricity. The market for power stations of any kind is simply imaginary[134-135].

The loss of cash-flow accident

Nuclear or fossil-fueled central power stations are, by their very complexity, extremely expensive to build—about a hundred times as capital-intensive as the traditional direct-fuel systems on

[134]For example, the SERI analysis,[216] whose implicit price elasticity is far from the largest seriously considered nowadays, assumed a two-thirds increase in real US GNP over the next twenty years, yet found the most plausible rate of change for US electricity demand in that period was around zero to minus one percent per year. The analysts' main difficulty, even without assuming more cogeneration, was figuring out how to dispose of all the surplus electricity.

[135]The point made in note 99 is worth reiterating: lower forecasts for electricity or primary energy demand do *not* imply that a given forecast nuclear capacity will make a proportionately larger supply contribution. Conventional forecasts of total primary energy demand are dominated by assumed growth in electrification; and, being in primary rather than delivered energy terms, they count each unit of electricity at about three times its delivered energy content. Lower primary demand forecasts thus tend to reflect lower electrical demand forecasts more than they reflect, for example, lower demand forecasts for direct heat or portable liquid fuels. For technical reasons,[121] only about half of total electrical demand is to be met with baseload (e.g. nuclear) plants, and nuclear plants in turn have to compete for the baseload power market with coal plants, cogeneration, etc. Thus, reasoning backwards from the demand forecasts to their supply components, lower demand does not leave room for unaltered nuclear supply and indeed often reduces it disproportionately. This is not the case with the end-use-matched soft technologies discussed in Chapter Seven: in general, lower primary demand forecasts imply that a given amount of soft-technology energy supply will yield a correspondingly larger fraction of total supply.

which the world's industrial economy has been built[136]. Coupled
with long construction times, this makes utility cash flow inherently unstable[137]. Paying the much higher cost of building new
plants generally entails raising the price of electricity during plant
construction. But this dampens demand growth below the forecast level on which the construction was predicated, producing a
shortfall of revenue that requires still higher prices to cover fixed
charges, so further depressing demand growth (or even, as in
Britain or Utah a few years ago, the *level* of demand). This "spiral
of impossibility" is exacerbated by many subtleties of utility finance and by attempts at subsidy. Its effect is that any utility,
whether public or private, regulated, unregulated, or perfectly
regulated, that keeps on building power stations will go broke.
The question is not whether its cash flow will collapse, but only
when. Many of the world's leading utilities are already in or
rapidly entering this position, leading to grave fears for their viability. Not surprisingly, major portfolio investment in US utilities
has virtually ceased, and the much more modest investment now
occurring—almost entirely from small investors—is likely to
cease with the next well-known utility that omits its dividend.
(Many utilities are therefore—improperly or illegally—using
short-term paper to raise enough money to pay their unearned
dividends.) Some utilities are already technically bankrupt[138], yet
are collectively too big for anyone, even national treasuries, to
bail them out. This problem is fundamental and inherent in the
nature of central-station (especially nuclear) technology—high
capital intensity, high complexity, long lead times. It can probably be solved, but only by cancelling construction and changing

---

[136]For details, see the sources cited in note 103.

[137]A. B. Lovins, "Electric Utility Investments: *Excelsior* or Confetti?" paper to
March 1979 E. F. Hutton utility investors' conference, updated and reprinted in
Journal of Business Administration (Vancouver) *12*(1), Spring 1981 issue (in press)
and concluding address (pp 168–78; see also panel, pp 124–29) in California Public
Utilities Commission, proceedings of the conference *Energy Efficiency and the
Utilities: New Directions* (at Stanford Law School, April 1980), PUC (San Fran-
cisco), 1980. See also *The Times* (London) 1, 1 March 1980, for a vivid British
example, and P. W. Shenon, *Wall Street Journal* 1, 9 October 1980, for a New
England one.

[138]To pick but one of many cases, Commonwealth Edison, the heavily nuclearized
Chicago utility, had in 1978 current liabilities about 2½ times current assets (total
net assets were nearly $8 billion), construction expenditures four times cash flow
after common dividends (which took up over a third of cash flow), and over six
years' net income tied up in nuclear construction. See I. C. Bupp (to whom this
example is due), "Some Background Information on the Financial Condition of
Certain Investor Owned Electric Utility Companies," 30 March 1980 typescript,
Harvard Business School, and R. Metz, "Utility Bonds and Ratings," *NY Times*
D6, 31 July 1980.

the utilities partly into conservation banks[139]. Indeed, matters may be even worse, because many analysts are coming to suspect that in the long run, a one percent increase in the price of electricity will reduce demand, at least in some sectors, by more than one percent ("price elasticity of demand bigger than minus one"). If this is true, then higher prices, in the absence of compensatory increases in population or income, will *reduce* the utility's revenues ("negative price elasticity of revenue"), because the utility would lose more money on the number of kilowatt-hours sold than it could make up by charging more for each kilowatt hour sold. If this is true, then building power stations is unprofitable not only in a cash-flow sense but also in a profit-and-loss sense, and an economically rational utility will seek to *reduce* its rate base and its prices. Even if this is not the case, the simple facts of today's utility industry—notably that new plants cost much more to build than old ones—mean that even if funding is available, building new plants is no longer in utilities' financial interest. Generating electricity, especially from new plants, has "ceased to be a commercially viable enterprise."[140]

Cinderella's pumpkin

These problems, singly and interactively, have taken their toll on industry morale[141], investor confidence, and resulting ex-

[139]The utilities should make loans at their internal cost of money (passing through any subsidies) to be spent at the borrowers' discretion on any fuel-saving measure cheaper than new power plants, and repaid at or below the borrowers' rate of return, so relieving their capital burden. Most such investments have such short lead times and fast paybacks that each utility dollar, during the period in which it would otherwise have been tied up in a power plant, can be re-invested about ten times over in successive efficiency improvements each of which yields typically five to ten times as much energy as the proposed power plant would have. The velocity of utility cash flow is thus so high—the revolving fund (set up "below the line," i.e. neither rate-based nor expensed) revolves so fast—that an energy program at least as large as the proposed plant construction program can generally be financed from real retained earnings without needing to go to the market for additional and very costly capital. For discussion, see Lovins.[137] Utilities with a fifth of US capacity are now developing or making conservation loans, though many of the rest are obdurate (J. Emschwiller, *Wall Street Journal* 23, 2 September 1980) and one pioneer, Tennessee Valley Authority, seems to be back-sliding: continuing undaunted with firm financial commitments to an enormous reactor program, to which TVA officials seem emotionally attached, is incurring such heavy carrying charges that TVA can neither afford conservation and solar programs of cost-effective size (whose annual budget would not cover three weeks' interest on nuclear projects) nor afford their loss of revenue. See L. Wann, *Chattanooga Times* 1, 19 and 27 August 1980.

[140]Quoted from I. C. Bupp in "A Dark Future for Utilities," *Business Week* cover story, p 108&ff, 28 May 1979.

[141]Most vendors—General Electric at San Jose is a salient example—have ex-

pectations. In only six years from 1973, nuclear forecasts for 2000 fell by a factor of five for the world[142], nearly four for FR Germany (no new orders since 1975)[143], and eight for the US (*minus* twenty-seven net orders during 1974–79, with at least eight more net losses just in the early weeks of 1980). It now appears that nuclear power, which today delivers about half as much energy in the United States as does firewood[144], is unlikely to get out of the firewood league in this century if ever. Nuclear forecasts worldwide are still plummeting—more for economic than for political reasons. The USSR, for example, achieved only a third of its nuclear goal for the 1970s, half for the past five years, despite the unlimited power of the State to crush dissent. The first Soviet pressurized-water reactor is five years behind schedule. It is equally revealing that the pattern of decline in official nuclear forecasts for the United States (Figure 2) and for Canada is virtu-

---

perienced a steady hemorrhage of staff in recent years and, even more ominously for long-term prospects, have found it all but impossible to attract first-class graduate talent, a problem now afflicting most universities' nuclear engineering programs too.

[142]For example, the IAEA in 1973 envisaged 3580–5330 GWe of world nuclear capacity in 2000; INFCE in 1978–80 forecast 850–1200 GWe. In its July 1980 Annual Report to Congress, the US Energy Information Administration estimated that 450–600 GWe would be the maximum physically possible outside the Communist bloc (which cannot begin to make up the difference) even if all constraints of siting, financing, and demand were removed. Interdevelopment Inc.'s independent forecast (*Nucleonics Week*, 22 May 1980) is 480 GWe of which 139 GWe would be in the US (the INFCE low assumption for the US was 255 GWe). The discrepancy between USEIA and INFCE arises partly because INFCE checked national forecasts for feasibility only to 1990, then took at face value governments' political puffs thereafter, which amounted to an impossible trebling of world nuclear capacity during 1990–2000. (Italy, for example, forecast at least 43 GWe but will have trouble achieving 5.) Given real constraints, we estimate that a world total (outside COMECON) of even 300 GWe is unlikely to be achieved. (*Cf*, for an advocacy view, M. Simnad, GA-A15797, General Atomic Co. (San Diego CA 92138), March 1980.)

[143]In November 1972, H. Krause (GfK Karlsruhe) and R. Randl (Bundesministerium für Bildung and Wissenschaft) estimated 179 GWe in 2000 (including 64 GWe of LWRs) at 199–227 in OECD/IAEA, *Management of Radioactive Wastes from Fuel Reprocessing* (OECD, Paris, 1973): see Fig 1, p 202. By spring 1977 this estimate had dropped to about 80 GWe: e.g. the GfK Karlsruhe estimates at 7 and 11 in H. Matthöfer, ed., *Schnelle Brüter: Pro und Contra* (Necker-Verlag, Villingen, 1977). The FRG official submission to INFCE in July 1978 forecast 52.4–71.4 GWe (47.5–66.5 GWe LWRs). US official estimates in early 1979, based on rigorous analysis of the "pipeline inventory" of plants under construction, were in the mid-forties of GWe and have since declined. The 1972–79 fall in forecasts for 1985 was from 61 to 18 GWe.

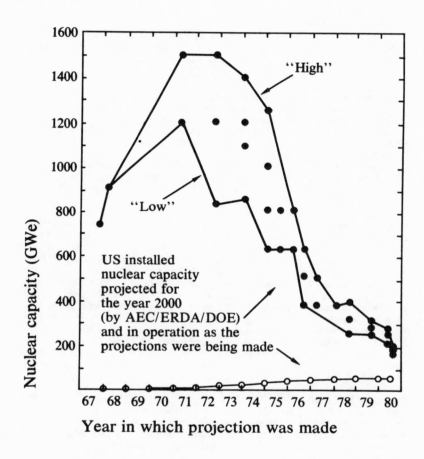

Figure Two: The decline and fall of US nuclear expectations for the year 2000 (solid dots), compared with currently operable US nuclear capacity (open circles).

Note: Forecasts since 1978 were prepared by the Energy Information Administration, US Department of Energy, on a different basis than pre-1978 forecasts. For nuclear capacity to be installed through 1995, EIA uses a ten-region input-output model to project electricity demand from GNP and population growth, then asses-

ally identical, even though there have been essentially no pro-
cedural barriers to building reactors in Canada. Clearly the cause
of the collapse is far deeper and more universal than mere US
regulatory hassles.

Despite intensive sales efforts, and subsidies often up to or
exceeding total costs[145], the drop in expectations for nuclear

---

ses nuclear capacity reactor-by-reactor, taking account of licensing and construction lead times and financial constraints. Post-1995 installed capacity, however, is
constrained only by 1980 domestic manufacturing capabilities, not by siting,
financing, or demand. Since pre-1978 forecasts supposedly consider how many
plants are likely to be installed, not just how many could be, the 1978–80 data
exaggerate nuclear potential relative to earlier forecasts. The form and earlier data
of this graph are due to C. F. Zimmermann & R. O. Pohl, *Energy 2*:465–471 (1977)
(Pergamon, UK). Year-end operable capacity data (open circles), from EIA, declined from a high of 49.4 GWe at the end of 1978 to 49.1 at the end of 1979 and to
49.0 in mid-1980.

[144]The US Domestic Policy Review of Solar Energy (TID-22834, February 1979, p
iv) estimated US primary wood consumption in 1978 was 1.3–1.8 q. Essentially all
of this was waste wood (bark, liquors, etc) burned at pulp mills with a nominal
efficiency of at least 70%, thus delivering 0.9–1.3 q: nearly all analysts accept the
higher figure. Not included is the estimated 1–2 q (a severalfold expansion since
1977-8) of small-scale firewood burning in tight stoves at a nominal efficiency of at
least 40%, yielding a further minimum of about 0.4–0.8 q. Given the prevalence of
unrecorded nonmarket firewood harvesting for private use, the higher figure may
even be conservative, even though the 1979 Gallup/Wood Energy Institute poll
estimated about 1.0 q: likewise for the pulp mills because of the many new cogeneration projects built since 1978. A total delivered energy around 2.1 q is thus not
unreasonable, and 1.3 q a bare minimum. In contrast, US nuclear power in 1980 is
likely to deliver (after nominal 10% transmission and distribution losses) of order
240 TW-h of electricity with a heat value of 0.8 q.

[145]See e.g. Wohlstetter *et al.*,[13] 77–78; Gall in *Reader*[20] at 173; Long,[21] *id.* 272–96.
Long points out that "Subsidy has been critical to almost all American nuclear
reactor exports": fifty of the sixty received ExImBank loans totalling over $6.5
billion, which had longer terms and, with one exception, a higher proportion of
subsidy than for any other US export. Such practices continue: on 27 September
1979 ExImBank agreed to finance 85% of the US export value of Korea's 7th and
8th nuclear plants at 8% annual interest over 22½ years, thus benefitting Westinghouse by hundreds of millions of dollars. (ExImBank loans for more than 15 years
are informally considered equivalent to grants.) Nuclear loans and guarantees are
about a fifth of ExImBank's total outstanding, though nuclear exports are scarcely
one percent of total US exports (within the "noise"). Other exporting nations,
particularly France and FR Germany of late, offer terms at least as generous;
some deals, notably by Canada, have amounted to paying the "buyer" to haul the
reactor away, especially when "commissions" are included. (Commissions on
Iranian reactors reportedly went as high as 20%: B. Mossavar-Rahmani, "Iran's
Nuclear Power Program: An Update," Rockefeller Foundation (NY) typescript,
July 1979.) Nuclear export subsidies are especially pernicious because they pro-

power has been even faster in developing countries, paced by Iran, which projected twenty-three gigawatts for 1994 and will probably get zero, and by Brazil, which projected seventy-five gigawatts for the year 2000 and now, with its external debt over fifty billion dollars and rising fast, is unlikely to want more than the two gigawatts that are already in serious difficulties. Total nuclear capacity in all developing countries in 1985 is now unlikely to be as much as thirteen gigawatts, or about the present FR German level. Even if giveaway offers tempt new customers (perhaps Mexico, Kenya, Turkey, Zaïre, even Bangladesh) to undertake the well-known problems of integrating gigantic, very costly, complex units into rather small grids in countries poor in infrastructure and averse to colonial dependency relationships, that extra "business" would be a tiny fraction of the loss elsewhere. It would not even be profitable business—only a way to inject export-bank funds via LDC treasuries into domestic vendors' ailing cash flows. It is hard today to find any respectable analyst who even bothers to defend reactor exports to developing countries. The World Bank, with a trivial exception, has yet to finance a nuclear development project. The failure of even such an eager exporter as FR Germany to secure a contract from Brazil without "sweetening" it with both enrichment and reprocessing plants, and unless the German government bore the entire financial risk for the first two reactors (probably all there will be), suggests the wisdom of Congressman Long's proposal that export subsidies be systematically abolished:

For those who profess faith that the profits are there, but perhaps hidden or in the future, here is a chance to prove that faith by putting up their own money. A major objection certain to be raised against curbing

---

duce no economic benefits even to the exporting nation. Under Lerner's Symmetry Theorem, every additional export produces an opposite and approximately equal import. The tendency of floating exchange rates to seek equilibrium cancels any balance-of-payments benefits of export promotion. (See Office of Management and Budget, *Interagency Report on U.S. Government Export Promotion Policies and Programs,* rev. ed., April 1975, Washington DC.) Employment gains likewise cancel or become negative unless the "import rebound" items balancing the export are less labor-intensive—which in the case of nuclear exports is extremely improbable. Resulting job losses may be billed to US taxpayers under the Department of Labor's "Trade Adjustment Assistance" program. Subsidies to exports divert domestic capital from higher-productivity investments, and encourage vendors to raise export prices and so capture the interest subsidy as additional rent. The only significant net economic effect is a transfer of jobs, profits, capital, and cash flow from non-nuclear to nuclear *domestic* industries.

United States subsidy of nuclear energy/weapon proliferation is its economic cost. This bears some resemblance to the objection that abolishing disease will have an adverse economic impact on doctors and nurses. Elimination of nuclear [power] proliferation would in any case be desirable, even without the nuclear weapon issue, simply because nuclear power is economically inappropriate for developing nations. . . .[146]

Indeed, the nation rich enough to afford nuclear power has yet to be found. The vendors and exporting nations—whose competitive commercial interests have supposedly stymied export restraint since they broke down the 1943 Québec Agreement, and inhibited new initiatives at the 1980 NPT Review Conference—have apparently been fighting only for the privilege of throwing away their money.

The collapse of nuclear markets has already sealed the fate of an industry tooled up to meet the inflated expectations of the early 1970s. Even with continued domestic and export subsidies, withdrawals by major firms seem inevitable[147]. While rhetorically the world nuclear enterprise is pressing forward, in reality it is grinding to a halt and even slipping backward as its back orders melt away. Thus

. . . the argument sometimes shifts subtly from the needs of a robust and inexorably expanding industry to the sympathetic care required to keep alive a fragile industry that is on the verge of expiring altogether.[148]

Future technologies whose time has passed

The industry's long-term hope has always been "advanced" plutonium technologies. Even though they have all the fundamental economic and political problems of once-through thermal-reactor fuel cycles—in spades—and offer in compensa-

[146]Long,[145] who represents a legislative program to this end. For support of his final proposition, see Richard J. Barber Associates, *LDC Nuclear Prospects, 1972–1990: Commercial, Economic and Security Implications,* ERDA-52, 1975; Z. Khalilzad, "Nuclear Power and Economic Development: Seven Cases," Pan Heuristics,[8] 1978; and a 1980 study in preparation by P. Hayes, L. Zarsky, & W. Bello, ERG.[130] For an update on Brazil, see N. Gall, *The Ecologist* 230&ff, Oct./ Nov. 1979.

[147]This could be either gradual (M. Lönnroth & W. Walker, "The Viability of the Civil Nuclear Industry," ICGNE,[65] 1980; see also T. Connolly *et al.,* "World Nuclear Energy Paths," *id.,* 1979) or rapid (W. Stoops *et al.,* "Nuclear Energy: Dark Outlook," Bache Halsey Stewart Shields (NY), 1979, summarized in *Energy Daily* 3, 18 December 1979).

[148]For history and sources, see Ch. 1 of GIR.[29]

tion only glamor and a hope of extremely long-term economic improvements far smaller than the "noise" in the price projections, plutonium cycles have long been credited by the credulous with the magical ability to "solve the energy problem." But they have not even gotten off the ground. Their first stage, recycling plutonium in thermal reactors, was supposed to pave the way for fast breeders, but was officially acknowledged in Britain and FR Germany in 1977–78 to save too little uranium to pay for the reprocessing and other costs.[148] Even the INFCE study, generally enthusiastic about plutonium, failed to find recycle inviting. Thermal recycle now appears to be moribund:

Experts representing or closely associated with the nuclear industry now refer to the "consensus" that plutonium recycled for light water reactors is of dubious economic attraction. The opposite notion—that such recycling was essential for economic reasons—was long stubbornly held and has been responsible for much of the appalling diffusion in weapons material which occured over the last decade.[149]

The groundwork for plutonium breeding—which has already inspired imitative "demand" for plutonium technologies in Argentina, Brazil, Pakistan, South Korea, Taiwan, and elsewhere—has quietly sunk into a morass of bad economics and unsolved technical problems. Even its most basic premise—that thermal recycle can significantly stretch the life of a fixed uranium stock—has proved on careful analysis[150] to be untrue for the growing nuclear programs of which it was posited.

Meanwhile, contrary to another argument once widely advanced for prompt reprocessing, INFCE has now concurred in the official positionsnof Canada, the US, and Sweden that reprocessing is not necessary for waste management (though as US arms controllers were reaffirming this abroad, Secretary Schlesinger was denying it on national television). Indeed, evidence is rapidly accumulating—most clearly in the Gorleben report and hearings[151]—that reprocessing LWR fuel probably makes waste

[149]H. Rowen & A. Wohlstetter, *op. cit.*[8]; *cf.* ref. 190.

[150]Notably by G. Rochlin *et al.*[29] For example, recycle saving 25% of uranium needs per reactor would stretch by three years the fueled life of a reactor program growing at 10%/y.

[151]*Op cit.*[29] and Deutches Atomforum e.v., *Rede-Gegenrede,* 1979 (a reprint of the state government's hearing transcript, though remarks originally made in English or French are printed in an unauthorized and not always accurate German translation).

management more difficult and more dangerous. This is because one or two percent of the throughput of plutonium (later greatly augmented by radioactive decay) and of similar very-long-lived transuranic isotopes must inevitably end up in low-level wastes[152], while the rest still exists and must ultimately be disposed of too. The high-level wastes are concentrated into a smaller volume—the price of which is more intense heat generation that interacts awkwardly with geological disposal media— but the total volume of long-lived wastes is greatly increased by the other types. And wholly new categories of intractable wastes are generated, including large releases of tritium (radioactive hydrogen which is both dangerous and hard to isolate), of long-lived and biologically active carbon-14, and of noble gases. It is partly to try to cope with these problems that proposed reprocessing plants are becoming rapidly more complex: the estimated real cost of reprocessing rose roughly thirteenfold during 1973–78 and is still rising.

For fast breeder reactors, that Holy Grail of nuclear power, the prospects likewise dim. Doubts about technical efficiency (the fast reactors built so far scarcely breed), safety[153], feasibility of reprocessing the fuel (intensely hot and radioactive, too high in fissionable content to be handled in normal plants without causing criticality accidents, and rich in insoluble metal granules[154]), and manageability of the tightly coupled plutonium fuel cycle persist, but have been overshadowed by a less arcane problem: on up-to-date data, the basic economics looks dismal for all countries until well into the next century, and probably well into its second half.[155] While the IAEA's Director-General insists that breeder

[152]See note 131. As Rochlin and GIR point out,[29] these and similar wastes are so voluminous that reprocessing expands by at least a factor of two, and in practice often by several factors of ten, the *total* volume of wastes requiring long-term isolation, compared with the total volume of unreprocessed spent fuel after it is "overpacked" in containers supposedly suitable for geologic disposal. (The industry claims to have such container designs for direct disposal of damaged fuel.)

[153]For a concise, not too technical summary of the main safety issues still outstanding, see A. B. Lovins, *New Scientist* 693–95, 14 March 1974.

[154]See note 32. Only trivial (kilogram) quantities of high-burnup breeder fuel have been reprocessed, after longer cooling times than would be economically tolerable in commercial cycles.

[155]B. G. Chow, "Economic Comparison of Breeders and Light Water Reactors," AC8NC113, Pan Heuristics[8] report to US Arms Control & Disarmament Agency, 1979. An update is in preparation. See also M. J. Prior's analysis prepared for the November 1978 South Bank Polytechnic conference, available from the author c/o NCB-IEA Services, 1415 Lower Grosvenor Place, London SW. 1. For precursors, see ref. 74, p 213, n 120.

cycles "must and will be developed", the money to do so, in an era of budgetary constraint, is ever more elusive. The US breeder program limps along with supportive rhetoric but (at least so far) successively deeper budget cuts.[156] The Kalkar project in FR Germany barely squeaked through the Bundestag, has ambivalent official support[157], and will not necessarily be finished. The next-stage British fast reactor receives periodic flurries of ringing speeches but in practice remains in indefinite limbo.[158] Super-Phénix in France has budgetary and technical problems[159], is wooing British money, must probably rely on British plutonium, and is unlikely to be rapidly succeeded by any larger version even if its present problems are overcome. Indeed, L. A. Kochetkov of the USSR State Committee on Atomic Energy, in a recent Lucerne colloquium, seemed to be siding with American speakers in discouraging French haste. While repeating official endorsements of the breeder concept, he noted that in the three experimental fast reactors built in the USSR over the past twenty years, there had been sodium fires in all three and serious fuel damage requiring the reconstruction of one.[160] The fourth is eight years

[156]To $384 million requested for FY1981—still a lot for a post-2050 "insurance policy" applicable to no more than a tenth of primary energy needs.

[157]See ref. 149. The Chancellor has confirmed (*Time*, 11 June 1979) that there is no commitment to the breeder. His party is split: see D. Nelkin & M. Pollak, *Transatlantic Perspectives 1*:8–10 (June 1979) and M. Dönhoff, *Foreign Affairs* 57:1052–64 at 1061 (Summer 1979).

[158]The Government is committed to a thorough public inquiry process whose nature is yet to be determined; but judging from the Windscale experience,[42] it is bound to destroy any remaining credibility either by being obviously "stacked" or by airing the weakness of the proponents' case. In theory, a decision could be made and safety clearance obtained (in secrecy) in about five years, but siting would offer formidable political problems.[283] Besides the general problems of the British nuclear program—stagnant or falling electricity demand, huge overcapacity, soaring prices, no approved reactor designs nor industry to build them nor money to build them with nor sites to build them on—the breeder offers such lavish extra problems that the UK appears unwilling to build the next one alone, and has been sounding out the US (to mutual embarrassment), France, and FR Germany about a possible partnership. See e.g. *The Times* 4, 7 July 1980, and *The Observer*, 29 June 1980 (noting Treasury opposition).

[159]None of these are noted by N. Wade in *Science 209*:884–89 (1980). President Giscard d'Estaing has reportedly told the breeder proponents that France cannot afford another big breeder for very many years at least.

[160]Panel discussion, afternoon of 17 October 1979, "The Breeder Reactor and Europe," Swiss Association for Atomic Energy (SVA, Bern) and Foratom. Of past US fast reactors, two worked satisfactorily while two others suffered serious accidents.[153]

behind schedule. On a realistic political assessment, prospects for
funding and siting the extremely costly next-stage fast breeder
projects range from only fair (in France and the USSR) to poor (in
FR Germany, Japan, the US, and the UK).

The rationale for fast breeders and the basis of their supposed long-term economic advantage over once-through thermal
reactors has always been their far lesser sensitivity to the price of
uranium—even though that is a small component of LWR power
costs anyhow, and breeders would have the compensating disadvantage of considerably higher capital cost. The premise that
uranium will become scarce and extremely expensive, during
periods of policy interest, however, depends on rapid nuclear
power growth which, as we have shown above, is no longer expected to occur. Arguments for rapid breeder development and
deployment are flawed even more deeply:

• The approximately fiftyfold improvement in uranium efficiency which successful fast breeders would achieve (if they can
be built and if plutonium losses elsewhere in the fuel cycle can be
greatly reduced) would take the best part of two centuries to be
realized, since it takes that long for the breeder's fuel cycle to
come to equilibrium[161].

• During the next fifty to eighty years, breeders' much
smaller uranium saving (only severalfold) could be achieved
much more cheaply and surely with uranium-efficient thermal
reactors instead[162]. Compared with present once-through LWRs,
anticipated design improvements for 1990 could save fifteen percent in existing and thirty percent in new LWRs. A presently
commercial heavy-water reactor (e.g. CANDU) with one-
percent-enriched uranium fuel and no reprocessing could save
forty percent. With uranium-235 and -233 recycle, but still throwing away the plutonium, it could save nearly eighty percent.

• These savings not only stretch finite uranium supplies, but
reduce sensitivity to uranium price. If uranium supply increases

[161]A simpler way of describing this problem is that in order to generate the
plutonium needed to start up one GWe of fast-breeder capacity, about 25–30 GWe
of LWRs must be operated for one year (or some equivalent combination of
capacity and time). The plutonium requirements of a breeder *program* are so great
that, in practice, both breeders *and* thermal reactors must operate simultaneously
over a long period for the latter to fuel the former. Their *combined* uranium
consumption therefore remains large for very many decades, even though each
breeder in isolation may need no fissionable uranium (^{235}U).

[162]H. A. Feiveson *et al., Science* 203:330–37 (1979).

only linearly with price[163], a forty percent uranium efficiency gain would increase by one hundred eighty percent—nearly a trebling—the total electricity that could be generated at a given uranium price per kilowatt-hour. The eighty percent uranium saving achievable with non-plutonium, non-breeder fuel cycles using presently commercial reactors would in this sense stretch uranium supplies twenty-threefold.

• As forecasts for uranium demand plummet, systematic exploration is producing sizeable uranium ore discoveries in many countries, thus tending to reduce the likelihood of either geological or political scarcities.

• If uranium scarcity were still a concern, a long-touted advantage of uranium over oil—its cheap storability—could come to the rescue. The carrying charges on a ten-year LEU stockpile (with uranium oxide at forty dollars per pound) would increase delivered electricity prices by less than one percent with the least, or by a fifth of one percent with the most, uranium-efficient thermal fuel cycles.[164] Stockpiling—which Japan is already doing—is thus far cheaper and surer than investing in breeders.

• Even neglecting all these arguments, whatever energy security could be achieved sometime in the 2100s through fast breeders would only address baseload electricity—a tiny part of any country's total energy supply—and would do so at the cost of the added vulnerability inherent in central-electric systems[165].

As the fallacious reasoning underlying a proposition to which thousands of influential nuclear bureaucrats have committed their careers seeps gradually into official consciousness, the extra proliferation costs of breeders are also becoming an embarrassment. Fast breeders require a plutonium inventory of about seven tons per electric gigawatt—both for the initial reactor core and for the "pipeline inventory" pre-placed in its fuel cycle to provide timely replacement fuel—before they can start up. As the Princeton University group (von Hippel, Williams, Feiveson, *et al.*) has pointed out, accumulating this inventory requires a com-

[163]This assumption is probably pessimistic: K. S. Deffeyes & I. D. MacGregor, *Scientific American* 66–76, 1980.

[164]Similar data are summarized by Feiveson *et al.*[162]

[165]Electricity cannot readily be stored in bulk, and the large and precise machines used to generate it must be exactly synchronized—through a frail network of easily severed aerial arteries. Large-scale accidental blackouts (recent examples include New York, France, and Israel) are trivial compared to what a few saboteurs could readily cause.

mitment to reprocessing about a decade before the first big
breeder is to operate, so as to allow time to build the reprocessing
plant. Because of the even longer times needed to build a breeder
population significant for national electric (let alone energy) supply, fast breeders require that a decision to reprocess be made at
least *forty years* before there is even a *possibility* of a uranium
shortage. Once the high cost of reprocessing has been paid, there
is a strong economic incentive to use the plutonium, and a potent
bomb material with insoluble safeguards problems begins to flow
in international commerce. Already, at least eight nations, including Argentina, Brazil, India, and Pakistan, are citing an alleged
need for breeders at some hazy time in the next century as justification for acquiring reprocessing plants now. In contrast, a
lower-cost, lower-risk "evolutionary strategy"[166] would not require even a decision about reprocessing until uranium-efficient
reactors were in widespread use and a uranium shortage was
nonetheless actually occurring. This is because such reactors can
begin with a once-through fuel cycle, then rapidly shift if necessary to uranium recycling. That option would have been left open
by storing the spent fuel (rather than irreversibly chopping it up
and dissolving it); and as Robert Newman, whose responsibilities
at Allied Chemical Corporation include the unlicensed Barnwell
reprocessing plant, remarked[167], it is straightforward to store
zirconium-clad spent fuel (as from LWRs or CANDUs) in pools
for a century or more.

Such cogent arguments are already leading in many countries to a comprehensive lack of enthusiasm for costly, difficult
breeder programs that could commit countries' scarce fiscal and
technical resources to erecting more milestones in a blind
alley—a commercial blunder akin (in von Hippel's simile) to per-
sisting in pushing Concorde while other nations develop jumbo
jets and sweep the market. A further resource squandered could
be political tolerance: further attempts to deploy breeders in an
already hostile climate could easily jeopardize the limited acceptance now enjoyed by thermal reactors[168].

[166]For example, that described in ref. 162. We are not endorsing this or any other
nuclear strategy; only pointing out that it better satisfies breeder proponents'
professed criteria than does their own program.

[167]At 270 in *Rede-Gegenrede*.[151]

[168]Many nuclear advocates implicitly admit this limited acceptance when they
argue that the rapid escalation of nuclear capital costs is due to unnecessary safety
regulations fostered by anti-nuclear organizations. (Those organizations will be
surprised to hear that the regulatory process is responsive to their wishes.) The
thesis carries the awkward implication that the regulators are incompetent play-

The demise of delusions

The loss of momentum for the breeder and for the nuclear programs it was to culminate is reflected at the highest political levels in all the main nuclear countries of OECD and beneath the surface throughout the Soviet scientific community. At various times in the past few years, the British, French, and FR German[169] Cabinets have been sharply split over whether the whole electronuclear program makes sense: Chancellor Schmidt has even speculated aloud that twenty billion marks may have been thrown out the window.

A supposed counterexample often cited—the outwardly vigorous nuclear program in France—on closer examination reflects to the core these political weaknesses. It is proceeding for the moment with a heavy mortgage[170], relying on an autarchic political structure whose stability and legitimacy it is hazarding[171]. Its survival depends on the timely solution of *all* of these formidable problems:

- Cracks in key reactor components are apparently growing,

---

things of an hysterical public; or, more fundamentally, that our political process is not a fit mechanism for deciding how to regulate nuclear technology—reactor safety should instead be left to the industry without "interference."

[169]See note 157. The present Finance Minister agreed in a conversation in 1977 that building more power stations was an uneconomic solution to the German energy problem. Whether it is economic or not, it no longer commands a politically interesting consensus: *Die Zeit* poll, p 3, 13 March 1979. The political fallout from the ÖKO-Institut's scenario for a nuclear- and oil-free FR Germany (F. Krause, "Energieversorgung der Bundesrepublik ohne Kernenergie und Erdöl," 1979, detailed in *Energiewende*[114]) forced the Government's Enquête-Kommission in 1980 to produce two nuclear-free energy scenarios, both of which assume a 2½-fold increase in real economic activity per capita during 1980–2030, but which nonetheless reduce the use of oil and gas by 47% and 77% (for Scenarios III and IV respectively) while increasing the use of coal by only 41% and 20% respectively—no more than in the nuclear scenarios (which reduce oil and gas by only 12% or 44%). See also A. B. Lovins, "Es geht auch ohne das Atom," *Die Zeit* reprint, 1978.

[170]This is the assessment of Bupp and Derian (*op. cit.*[33]), widely regarded as careful and unbiased students of French nuclear politics. Nelkin and Pollak[157] concur.

[171]Sadruddin Aga Khan, "The Nuclear Power Debate in Western Europe," *Bulletin of the Atomic Scientists* 11-12, September 1979, and declaration of the Groupe de Bellerive (Geneva), 31 May 1979. For similar international perspectives, see L. Gerlach, "Energy Wars and Social Change" and "Can Independence Survive Interdependence?" (Dept. of Anthropology, U. of Minnesota, Minneapolis 55455, 1979) and A. B. Lovins, "Democracy and the Energy Mobilization Board," *Not Man Apart* (FOE Inc[29]) 14-15, February 1980.

and no method of repairing them effectively is known. They may reach dangerous size in a few years. LWR reliability has been disappointing.

• Even ignoring its serious loss-of-power accident in 1980, the Cap La Hague reprocessing plant essential to the whole French fuel cycle does not, for all practical purposes, work. Its increasing contamination and maintenance problems are likely to stiffen the opposition of the main nuclear union (Conféderation Française Démocratique du Travail).

• The waste problem must be solved in demonstrable fact, not in unverifiable claims, and including a viable disposal site.

• Export markets must be found to keep the monopoly reactor vendor Framatome solvent: the lost patron in Teheran (who consistently bought French reactors at about twice their internal price, and thoughtfully buoyed up the franc by advancing $1 billion in cash for Eurodif shortly before the French elections) will be hard to replace.

• Rapidly growing electrical demand must be maintained and artificially stimulated—through economically ruinous electric heating contrary to express public policy, there being no other marginal markets of any size available—to keep Électricité de France solvent (the forgiveness of five milliard francs of ÉdF debt to the Treasury in early 1980 will only help temporarily).

• Politically acceptable reactor sites must be found by some means more lasting than having central-government prefects overrule local governments.

• Public acquiescence must be won by some means more legitimate than enforcing the edicts of a governmental and technical elite that is far from monolithic[172].

Each of these problems in isolation might, with considerable luck, be soluble. But the chances of avoiding all hazards—technical, economic, and political—look slim indeed. In France as everywhere else, wherever one looks, the message is the same: no nukes.

[172]The Ministry of Finance has been desperately unhappy with the program for years. It has probably cost over $40 billion to date. A senior Cabinet member asked one of us (ABL) in 1976 to set up a soft-path study for France to test his suspicion that it would look far more sensible than Government policy. (The study was officially agreed, but owing to high-level bureaucratic stalling, is still to get underway despite much negotiation within several Ministries; meanwhile, four less complete private studies have been done and published.) Critics of the program now include the former ÉdF research director, prominent economists and physicists in the bosom of elite universities, the main nuclear labor union (CFDT), the Select Committee of the National Assembly, and increasingly the Socialists (whose last election platform included abandonment of the breeder program

forthwith). Some well-placed French nuclear officials who put the official line vigorously to other governments argue against it within their own, and some are even anti-nuclear activists in their private lives. The Government's task in enforcing a policy with dwindling internal support is unlikely to be simplified by recent developments: the December 1979 national power failure illustrating the grid's fragility; the 15 April 1980 fire which interrupted all electrical power to La Hague (luckily without catastrophic consequences), an accident the operators had just been insisting was impossible; the Government's 1980 insistence on shipping a half-dozen bombs' worth of HEU to Iraq; the Government's need to bribe localities to accept reactors by reducing their electric bills 15% (a practice which, as in Japan, is giving rise to adverse inferences); and a local government's leaking in 1979 of what appears to have been the official emergency plan in case of a major accident: armed troops were to surround the contaminated area and shoot anyone trying to *leave*.

Chapter Six

The Fatuity of US Policy

Magnificently constant in the face of flux, the policy of the United States has been to pretend that the nuclear collapse is not happening, or that if it is, it shouldn't be and deserves no support: indeed, the illusion that it is not happening has been actively propagated. President Carter and Secretary Schlesinger repeatedly projected onto all other countries, even in Summit statements, their own belief in the necessity of nuclear power even after many others had begun to lose faith. The protracted tenure of Dr. Schlesinger and his deputy, Dr. O'Leary (now an official of Three Mile Island's owners), did almost irreparable harm to the accuracy of foreign perceptions of the real status of US nuclear energy and offered ideal ammunition to those anxious to cite the fuel-rich US as authority for bolstering sagging nuclear programs in fuel-poor countries. US promotional rhetoric gave the nuclear industry a license to present on each side of the Atlantic a false but largely uncontested image of a nuclear enterprise in the bloom of health on the other side.

This rhetoric has been reinforced by consistent action. Secretary Duncan has apparently committed two-fifths of the US energy research budget for the next five years to nuclear power, and is proposing major shifts of conservation and solar funds to fast breeders. Far from accepting the accelerating collapse of the US nuclear program as a fact to be reflected in policy, the Carter Administration sent to Congress a bill to "streamline" (bulldoze through) reactor licensing[173]; sought more reactor export subsidies and looser export controls; and began a gratuitous five-billion-dollar expansion of centrifugal enrichment capacity[174] despite plummeting demand forecasts and an INFCE-acknowledged glut. Repeatedly mandated programs of non-nuclear energy aid remained derisory and misdirected: a study meant to identify non-nuclear opportunities for Egypt concluded, not surprisingly, that what Egypt most needed was an American reactor. The Department of Energy was simply preaching what it practices. The

---

[173]This implied acceptance of the industry's view that its problems are artificial and political rather than real and economic—and rejection of DOE's own analysis (by W. Mooz of RAND) showing that there is no significant correlation between licensing delays and reactor costs (an unsurprising finding, since those costs are not sunk until a construction permit has been obtained).

[174]This most proliferative method of enrichment was adopted, regardless of its bad example, as an electricity-saving measure—opening the way for France to argue that it viewed plutonium technologies as an electricity-saving measure too. The US Energy Research and Development Administration had itself classified

State Department, wrongly convinced that once-through LWRs are not significantly proliferative, proclaimed that *not* using nuclear power (in that form) would *worsen* proliferation and *reduce* national security.

Were it not for a widely shared and uncommonly persistent ignorance of non-nuclear energy options within the Administration, especially the State Department, informed analysis of a full range of opportunities might have led President Carter to emphasize the inability of nuclear power in any form and in any country to provide significant oil relief or to help with balance-of-payments or export-industry problems. Instead, in his 7 April 1977 statement, he went out of his way to stress that

Many countries see atomic power as their only real opportunity to deal with the dwindling supplies of oil, the increasing price of oil and the ultimate exhaustion of both oil and natural gas. Our country is in a little better position. We have oil supplies of our own and we have very large reserves of coal. But even coal has its limitations so we will ourselves continue to use nuclear power as a share of our total energy production. The benefits of nuclear power, particularly to some foreign countries that don't have oil and gas of their own, are very practical and critical.

Vince Taylor comments[175]:

This erroneous belief, based on a mistakenly inflated perception of the potential contribution of nuclear power in other countries, . . . has enormously handicapped efforts to gain international agreement to halt development of reprocessing.

While President Carter did raise eyebrows by remarking in the INFCE opening plenary that

I have a feeling that the need for atomic power itself for peaceful purposes has perhaps been greatly exaggerated, and I hope that all of the nations represented here and others will assess alternatives to turning to this source of power, if for no other reasons than because of economic considerations. . . . [T]here is a tremendous cost even for the potential peaceful use of atomic power.[176]

plutonium recycle as an energy conservation initiative!

[175]V. Taylor, "A Review of Recent Efforts to Halt the Spread of Nuclear Weapons: Lessons for the Future", unpublished 25 January 1978 typescript available from Taylor c/o UCS[87]. We gratefully acknowledge our debt to this analysis.

[176]For numerical debate, see the first two *Science* letters cited in note 103. Both Candidate Carter (May 1976 UN speech[5], reprinted at 73, *Reader*[20]) and President Carter in this speech asked whether nuclear power is necessary, but neither ever put in train the analysis needed to answer the question.

He continued, "Even so, we recognize that there will be a need, and we are eager to cooperate." The resulting communiqué established as a central premise of INFCE that nuclear energy for peaceful purposes should be made widely available to meet the world's energy requirements—just the question that should have been examined. The US delegation, dominated by nuclear devotees and virtually devoid of non-nuclear energy experts, never pressed for the end-use assessments that would have shown the economic absurdity of the national extrapolations of nuclear "need." The most critical question was thus begged from the start. Even in August 1980, the US responded to criticism of its supposed lack of vigor in pushing nuclear power by emphasizing at the NPT Review Conference, not that the merits of the technology were no longer obvious, but rather how many countries' nuclear programs were benefitting from American exports of technology and fuel[177].

That the Carter Administration spent four years muffing a unique opportunity to educate the world about past mistakes in energy policy should not deprive it of credit for some important and partly successful initiatives. A polylogue (or Babel) is now underway. The luster of breeder programs has worn off and that of thermal plutonium recycle all but vanished. Exporting reprocessing and enrichment plants is no longer a normal practice within the London Suppliers' Group. The South Korean and Pakistani "purchases"[178] of such facilities (and the Iranian entitlement to them via a nuclear "most-favored-nation" clause linked to US-Japanese concessions) appear to be dead, and their export to Brazil is cast into doubt[179]. (Such exports in the future are apparently to take more devious forms or be replaced by franker exports of directly usable bomb *materials*.) NRC votes are split (though overridden by the President) on such matters as exports to Spain, and fairly solid, with key Congressional sup-

[177]D. Cook, *LA Times* I:4, 13 August 1980.

[178]"Purchase" is a euphemism: as a senior French official remarked before Pakistan withdrew its request, a painless way to scuttle the deal would be to ask Pakistan to pay for the plant.

[179]It appears that functional reprocessing technology is not being delivered to Brazil. The enrichment technology planned for 1986 operation at Rezende is unattractive. (Both plants, for a nuclear program that now seems likely to amount to two plants, seemed to Chauncey Starr like selling a car with an oil refinery to go with it.) Bechtel Corporation, without authorization, offered Brazil gas-diffusion technology in 1975 and was forced to withdraw the offer. A German attempt to deliver centrifuges in the early 1950s was apparently foiled (N. Gall, *Foreign Policy 23*:155-201, Summer 1976). Some Brazilians assert, and the Chairman of the UKAEA denies, that six small British research reactors were shipped to Brazil in 1969 and have not been heard of since.

port, in favor of a fuel embargo against India. HEU research reactors are being redesigned. Phony solutions—CIVEX[180], the French method of chemical uranium enrichment, tandem cycles, "denatured" plutonium and thorium cycles—have been discredited. Weaknesses in NPT/IAEA safeguards are better appreciated. NPT ratifications have reached one hundred fourteen. Most importantly, the world is more sophisticated and more scared.

Yet far greater gains were sacrificed by internal inconsistencies and ambiguities in US policy, exploited by a still powerful domestic industry that remains the core of the world nuclear lobby. The US is of course not the only country to have an incoherent nuclear policy: Soviet bureaucrats once promised India heavy water forever before they were overridden. But the incoherence of the most vital policy initiatives on proliferation since 1953, made by a country whose pluralism supposedly enriches the policy process, is especially deplorable. Many of the same initial errors are still being repeated through failure even now to appreciate them. Fuzzy language—does "foregoing" nuclear power mean phasing out existing plants or merely not building more?—is encouraging fuzzy thinking. Issues that should be reticulated—military nuclear decisions (targeting doctrine, neutron bomb production, MX missiles, cruise missiles), NPT Article VI obligations, horizontal proliferation—are isolated and considered piecemeal. Most disturbingly, much of the unclarity and inconsistency arose from the original statements, made by the most senior sources, of nonproliferation policy—a subject that above all others demands careful formulation.

The reprocessing debacle

President Carter's 7 April 1977 statement of US plutonium policy, for example, neatly self-destructed on the most basic of issues: whether the US encourages or discourages reprocessing. Despite the risks of the uncontrolled spread of bomb capacity via reprocessing, he said,

We can't arrest it immediately and unilaterally. We have no authority over other countries. . . . We are not trying to impose our will on those nations like Japan, France, Britain and Germany, which already have reprocessing plants in operation. They have a special need that we don't

[180]In this hypothetical plutonium cycle, proposed by Chauncey Starr and Walter Marshall, certain medium-lived fission products are left mixed with extracted plutonium to inhibit its misuse for a few years[26]. The cycle would take many decades to implement, is no barrier to governments, and looks otherwise unattractive.

have in that their supplies of petroleum products are not available.*** Obviously, the smaller nations, the ones that have established atomic power plants, have to have someplace either to store their spent fuel or to have it reprocessed, and I think that we would very likely see a continuation of reprocessing capabilities within those nations that I have named and possibly others. We in our country don't have this requirement.

As Vince Taylor remarks[181],

A series of statements less helpful to his own cause [is] difficult to imagine. In effect, the President laid out a line of attack on his own policy that, if based on correct premises, would completely destroy the rationale for his own policy, and then he emphasized the validity of the attack before his critics even had the chance.

Even worse, the premises that the President endorsed were *not* correct. From his self-effacing statements one would never guess that virtually all the spent fuel in Japan (and, to a lesser extent, in Europe) whose reprocessing was in question was and is subject to US veto or control under existing agreements that require US consent for it to be "retransferred" for this purpose. It is precisely that veto power that would have to be exercised, at least *in terrorem,* if reprocessing were to be prevented—and that today looks increasingly notional. Further, at the time he endorsed supposedly existing reprocessing, there was no reprocessing plant for oxide fuel operational anywhere in the world. The small German experimental plant was closed; a small multinational pilot plant in Belgium had long been closed; Japan was building a pilot plant that had not yet opened (it did later after the US granted special retransfer permissions); the English oxide head-end at Windscale had been shut down since a 1973 accident; and the oxide head-end at La Hague, after reprocessing about 75 tons (scarcely over two reactor-years' worth) of relatively low-burnup oxide fuel in 1975, had been closed down to free subsequent stages of the plant to cope with a backlog of corroding metallic fuel[182]. It is only this type of fuel that was being reprocessed in Britain and France; and while this type, produced by a class of gas-cooled reactor that has not been ordered for years and is now considered obsolete, requires reprocessing because otherwise it cannot be safely

---

[181]See ref. 175.

[182]"Magnox"-clad fuel[31] stored in water corrodes in a few years: hence the great difficulties, and union unease at occupational hazards, which constipation at Windscale and La Hague is causing as technical problems in the reprocessing plants cause accumulation of fuel inventories rotting in ponds.

stored[183], that is not the case for the water-cooled reactors now in worldwide use, whose stable ceramic fuel (uranium oxide clad generally in a zirconium alloy) can be stored indefinitely without reprocessing. Thus "on the definition that really mattered, none of the four countries cited by Carter had reprocessing plants in operation."[184] And finally, the President's linkage of reprocessing with energy security flew in the face of the analyses on which his subordinates were later to attempt to rely in explaining his policy to its critics.

Although the President's key sentence referred to the risk of spreading "sensitive technologies which entail direct access to . . . weapons usable material", he said nothing further about the material itself, leaving dangerously unresolved the ambiguity about whether it is reprocessing plants or their plutonium products that are of prime concern. This key ambiguity was later deepened by the Administration's qualified support[185] for reprocessing with palliative variants such as coprocessing[186], other non-Purex processes, and multinational plants.

Since the British knew that the President's endorsement of their reprocessing must have taken account of their previously announced plans for the vast expansion of the Windscale plant to provide oxide-fuel export reprocessing, they naturally took the opportunity to bolster their proposal, which at the time enjoyed far from complete Cabinet support, by cynically misconstruing his speech as a hint that if they expanded the plant, the US would grant the necessary retransfer permissions. A medium-level State Department "clarification" was so weak that it was widely taken

---

[183]At the Wylfa reactors in North Wales, Magnox spent fuel is stored in dry carbon dioxide gas, not in a water pool, and does not significantly deteriorate. It may be possible to arrest corrosion of pool-stored Magnox fuel by transferring it to dry gas storage, but so far nobody seems interested.

[184]See ref. 175.

[185]L.V. Nosenzo's testimony to USHR Committee on Science and Technology, Subcommittee on Energy Research & Production, 31 October 1979, contemplates new reprocessing plants, "if and when…justified", which "should incorporate appropriate technical and institutional barriers to proliferation", such as

> . . . co-processing, co-conversion, mixed oxide fabrication at the plant site and advanced safeguards. Retention of fission products in the reprocessing stream or pre-irradiation and 'spiking' might also be considered. These latter steps create special handling, safeguards, and accounting problems that need to be carefully weighed against non-proliferation benefits. . . .

They are also known not to work[36].

[186]Producing pre-mixed oxides[34] or their nitrate precursors, rather than separate plutonium and uranium output streams.

as confirmation. Japan, which was largely financing the expansion of which it is to be the main customer, applied concerted pressure from the other end by making retransfer approvals for its Tokai Mura pilot reprocessing plant and for two utility shipments (one to Britain and one to France) a test of US-Japanese bilateral relations. The US did not respond that it viewed the matter similarly, but granted the approvals subject to face-saving and essentially meaningless conditions. The Windscale and La Hague expansions, the former still only on paper and both reversible even today (albeit at higher political cost than in 1977) by a gesture of US determination, are growing from infancy to adolescence, gaining momentum and committing resources as US policy rots from within. By late 1979, Japan was sufficiently encouraged by US leniency to announce plans for a wholly new, full-scale reprocessing plant to be commissioned around 1990. The US was not heard even to whimper.

At first, the qualifications and accommodations meant to make the 1976–77 US policy initiatives more palatable to allies were so framed as to be mistaken—or, with some ingenuity, mistakeable—for the policy itself. Acknowledgments of the strict diplomatic "right" of sovereign states to reprocess fuel of non-US origin for existing plants was taken to foreshadow US approval of retransfers of US-enriched fuel for future reprocessing plants. Short-term approvals of limited retransfers were taken to indicate a policy of future approvals without limit—especially when the "case-by-case" and "showing of need" procedures turned out in practice to mean every case and every "showing", however transparently trumped-up and unpersuasive. Expedient exceptions evolved, then supplanted their rules. Other nations have found it impossible to avoid the conclusion that US failure to correct these misinterpretations emphatically and at the highest level means they are de facto the new US policy, and that previous implications to the contrary were mere rhetoric for domestic political consumption. In short, the 1977 presumption against reprocessing of US-enriched spent fuel at first admitted exceptions in case of urgent need, then all exceptions asked for; then, in 1980, the ship deserted the sinking rats: Ambassador Gerard Smith, in a still-classified memorandum[187], reportedly asked that the exceptions be formally made the rule. Thus US complicity continues in the commitment of resources, time, and national

[187]R.J. Smith, *Science* 208:478 and :1352-3 (1980). For history, see Senator Glenn's letters to President Carter, 8 March (with others) and 15 September 1978. The US nuclear industry is now using this apparent acquiescence in reprocessing abroad as an argument for reprocessing at home. The State Department is trying to shield its policy collapse from independent review.

prestige to still more nuclear Concordes which threaten in the 1990s to unleash upon the world a veritable flood of commercial plutonium.

Breeding false hopes

At face value, the US initiatives of 1976–77 were a relatively timid attempt to win a deferral or, in due course, an abandonment of thermal plutonium recycle in return for an offer of continued support for "research and development" involving the more distant prospect of fast breeder reactors. Yet this activity ostensibly justifies present reprocessing commitments on a scale and with an immediacy indistinguishable from those of thermal recycle. While some US officials apparently hope that more mature reflection, during the time won by deferring recycle, will consign breeder programs to deserved oblivion, the same officials' emphasis on the legitimacy of initial, "experimental" breeder deployment in any country which, in its sovereign subjectivity, considers this advantageous is a rationalization implicitly supporting the result it anticipates. From the start, the US, consolidating the early disadvantage of its doctrinaire pro-nuclear position, has "left unchallenged—apparently in the belief that they are not susceptible to challenge— . . . the most outrageous assertions of other countries about the necessity of the breeder."[188] Other countries correctly argued that the US had long encouraged their breeder programs, then fallaciously argued that those programs remain necessary and desirable. Rather than rebutting the fallacies, US spokesmen confirmed them, re-emphasizing the falsehood that breeders could "eventually make a substantial contribution to energy needs and independence from imports"[189] and amiably agreeing that the US, too, finds breeders an essential "insurance policy". As Assistant Secretary Pickering described the position[190]:

[188]See ref. 175. J.S. Nye, in his 3 October 1977 Bonn speech "Nuclear Power Without Nuclear Proliferation," stated: "We are not antibreeder. . . . Indeed, even without the Clinch River Breeder, President Carter proposed to spend some $450 million in this fiscal year on breeder research."

[189]T. Pickering, 12 March 1979 speech to Atomic Industrial Forum (Atlanta). Likewise, Nosenzo[185] states:
> Devotion of resources in the near-term to plutonium production and development of [the breeder] is . . . justified only in states with significant economic resources and that look to nuclear power to supply a large percentage of their energy needs. . . .

but many will read this without the "only".

[190]T. Pickering, response to ref. 8, sent 3 October 1979 to Senator Glenn.

We are, as in 1977, still seeking a deferral of commitments to commer-
cialization of plutonium use, at least until such time as they may become
advantageous on economic and resource grounds and less susceptible to
non-proliferation risk (which in all or most countries is not soon and
maybe never, particularly in the case of thermal recycle). . . . Along with
other energy options, we are engaging in a fast breeder R&D program
required to establish and evaluate options and clarify technical, proliferation and other questions as a basis for future decisions.

Carefully read, this statement is subject to almost eliminative
qualifications. The economic criteria proposed for breeder decisions and for their timing are so weak and vague that almost any
nation can meet them, as India has already claimed to do. If a
nation with America's wealth, skills, and fuels thinks it needs a
breeder program "to establish and evaluate options", countries
lacking those advantages can hardly be expected to reach a different conclusion. If a country as concerned with the risks of
proliferation as the United States claims to be does not internalize
their cost in deciding what is "advantageous on economic and
resource grounds", it can expect other nations, too, to value
those costs implicitly at zero.
    Throughout the short unhappy life of the Ford-Carter anti-
proliferation policy, internal equivocation, even disloyalty, has
undercut efforts at home and credibility abroad as domestic
plutonium advocates in and out of government have informally
encouraged other governments to withhold cooperation until US
policy "extremists" (i.e. those seeking to carry out what appeared to be clear Presidential directives) could be brought to
heel. As officials loyal to the expressed policy found themselves
the repeated victims of incremental, unannounced shifts in that
policy, formulation and implementation passed gradually into less
sympathetic hands. Promise began to wither short of fulfillment.
As the Nuclear Non-Proliferation Act's requirements (which the
Administration had opposed) for full-scope safeguards and
EURATOM renegotiations ripened, they were threatened with
waiver.
    In 1976–77, many officials were reluctant to say
squarely—because the implications scarcely bore thinking
about—that bomb materials are dangerous and cannot be
safeguarded, hence that fast breeders and reprocessing are proliferative per se. They had therefore retreated early to weaker
arguments against embracing the inevitable *prematurely*—as determined by infinitely arguable economic calculations valuing
bomb risks at zero. By 1979, the metamorphosis to mush was
complete. Internationally supervised storage of spent fuel and of

"excess" plutonium beyond that "required" for breeder development was no longer described as "essential" but merely as "preferable." The State Department was saying less about prematurity, more about US enthusiasm for unabated breeder development with a view to limiting later deployment to large and wealthy countries[191]; less about not doing things acknowledged[192] to be unsafeguardable, more about cosmetic "multinational control" of those things; less about timely warning, more about vague "institutional arrangements". Though the US position that separated plutonium is not safeguardable in principle is claimed not to have changed, it is no longer articulated. Despite an expressed belief that "existing reprocessing capacity is adequate for a substantial period"[192], manyfold expansions are being given at least tacit encouragement. In practical effect, the emerging post-INFCE policy differs only in detail and efficiency from that of the Nixon Administration—save in its degree of forthrightness about its goals and methods.

Finding the fulcrum

The officials responsible for these blunders were not necessarily fools or knaves; but they were beyond doubt prisoners of the illusion, propagated for so long by their own agencies, that nuclear power is necessary and its expansion inevitable. This illusion was reinforced by the appearance of outrage and solidarity—an appearance skilfully orchestrated by the US nuclear industry—that representatives of other nations mustered whenever the adequacy of the emperor's new clothes was questioned. Yet the State Department did not know, and even today seemingly does not want to know, that however monolithic this policy front may appear, every national nuclear power policy is riven from top to bottom by doubt and dissent. Whatever the United States has done, in policy or in rhetoric, has helped one side of those internal debates and hurt the other. The State Department, maintaining a meticulously lopsided neutrality, has never appreciated that the most powerful US lever for affecting

[191]Thus intensifying developing countries' resentment at supplier discrimination (Chapter Nine). Wohlstetter *et al.*[13] list fast breeder projects operating, being built, or planned (as of a few years ago) in seven non-weapons states: Brazil, FR Germany, India, Iraq (like Brazil, planned under a 1975 French contract), Italy, Japan, and Spain. Many other developing countries claim to contemplate breeder programs, citing as authority the OECD countries' programs and the 1976 IAEA projections that by 1990 some 46 countries would "need" plutonium.

[192]Nosenzo[185] states that "the NPT, existing safeguards methods and existing institutional arrangements, cannot adequately deal with a situation in which separated plutonium or other weapons-grade material is in widespread use. . . ."

foreign nuclear policies in either direction is not blunt instruments like fuel supply, but rather the *political example* of stated and applied US energy policy in its broadest terms. The greatest instrument of influence still lies unused and all but unseen. It is only when a lesser nation grasps it—as in the Austrian referendum, with its political fallout in Switzerland, FR Germany, and Scandinavia—that governments notice that the power of example, a power they hope to harness by citing France, can work both ways. US technological dominance of the nuclear arena, though still preeminent, is no longer hegemonic; but US political dominance of world energy policy still is essentially hegemonic, and has so far been exercised in exactly the wrong direction.

Ignoring the profound influence of the US example on internal politics abroad, hence on how other nations' domestic political constraints permit them to *use* their technical capabilities, advocates of continuing subsidized nuclear exports and services have argued that if the United States does not supply proliferative capabilities and support nuclear power by offering technologies and materials, others will, so the US might as well—and, simultaneously, that since others can, the US has no "leverage" to justify abstention and should therefore again ship the same items. The former argument—the same discreditable one used to defend eighteenth-century British slaving as essential to protect the slaves from the less humane French—presumes that others will ignore the mutual advantages of restraint; it would be more persuasive if any country had found nuclear exports profitable; and above all it assumes that foreign governments have complete freedom of action without regard to the domestic politics that the US example would influence. The latter argument reflects the inconsistent view—embodied, despite outwardly strict statutory language, in actual US behavior towards proliferators (India, Israel) and reprocessors (Japan, UK, France)— that "we can retain our leverage only if we never use it. A lever is a form of abstract art rather than a tool giving us a mechanical advantage."[193]

Today the United States proclaims itself anxious to be seen as a "reliable supplier" of nuclear fuels and equipment, swells the enrichment glut to take on new fuel export contracts, and seeks via an international Fuel Bank to make those export commitments irrevocable. Yet at the same time the US asks itself, half

[193]Rowen and Wohlstetter, *op. cit.*[8] The USHR Committee on International Relations likewise called for aggressive US leadership in its report 94-1469, 2 September 1976. The US did exert strong and so far apparently successful leverage on South Korea, but it was not nuclear leverage. With such client states, nuclear leverage is not needed; with others, it apparently cannot be used.

aloud, how much "leverage" it can obtain by exporting more US-fueled reactors as hostages to later sanctions, i.e. with an eye to later becoming an "unreliable" supplier. Having reawakened to some basic facts of nuclear physics and proliferation politics, the US sought to assert some slight "leverage" via fuel supplies—the bare hint of whose exercise reversed French and German positions on export of fuel-cycle facilities—and now seeks both to expand the potential scope of that leverage and to renounce forever its potential application. But both instruments, fuel exports and reactor exports, leave the US in the unpalatable position of proliferating vigorously in the name of nonproliferation, sacrificing for a weak and counterproductive physical lever-age[194] a strong and positive political leverage.

How real is that political leverage, that ability to influence by announced energy policy the domestic political currents and the perceived competitive environment of other countries? An event in 1979 strikingly illustrates the political vulnerability of major nuclear projects and vindicates those who urged the State Department to bolster its lukewarm opposition to proposed European reprocessing expansions. While the Department, citing sensitive alliances, was fumbling low-cost opportunities to scuttle nascent reprocessing projects in the UK, France, and Japan be-fore still-fluid political commitments had solidified behind them, the FR German government was making an apparently firm commitment, allegedly crucial for national survival, to build an enormous reprocessing and waste-disposal plant at Gorleben in Lower Saxony. Yet behind the outward solidity there were doubts[195], and to defuse local opposition and preserve his own

---

[194]As Senator Ribicoff notes (*Foreign Affairs* 54:764, 1976), only Canada has had the political determination to be "the first nuclear supplier to place itself at a commercial disadvantage [for nonproliferation goals] . . . an example that serves to discredit US . . . policy." Canada, which supplies most of the uranium en-riched by the US for export, cut off uranium and heavy-water supplies to India and Pakistan, and caught even major European allies in tightened safeguards. *Cf* B. Goldschmidt & M. B. Kratzer, "Peaceful Nuclear Relations: A Study of the Creation and the Erosion of Confidence", ICGNE[65], 1978.

[195]Bonn had long assumed that reprocessing was the only way to deal with spent fuel, and had studied no other options. Reactor licensing was legally constrained without some appearance of progress towards solving the waste problem, and for the tottering domestic vendor Kraftwerkunion to stay in the nuclear business, export orders were deemed essential which apparently could not be won without "sweetening" with offers of reprocessing (i.e. plutonium-exporting) services, which Bonn therefore had to appear to be preparing to provide. (Assurances had been given that Gorleben was not for export use, but doubtless its large excess capacity could create an economic argument for breaking that promise later.) Under this compulsion, although the German chemical industry had previously

political options, the Governor of Lower Saxony commissioned a technical review by an ad hoc panel of twenty independent experts from five countries. Their report was so comprehensively devastating, and emerged so unscathed from six days of unprecedented and highly publicized adversarial hearings in Hannover[196], that neither the Chancellor's own party in Lower Saxony nor, privately, the project's promoters could defend it, and Bonn had to cancel it outright. If a mere report and hearing with no official resources behind them can be the catalyst that nucleates enough domestic opposition to kill a supposedly irrevocable national commitment, what political leverage might a country—especially the United States—apply even within the context of a wider bilateral agenda, by the example of its whole energy policy? It is to this realm of "insurmountable opportunities"[197] in energy policies—innovations that both meet pragmatic goals and fire the imagination—that we turn next.

---

declined to enter the reprocessing business on economic grounds, Bonn told the waste-management consortium DWK to whip up a quick safety/feasibility report, which other Federal agencies rubber-stamped, for an $8 billion integrated fuel-cycle center: a reprocessing plant more than twice as big as the proposed Windscale expansion, plus plants for mixed-oxide fuel fabrication (for thermal recycle and perhaps breeder fuel), waste treatment, and final disposal on-site in underground salt beds. Salt implied a site in Lower Saxony, whose Christian Democratic governor, Ernst Albrecht, chose a site at Gorleben within catapult range of the East German border—a polite way of saying he didn't want it. Bonn, desperate to have the plant approved, abandoned its previous site criteria and said Gorleben would be fine, but Albrecht would have to find that it could be safely built. Albrecht, not overeager to help the Social Democratic Federal government out of a hole, commissioned the Gorleben International Review[29] as a gesture towards local opponents.

[196]The hearings[151], precisely contemporaneous with the Three Mile Island accident, were chaired by Carl-Friedrich von Weizsäcker at the personal request of Chancellor Schmidt. Governor Albrecht attended consistently and often interjected incisive questions. Probing and extensive TV and newspaper coverage intensified local concerns, leading to a peaceful demonstration by 100,000 of Albrecht's constituents, largely members of his own party—conservative farmers who rightly suspected Bonn had misled them about the project's "necessity"and risks. DWK declined to defend their own report, imported US and other non-German advocates largely unfamiliar with the papers to do so for them, and were reduced to watching the hearings on closed-circuit TV from another room in the same building and issuing press releases saying they didn't take the safety report too seriously themselves. Some DWK officials privately agreed with much of the GIR critique. The hearings discredited all the Federal nuclear agencies, confirmed the need for critical international review of major nuclear proposals, and marked a major—and apparently irreversible—innovation in German process.

[197]W.K. Davis (Bechtel Corporation), 6 December 1979 speech as summarized by British Nuclear Energy Society, *Energy World 67*:15 (February 1980). See also D. Rose & R. Lester, *Reader*[20] 391.

Chapter Seven

How To Save Oil

To this point we have been balancing the dangers of nuclear power's crucial contribution to the spread of nuclear bombs against its necessarily limited role in total energy supply and against the mounting evidence that even in that limited role nuclear power does not make economic sense. (It also raises serious safety and social issues on which it is hardly necessary to dwell.) The balance is overwhelmingly negative, and should in itself lead one to conclude that it is time to phase out nuclear power once and for all. This dawning realization has already made the future of fission power so precarious that a change in policy by the United States or by several other countries would start a political chain reaction of similar shifts worldwide: the more so because the issue is not whether to maintain a thriving enterprise, but rather whether to accept the verdict of the very calculations on which competitive market economies rely.

But to make a fully rounded presentation, we need to consider what is affirmatively needed to meet the world's energy needs, and especially to relieve the dependence on dwindling, insecure, and unsupportably costly oil imports that is now among the world's leading sources of hardship and instability. The world economic and political system is indeed headed toward disaster from too little oil and too many bombs. We agree with proponents of nuclear power that these problems are related. We seek, however, not to exacerbate them—by inefficiently replacing oil while expeditiously spreading bombs—but to solve them jointly by rapidly reducing reliance on both oil *and* uranium.

Many nuclear advocates assert with some heat that both national and world security require widespread pursuit of vigorous nuclear power programs to "validate the nuclear option"—or at least "keeping the nuclear option alive" by continuing to expand it (a self-fulfilling prophecy of the inevitability of the "option"). To do otherwise, they assert, exchanges for the "trivial" risks of extra proliferation "the risks [of war] in a world struggling for growth in the face of inadequate and poorly distributed sources of energy."[197] This perilous policy ignores the contrary evidence that nuclear power in fact heightens these oil-linked risks of war in three ways:

• it slows the displacement of oil by foreclosing or retarding cheaper and faster options—especially sources of energy (mentioned below) which, unlike fossil fuels or uranium, are distrib-

uted freely, equitably, automatically, and daily throughout the world;
- it creates serious new international conflicts over uranium, fuel-cycle services, and technologies; and
- it unavoidably and incontinently spreads bombs, innocent disguises for bombs, and the ambiguous threat of bombs that motivates rivals to acquire them, thus reducing (as we shall argue in Chapter Nine) the security even of those nations that do acquire them.

These extra risks are far larger than all those that currently dominate the debate about which energy sources to choose[198]; and if one adds them up and imagines how they feed on each other, a more destabilizing formula could hardly be imagined. How, then, can the oil saving so central to security and world peace be reliably achieved without nuclear power? Broadly speaking, the important oil-saving measures are distressingly simple: stop driving Petropigs and stop living in sieves[199].

[198]This is vividly illustrated by J. P. Holdren[130] in "Cross-Cutting Issues in Integrated Environmental Assessment of Energy Alternatives: Distribution of Costs and Benefits", ERG-WP-80-10, March 1980, Table 1. For example, if the extra proliferation caused by nuclear power increased by 10% the probability of a thermonuclear war killing 10^9 people during 1980-2010 only (ignoring subsequent risks), and if that probability were already 0.1, then the incremental 10^7 deaths, distributed over perhaps 500-1000 q (1 q $\equiv$ 10^{15} BTU of primary energy), would yield of order 10,000-20,000 deaths per quad. The Rasmussen Report's best estimate is only 4 cancer deaths per quad from reactor accidents (neglecting sabotage), with most upper-limit estimates in the literature only one or two orders of magnitude larger. Total nuclear risks integrated over all future populations, based on official assessments that neglect proliferation and sabotage risks (and dominated by long-term radon releases from present tailings-disposal practice and carbon-14 emissions), are about 1,200-8,000 deaths per quad: Ramsay & Russell[130]. In contrast, if CO_2-induced climatic change from burning a tenth of world coal resources (about a 50% increase in atmospheric CO_2 content) risked a 10% chance of a famine killing 10^9 people, a 50% chance of one killing 10^8 people, and a 40% chance of no significant deaths, the risk would be about 6,500 deaths per quad. The 80% confidence interval for deaths from SO_2 releases (3%S coal, 80% removal) is 0-500 deaths per quad: the same order of magnitude as is plausible for subnational acquisition of nuclear bombs (one bomb per decade to 2010 with 10^5 deaths per bomb would be $\geq$300 deaths/q).

[199]This Chapter and the next one necessarily simplify a complex subject, attempting to summarize its flavor without being able to do justice to its rich technical detail. Supporting data and primary references can be found in the back issues (1978-) of the bimonthly journal *Soft Energy Notes*, available from IPSEP, 124

Recycling the Petropigs

Cars use about half of all US oil, about a sixth of European and Japanese oil[200]. The one hundred million US cars, a third of the world fleet, use a ninth of all world oil consumption. An average car today gets, in round numbers, about fifteen miles per US gallon in North America, about twenty to twenty-five in Europe and Japan. The average new domestic car sold in the US in 1979 got about nineteen, the average import about thirty-two—a sixth better than the Congressionally mandated average standard for 1985 models[201], and a little better than a tanklike diesel Mercedes gets today. A diesel Rabbit, with only a tenth less interior space than the average US model-year 1978 car, averages about forty-two miles per gallon, its successor model about sixty-four. Volkswagen has already tested a four-passenger advanced diesel car with measured EPA composite efficiency of

---

Spear St, San Francisco CA 94105. Issues 1-7 are reprinted free by USDOE as DOE-PE-0016/1, available from Office of Solar Policy, Office of Policy & Evaluation, Mail Stop 7E-088, USDOE, Forrestal Building, Washington DC 20585. Other primary sources are cited in A. B. Lovins, "Economically Efficient Energy Futures"[97], *Soft Energy Paths* [74], and "Soft Energy Technologies"[103].

[200]In Europe, most of the oil is used for low-temperature heating (which is, for example, half of all delivered energy needs in FR Germany[104]) and for industrial heat. In Japan, industry dominates, and oil must be saved chiefly by efficiency improvements there—for which there is surprising scope, since energy has been subsidized even more heavily in Japan than in the US, and cost less in Japan until 1973. (See Mitsubishi Research Institute Inc (1-8-1 Yuraku-cho, Chiyoda-ku, Tokyo 100), "Assessing Incentives Created by the Japanese Government to Stimulate Energy Production", final report to USDOE, showing a 1946-76 net subsidy totalling 37 x 10^{12} Yen in 1976 Yen, and Institute of Energy Economics, "Present State and Future Potential of Energy Conservation in Japan", 1979, summarized in *Soft Energy Notes* 3(l):12-13 (February 1980).) The main transitional role of coal, too, should be to replace oil and gas under industrial boilers, especially with cogeneration[117], not in new power stations. This will not entail a vast expansion of world coal-mining or trade if cost-effective efficiency improvements are done first. Indeed, even the early stages of expansion of coal-mining in much of the American West have already outrun their domestic market as higher energy prices spur efficiency gains.

[201]The 1985 standard, averaged over each manufacturer's sales, is 27.5 mi/US gal EPA composite, but since the EPA test overstates actual efficiency, the average on-the-road efficiency may only be about 20 mi/gal. (Further, there are effectively no fuel efficiency standards for light trucks, whose US sales are 30% those of cars and whose efficiency averages a fifth worse.) If every car sold in the US in early 1980 had been as efficient as the best in its class, the average car sold would have gotten an EPA mileage of not 21.4 but nearly 37 mi/gal.

seventy to eighty miles per gallon[202]. A big, comfortable car using either an infinitely variable transmission[203] or a diesel-electric series hybrid drive[204] would readily do better than that, as European prototypes have already done, even without using existing technologies for very lightweight but crashworthy body design[205]. A car fleet only as efficient as present imports to the US—which need not entail any loss of size, comfort, or performance—would displace about half as much oil as the US imported in 1979 from the Gulf. A fleet of cars and light trucks averaging a hundred

[202]The compact car has a 1.2-liter supercharged diesel which shuts off on idle or coast, then restarts in 0.2 seconds when the accelerator is depressed. VW is developing, in a four-year program with FR German Government aid, a subcompact/compact (larger than the Rabbit) low-drag car with 1430-pound curb weight, a similar small diesel, composite efficiency over 65 mi/gal, and safety and emission characteristics within all US requirements. See F. von Hippel, "Forty Miles a Gallon by 1995 at the Very Least!," PU/CEES-104, 1980, Center for Energy & Environmental Studies, Princeton U., Princeton NJ 08540; R. H. Williams, "A $2 a Gallon Political Opportunity," PU/CEES-102, 1980; and *Soft Energy Notes 3* (4): 2-5 (August/Sept. 1980). VW has turned over to USDOT for testing an experimental safety car with composite 60 mi/gal, 1.5-liter turbocharged (20 extra horsepower) 4-cylinder diesel Rabbit engine with 5-speed manual transmission, 2072-lb (942-kg) curb weight, very low emissions, 0-60 mi/h acceleration in 13.5 s, and excellent passenger protection in 40 mi/h crashes. (The 64 mi/gal version mentioned in the text is a turbocharged diesel Rabbit with the engine downsized for unaltered performance.) See Volkswagen of America (Englewood Cliffs NJ), undated "IRVW" press release. British Leyland has reportedly achieved 100 mi/gal with a Rabbit-sized car having a fairly conventional powerplant but exceptionally low rolling resistance, though the test conditions may be different.

[203]These are typically 90+% efficient and permit the engine to run at constant speed in its optimal-efficiency range. One model, developed with Borg-Warner, is about to be adopted by Fiat; some even simpler ones are undergoing prototype tests.

[204]In this design, a diesel engine runs a generator which charges a few ordinary batteries which run drive motors. The batteries power acceleration and recharge with deceleration. The diesel, meeting only the average load at constant speed and torque, is small, clean, and extremely efficient. (It can also be replaced by a fuel cell.) Neither conventional fueled cars nor pure-electric cars (in the absence of very cheap photovoltaics) are likely to be able to compete even in principle with the series hybrid—the latter because the hybrid replaces over a ton of high-density batteries with an inherently lighter, smaller, cheaper, longer-lived motor-generator set, yet provides all the same advantages.

[205]Estimates at the CalTech Jet Propulsion Laboratory suggest that a large, crashworthy car with energy-absorbing crushable foam components need weigh only about 1200 pounds (or about 800 pounds if juggernauts are not on the road to crush it, or if speed limits are replaced on multi-lane roads by kinetic-energy limits in which allowed speed varies roughly as the inverse square of vehicle mass). Most recent studies of car safety as a function of size and mass neglect the small cars' greater maneuverability and what can be done with good design[202].

miles per gallon—not at all an unrealistic prospect[206]—would save over five million barrels of oil per day, or about two-thirds of all 1979 US net oil imports.

For any country, accelerated turnover of the car and light truck stock would provide major, quick and cheap[207] relief of oil import dependence—and great benefits to a domestic industry now under such siege that within this decade only five automakers may be left in the world. The car stock normally takes about ten years to turn over, and the collapse of trade-in value for North American gas-guzzlers has only accelerated their filtering down to poor people who can least afford to run or replace them. But these obstacles can be overcome. Rather than building synthetic-fuel plants, it would be much quicker and cheaper to save oil by using the same funds to pay anywhere from half to all of the cost of giving people *free* diesel Rabbits or Honda Civics (or an equivalent American car if Detroit would make one) in return for scrapping their Brontomobiles to get them off the road. Alternatively, it would be quicker and cheaper to save oil by giving cash grants approaching two hundred dollars for every mile per gallon by which a new car improves on a scrapped gas-guzzler[208]. For

[206]Based on a calculation from first principles by C.L. Gray Jr. *et al.*: *Soft Energy Notes, op. cit.*[202]. Details will appear in the SERI study [216].

[207]Retooling Detroit for two generations of cars over the next decade would normally cost of order $50 billion (von Hippel[202]). If a crash program to do so with greatly altered designs—similar to the US car industry's switch to jeep and tank production in less than a year at the start of World War II—incurred *additional* retooling and retraining costs of $100 billion, surely an overestimate, it would still be worthwhile. US oil imports, at least three-quarters of which are attributable to cars and light trucks, will be nearly $100 billion in 1980 alone. An extra charge of $100 billion spread over a completely new fleet (100 million cars and 30 million light trucks) would average $770 per vehicle. A new car driving 10,000 mi/y and getting 100 mi/gal rather than the present 15 mi/gal would save 567 gal/y, yielding a *one-year payback* if the fuel saved cost $1.36/gal—about the present price of gasoline that averages costly foreign oil with cheaper domestic oil.

[208]An average US car annually goes about 10,000 miles and uses about 17 barrels of crude oil equivalent. A marginal one-mile-per-gallon improvement saves about one barrel per year and gives, at a $200 cost, a five-year payback against delivered synfuels (over $40/bbl): see e.g. *The Economist*, 6 October 1979 (Bechtel estimates $40–60/bbl). The worst cars would pay back faster; better ones, more slowly. A bounty should also be offered, based on inefficiency and expected remaining lifetime, for scrapping gas-guzzlers without replacing them. Scrapping in either case should probably include a requirement of metal recycling, since the energy needed to build a big car from virgin materials is about the same as its present average fuel consumption for one year. For a more sophisticated study of the cost of marginal efficiency improvements, see the TRW analysis by Gorman and Heitner summarized in *Soft Energy Notes*[202]. A seemingly contrary 1980 conclusion by the Mellon Institute's Energy Productivity Center[113] assumed competition with $27/bbl synfuels, a most implausible prospect.

once, what is good for General Motors might be good for the world. For a US car industry that has lost money on its 1980 model year and sees imports about to take thirty percent of its domestic market, and for a United Auto Workers union hit hard by plant closures, there is clearly an incentive to promote such measures. Replacing all US cars with hybrids getting a modest sixty miles per gallon (achievable now using off-the-shelf components in a big, nearly two-ton car) would save almost four million barrels of oil per day—half the 1979 rate of net US oil imports, greater than imports from the Gulf, two and a half Alaskan North Slopes, eighty big synfuel plants, or several pre-1979 Irans. (Similar action with light trucks would save a further one and a half million barrels per day, about equivalent to one North Slope.) Precisely the same logic applies in other countries.

Stuffing up the sieves

Analyses in the United States, United Kingdom, and Denmark have shown that an elementary program of systematically applied building "retrofits" (making old buildings efficient), cost-effective at present fuel prices, would save half to two-thirds of space-heating energy without coming anywhere near technical or economic limits.[209] The US alone could save half its space-heating oil and gas—equivalent to two and a half million barrels of oil per day—by the mid-to-late 1980s, much of it just by stopping up the holes, totalling a square yard, in each typical dwel-

[209]See A.H. Rosenfeld et al., "Building Energy Compilation and Analysis," LBL-8912, Lawrence Berkeley Laboratory (Berkeley CA 94720), 1979 (updated version to be published late 1980, *Buildings and Energy*) and the detailed national studies by Sant[113], Leach[114] (relying on a separate volume chiefly by R. Romig), Krause[114], and Nørgård[114].

[210]M. Ross & R. H. Williams, "Drilling for Oil and Gas in our Buildings,"PU/CEES-87[202],1979, and its cited case-studies, including the remarkable Twin Rivers retrofits by the Princeton group (R.H. Socolow, ed., *Saving Energy In the Home*, Ballinger (Cambridge MA), 1979).More precisely, US buildings currently use for all purposes about 13 q/y of directly burned oil and gas—about 80% of it for space heating—and about 14½ q/y of primary energy to generate electricity—about 12% of it for space heating. The August 1980 Santa Cruz Summer Study of the American Council for an Energy-Efficient Economy, chaired by Jack Hollander (90-3132 Lawrence Berkeley Laboratory, Berkeley CA 94720) analyzed in detail how comfort-increasing efficiency improvements, all cost-effective at the margin and nearly all cost-effective at present rolled-in prices, could save more than 10 q/y—possibly as much as 21 q/y—by the year 2000, roughly half of it by 1990. (Several q/y of additional savings could be achieved by renewables.) At a real fixed charge rate of 6.7%/y, empirical retrofit costs range from about $6/bbl for well-designed to about $19/bbl for relatively sloppy programs in houses, and run about $6-7/bbl or $1/ft² for commercial buildings. The proceedings of the Summer Study are to be published in book form and contain extensive backup data and citations.

ling.[210] Improved heat-tightness so far—seventeen percent better
for American gas-heated dwellings during 1972–79, twenty percent for FR German oil-heated single-family dwellings during
1973–79—illustrates the thesis but has barely scratched the surface. Savings around ninety percent, and some of essentially a
hundred percent of space-heating energy, are now fairly common
in cleverly designed new buildings, and savings of a similar order
are being cost-effectively achieved in some retrofits.[211] Indeed,
adding an external vapor barrier, superinsulation, air-to-air heat
exchanger, and new façade to a typical single-family English
house, to a level that eliminates space-heating requirements, still

[211]See e.g. "Low Energy Passive Solar Housing Handbook," Division of Extension and Community Relations, U. of Saskatchewan (Saskatoon S7N OWO),
October 1979 (which gives detailed instructions for building both new and retrofit
superinsulated houses); ref. 107; R. S. Dumont *et al.*, "Measured Energy Consumption of a Group of Low-Energy Houses", Dept. of Mech. Eng., U. Sask.,
May 1980 (describing fifty houses using an average of two-thirds less space-
heating energy than the pre-1970 electrically heated stock); G. Dallaire, *Civil
Engineering* 47-59, May 1980; W. Shurcliff, "Superinsulated Houses and
Double-Envelope Houses" (19 Appleton St, Cambridge MA 02138), a 1980 compendium of recent data; L. Palmiter & B. Miller, "Report on the October 13-14,
1979 Saskatchewan Conference on Low Energy Passive Housing", National
Center for Appropriate Technology (Butte MT), 1979 (including accounts of re-
trofits for about $3000 and superinsulation of new houses for essentially no extra
capital cost); E.H. Leger & G. S. Dutt, "An Affordable Solar House", 4th Nat'l
Passive Solar Conf. (Kansas City), 1979, from Vista Homes, (PO Box 95, E
Pepperell MA 01437); W. Shick *et al.*, "Details and Engineering Analysis of the
Illinois Lo-Cal House", Small Homes Council–Building Research Council, U.
Ill., Champaign IL 61820, 1979; L. Lange, "The First Annual Pasqua House
Report", Enercon Consultants Ltd (Regina, Sask.), 1980; D. A. Robinson, "The
Art of the Possible in Home Insulation", *Solar Age,* October 1979; W. Shurcliff,
"Window Shutters and Shades", 1980, Brick House Publishing Co (Andover MA
01810); R. Korda, "What About Windows?", Center for Community Technology
(1121 University Ave, Madison WI 53715), 1978; "How To Build a Superinsulated
House", Cold Weather Edition (Box 81961, College AK 99708), 1979; and the
compendia in *Soft Energy Notes* 3(1):18-28 (February 1980) and 3(4):22-23
(August/September 1980). The latter notes that compared with a 1976 US average
space-heating requirement for houses around 15 BTU ft^{-2} °F-d (3l3 kJ m^{-2}°C-d^{-1}),
standard superinsulated designs (Phelps Lo-Cal, Pasqua, Leger) need only 0.85-
1.3 (17-28), and the Saskatchewan Conservation House, without special efforts to
maximize passive solar gain, needs only 0.22 (4.5)—a saving of over 98% at an
extra capital cost of about $2500 (1978-79 $). Similarly, Gulf Canada Square uses
5.4 W/m^2, most other Toronto offices ~ 70. Contrary to an often-heard objection,
major savings are also obtainable even in countries with a relatively efficient
building stock: the Ulvsunda project in the Stockholm suburb of Bromma, for
example, has roughly halved heating-oil use in three years by retrofitting apart-
ments, and is still far from the efficiency levels now achievable. (Many Swedish
retrofits have been unnecessarily costly because the money was spent for other
purposes than saving energy, or was spent in the wrong order—triple glazing
before window shades and air recuperators[107].)

costs several times less than building a new power station to do the same task.[212]

Adding up the savings

In short, just the two largest single terms in improved US energy productivity, just in the 1980s, and pursued to a level far short of what is technically feasible or economically optimal, would together displace virtually all US oil imports (at the 1979 net rate[213]). They would "supply" energy at more than six times the rate deliverable by the maximum US nuclear capacity physically achievable in the same period[214]—at a small fraction of the cost. And they would do this before a reactor ordered today could deliver any energy whatsoever[215].

As the first glimmerings of this opportunity penetrate official consciousness, projections of future needs for energy, hence for major facilities to supply it, have dropped precipitously, affected relatively little by reduced expectations of economic growth. One way of illustrating this is a matrix of various analysts' estimates of approximately how much total primary energy the United States would need in the year 2000:

[212]Calculation by D. Olivier[114], personal communication, March 1980. For a less thorough US example, see F. S. Langa, *New Shelter* 41-48, April 1980, Rodale Press (Emmaus PA).

[213]In 1979 this rate averaged about 7.8 million barrels per day and was falling fast; the 1980 average should be about 6.3. The 1977 and 1978 levels were 8.6 and 8.0 respectively.

[214]The EIA "Supply Model" (see Fig. 1 caption) predicted in early 1980 a maximum feasible US nuclear capacity of 155 GWe in 1990. At the cumulative average capacity factor (for reactors >800 MWe) of 0.55 and a 90% transmission and distribution efficiency, 155 GWe would deliver 673 TWe-h/y or the heat equivalent of 1.14 million barrels of oil per day (1 bbl = 5.8 GJ). Improving 100 million cars from 15 to 60 mi/gal, if each is driven an average of 10,000 mi/y, would save 3¼ million barrels of gasoline, or about 3.6 million barrels of crude oil, per day. Improving 30 million light trucks (each driven 9,400 mi/y) from 12 to 60 mi/gal would save an extra 1.4 million barrels of crude oil per day. These savings plus 2½ Mbbl/d from weatherization[210] would total 7.5 Mbbl/d, or about 96% of the early-1980 rate of net oil imports, or about 6.6 times the maximum nuclear delivered-energy contribution, or over twice the nuclear contribution if that were wrongly assumed to substitute directly and entirely for oil-fired power stations. (Such stations actually burned about 1½ Mbbl/d in 1979[81].) Of course this calculation omits all other oil savings, including those from the 1980s' near-doubling of jet aircraft efficiency.

[215]According to the US Energy Information Administration, a US reactor typically needs 9.4–12.7 (mean 10.5) years to build, of which around 7.2–9.2 years is actual construction (including a half-year each for site preparation and power

Selected estimates of approximate US primary energy demand in 2000

$$(q/y \equiv 10^{15} \text{ BTU}/y \sim 10^{18} \text{ J}/y \sim 33 \text{ GWt})$$

Year in which analysis was published	Beyond the pale	Heresy	Conventional wisdom	Superstition
1972	125^a	140^b	160^c	190^d
1974	100^e	124^f	140^g	160^h
1976	75^a	$89^i - 95^j$	124^g	140^h
1978	33^k	$63^m - 77^m$	$95^n - 96^m - 101^p$	$123^q - 124^r$

Column header (spanning): Sociological category of analyst

[a]A. B. Lovins speeches (in 1972, J. P. Holdren was perhaps the only analyst estimating below 100 q/y)
[b]Sierra Club (a major national conservation group)
[c]US Atomic Energy Commission
[d]Federal Power Commission, Bureau of Mines, other Federal agencies (some were reportedly as high as 300 q/y, and Exxon was about 230 q/y)
[e]Ford Foundation Energy Policy Project, "Zero Energy Growth" scenario
[f]Ford Foundation Energy Policy Project, "Technical Fix" scenario
[g]US Energy Research & Development Administration (forerunner of USDOE)
[h]Edison Electric Insitute (and, generally, Electric Power Research Institute)
[i]F. von Hippel & R. H. Williams (Princeton University)
[j]A. B. Lovins, *Foreign Affairs*, October 1976
[k]J. Steinhart (University of Wisconsin) for 2050 with lifestyle changes
[m]CONAES Demand & Conservation Panel (*Science*, 14 April 1978), scenarios I–III (II and III are pure technical fixes) for 2010 assuming doubled real GNP
[n]USDOE Domestic Policy Review of Solar Energy, assuming world oil price (1977$) of $32/bbl by the year 2000 (this is scarcely below the *1980* price)
[p]A. M. Weinberg (Institute for Energy Analysis, Oak Ridge), "low" case
[q]As ref. n, but averaging the $18/bbl and $25/bbl cases
[r]R. Lapp (prominent US advocate of nuclear power and of fixed energy/GNP ratio)

Source: A. B. Lovins as cited by E. Marshall, *Science 208*:1353–56 (20 June 1980), with typographical errors corrected and refs. *n* and *q* added

Such a matrix shows a pleasingly symmetrical pattern: every two years, entries drop one slot towards the lower right, gaining one notch in respectability. Today the highest official estimates of US

ascension) after 2.2-3.5 years of licensing. We do not count here the several years' operation needed to recoup the energy invested in the reactor and its first fuel load, according to Westinghouse and EdF data (see Part Two, Appendix in A.B. Lovins & J. Price, *Non-Nuclear Futures*, Ballinger (Cambridge MA), 1977 and Harper Colophon (NY), 1980).

energy needs in the year 2000 are below the lowest, most heretical unofficial estimates made in 1972. The lowest government estimates, still assuming a two-thirds increase in real GNP during 1980–2000, are less than half as large, and more than a quarter *below* today's level—nearly a half below it in terms of nonrenewable fuel consumption[216]. The downward trend continues as new studies incorporate greater detail, identifying more opportunities for saving in hundreds of individual sectors, and take account of rapid recent technical progress in raising energy productivity to an economically efficient level. This level is at least several times that now prevailing in the most energy-efficient countries: at least a fourfold improvement in West Germany, more than sixfold in the UK, arguably more in the US[217].

Comparing the rates

Far from being uselessly slow, efficiency improvements are the fastest-growing energy source today. Of all new energy "supplies" to the nine EEC countries during 1973–78, about ninety-five percent came from more efficient use and only five percent from all supply expansions combined, including North Sea oil and nuclear power—a ratio of about nineteen to one in favor of conservation[218]. In Japan, the corresponding ratio rose to about ten. In the United States it averaged about two and a half during 1973–78 but rose to nearly forty in 1979, when real GNP rose 2.3 percent while energy use increased only 0.06 percent, implying that some ninety-seven percent of economic growth was

---

[216]These estimates are from the 26 May 1980 review draft of the Solar Energy Research Institute's detailed report "A New Prosperity: Building a Sustainable Energy Future", commissioned by Deputy Secretary Sawhill and due to be published by SERI[227] in final draft in late autumn 1980. In essence it seeks to calculate, with due attention to conservative estimates of achievable rates, a "least-cost strategy"[113] for 1980-2000. See also "Low Energy Futures for the United States", DOE/PE-0020, 1980, for precursors. Neither report considers accelerated turnover of the vehicle fleet.

[217] See the citations in notes 114 and 116. The UK and US are not among the most energy-efficient countries today. Asymptotic (post-2050) US demand, even assuming considerable economic growth, could be as low as 10-15 q/y: see "Economically Efficient Energy Futures"[97].

[218]Data from J. Saint-Geours *et al.*, "In Favour of an Energy-Efficient Society", EEC (Brussels), 1979, Annex 2, p 1 (*cf.* p 2); and, for US data, Sant[113] and V. Taylor, "The Easy Path Energy Plan", 1979, available from UCS[87]. The energy "supplies" from conservation calculated in this paragraph are the difference between the energy actually used to produce economic output in a given year and the energy that would have been needed to do so at previous levels of technical efficiency.

fueled by efficiency improvements[219]. This is remarkable progress in view of the more than $100 billion in annual tax and price subsidies which underprice fuels and power by an average of more than a third. The savings should accelerate as price increases take hold (it was not until 1979 that real US gasoline prices rose above their pre-embargo level). During 1973–78, total US efficiency gains yielded twice as much energy-"supplying" capacity, twice as fast, as synthetic-fuel advocates claimed they could do with their option—which, if it worked, would have cost about ten times as much. Even this ten percent gain in national energy efficiency was less than a third of what would have been worthwhile at 1978 energy prices[220]. The 1973–78 efficiency gains in US industry alone yielded twice the 1978 "supply" of Alaskan oil, but left the oil in the ground. By 1979, total post-embargo savings were at least five million and probably six million barrels of oil per day, nearly halving the severity of the US oil-import problem from what it would have been at 1973 levels of efficiency.

In a crisis the normal reflex is to abandon competition among many solutions in favor of single but dramatic nonsolutions (as in the 1979 post-gas-line White House hysteria for synthetic fuels). But these examples show that the centrally managed supply programs are being far outpaced by millions of individual actions in the market—actions by people seeking to save money by saving energy. There are three further structural reasons why efficiency gains (and the soft technologies discussed below) can displace oil far faster than other types of investments:

• The soft-path investments have construction times per unit that are measured in days, weeks, or months, not ten years.
• They diffuse into a vast consumer market, rather like citizens'-band radios, snowmobiles, and pocket calculators, rather than requiring tedious "technology delivery" to a narrow, specialized, and dynamically conservative utility market.
• The institutional barriers that hold back their dozens of technological categories are largely independent of each other: microhydro is held back by regulatory problems, air-to-air heat exchangers by the need to retread the building industry and building inspectors. Because these and analogous problems are not generic—like the major-facility siting problems that hold back all hard technologies everywhere at once—dozens of relatively

[219]Early data suggested that US primary energy use in 1979 *declined* 0.2%; the difference is well within the statistical "noise".

[220]As calculated by Sant[113], whose data are conservative.

slowly-growing individual wedges of efficiency improvements and soft technologies can independently add up by strength of numbers to very rapid total growth.

The problems of implementing a soft energy path (Chapter Eight) via desubsidization, tariff reform, replacement-cost pricing (or equivalent rules for allocating capital), and purging of institutional barriers are difficult problems—though easier than the alternative. Their solution, though no longer mysterious, is still at an early stage of practical application. Yet price incentives have already accelerated efficiency gains and the use of renewable sources far beyond the rate anyone dared hope for. Still faster implementation could be achieved by reinventing and adapting the institutional innovations used in the past for major national changes in capital stocks, such as the changes of electrical voltage in Sweden or of frequency in Toronto[221] and Los Angeles, the advent of North Sea gas, smokeless fuel, decimal coinage, and indoor toilets in Britain, and right-hand driving and district heating[222] in Sweden. (Many social action programs in Asia provide even better examples but are less apposite for industrial countries.) It is chastening to recall that when the Swedish government in 1767 commissioned development of the Cronstedt recirculating stove, five times as efficient as the open fires that were causing a firewood crisis, the solution was perfected and published within eight years; mandatory conversion was rapid throughout Sweden; and soon the stoves were all over Northern Europe[223].

Different countries can and will improve their efficiency and switch to renewables at different rates. Those that get a head start will merely improve their self-reliance and their competitive position at the expense of the slower and less astute. Mistakes will be

---

[221]Metropolitan Toronto and Montréal converted from 25- to 60-Hz electricity one neighborhood at a time using fleets of specially equipped vans (with machine shops and other facilities) that were left over from cleaning up after the Normandy invasion and were staffed by resourceful people good at improvising. Similar "conservation caravans" could be used for efficiency and solar retrofits.

[222]During 1975-85, all towns over 100,000 population (except Stockholm, which will take longer) are replacing most of their single-house oil furnaces with pressurized hot water distribution in insulated pipes. Connection is voluntary but there is a strong incentive in cost and reliability. The load is aggregated from the bottom up; one does not simply build a town heating plant and lay pipes from it. Sweden is the world leader in innovative district-heating technology.

[223]H. Larsson, "Vedeldning genom tiderna", report 5, Tekniska Högskolornas Energiarbetsgrupp (Fack, 10072 Stockholm), 1979.

made, but reliance on a large number of diverse, relatively simple measures already known to work, with small unit costs and short lead times, reduces the risk and the cost of failure, and allows rapid corrections. Our least-cost policy for saving oil does not pit national against world or regional interests in oil security, but advances interests at all levels: oil saving, unlike oil exploitation, is not competitive but cooperative and reinforcing. (Oil-exporting nations concerned with the economic, military, and social problems of excessively rapid oil depletion may even wish to offer preferential prices or supply guarantees to oil importers whose efficiency gains best ease mutual problems and keep exporters in business longer.) The problems of implementation are mainly problems of pluralism; they are messy and localized rather than intractable and centralized. But any energy policy entails tough problems, and nations must decide which kinds of problems they prefer. There is no free lunch, though some lunches are cheaper than others.

Long-term global prospects

Developing countries should be able to achieve the same ultimate energy efficiencies as industrialized countries, but faster and cheaper, because they can use the most efficient technologies from scratch (the world's most efficient steel mill is said to be in Kenya), rather than having to install them by slow and costly retrofit of existing plants. On this basis, preliminary estimates suggest that a completely industrialized world of eight billion people, with a standard of living somewhat above today's Western European average, need use no more total energy than the world uses today[224]. This energy need—less than a tenth electricity, about a fifth liquid fuels for vehicles, the rest heat—lends itself to supply entirely from well-known "soft technologies": diverse renewable sources that are relatively understandable to the user (though they can still be technically very sophisticated) and that supply energy at the scale and quality appropriate to

---

[224]"Economically Efficient Energy Futures"[97]. (Such levels of population and material throughput may be impossible or undesirable on grounds other than energy availability.) Third World analysts are right to attribute the world's energy crisis to the North, but the absolute amount of waste in the North is irrelevant to the merits of efficiency-improving investments in the South. Their scope and attractions are immense; see e.g. pp. 9-13 and refs. 37-44 of "Economically Efficient Energy Futures"[97]; World Bank Staff Working Paper 346, "Prospects for Traditional and Non-Conventional Energy Sources in Developing Countries," 1979; E. Cecelski et al., "Household energy and the poor in the third world", Resources for the Future (Washington DC), 1979; and numerous articles in *Soft Energy Notes*[199].

each task, so as to minimize the costs and losses of energy distribution and of energy conversion respectively[225].

The four years since the emergence of the concept of a soft energy path—a coherent strategy combining soft technologies and transitional fossil-fuel technologies with major efficiency improvements within a noncoercive policy framework[226]—have seen astonishingly rapid analytic and practical progress. As a result of thousands of studies and experimental projects, what was controversial has become widely accepted. Economic claims once made with caution can now be made with confidence. Findings extrapolated from early analyses in a handful of countries are now bolstered by dozens of far more detailed studies in about fifteen countries and many localities—and, increasingly, by practical demonstrations on a significant scale[227].

[225]For an introductory treatment, see *Soft Energy Paths*[74] and "Soft Energy Technologies"[103]. The original statement of the thesis was A.B. Lovins, "Energy Strategy: The Road Not Taken?", *Foreign Affairs* 55:65-96 (October 1976).

[226]Besides these three technical elements, a soft path is defined by its avoidance of the political costs that characterize a "hard energy path"—one based on the increasingly rapid conversion of depletable fuels to premium forms in more centralized plants. Those costs include centrism, autarchy, vulnerability, technocracy, and inequitable allocation of energy and its social costs. The policy instruments of a soft path are instead noncoercive and market-oriented. It neither assumes nor requires that car efficiency, for example, be improved by the particular means mentioned above. Our soft-path analysis assumes rapid, undifferentiated, and worldwide economic and industrial growth; no significant changes in social goals, composition of economic output, or patterns of settlements, political organization, or behavior; and implementation only through "technical fixes"—i.e. presently proven, presently economic technical measures with no significant effects on lifestyles. (That is, we assume the "insulating the roof" kinds of energy savings rather than the "freezing in the dark" kinds; the two are often confused.) Readers who consider today's values or institutions imperfect are welcome to assume instead some mixture of technical and social change which would simplify implementation, but as a conservatism, we have not done so; we assume a "pure technical fix".

[227]Many are summarized in *Soft Energy Notes*[199]. See also the proceedings published by the Solar Energy Research Institute (Golden CO 80401) of the First (Boulder, 1979) and Second (Seattle, 1980) National Conferences on Community Renewable Energy Systems (the first, published by SERI in 1980, is entitled *Community Energy Self-Reliance*); "Renewable Energy Development: Local Issues and Capabilities", DOE/PE-0017[199], 1980; J. Ridgeway, *Energy-Efficient Community Planning*, JG Press (Emmaus PA), 1979; Office of Consumer Affairs, USDOE, *Energy Consumer*, February/March 1980 (special issue on community energy activities); and project lists from the Center for Renewable Resources (1001 Connecticut Ave NW, 5th floor, Washington DC 20036), including the 1980 survey *Shining Examples*; from the Institute for Local Self-Reliance (1717 18th St NW, Washington DC 20009); and from the Institute for Ecological Policies (9208 Christopher St, Fairfax VA 22030), whose *County Energy Plan Guidebook* is being widely used.

From this broader base of information it is now possible to confirm that if carefully selected and efficiently used, the best soft technologies already in or entering commercial service, and matched to local needs and climates, are sufficient to meet virtually all long-term energy needs in every country so far studied, including the US, Canada, UK, FR Germany, France, Denmark, Sweden, and Japan: a suggestive list, as it includes countries that are simultaneously cold, cloudy, densely populated, and heavily industrialized. The same finding has been broadly confirmed on a world scale by both regional estimates and a worldwide scoping calculation embodying case-studies, both assuming a much lower than economically efficient level of energy productivity[228]. Further, the foregoing statements assume no technologies yet to be developed, but only the best *present* art in passive and active solar heating, passive solar cooling, high-temperature solar heat for industry (collectable even in cloudy winters[229]), converting farm and forestry wastes to liquid fuel for vehicles, both present and small-scale new hydroelectricity, windpower, and in some cases other simple devices such as woodburners, biogas plants, and low-temperature heat engines[230]. The appropriate mix of

[228]Analyses by T. B. Taylor and B. Sørensen, summarized in "Economically Efficient Energy Futures"[97].

[229]Though cloud reduces the intensity of solar radiation, the thermodynamic quality of the light is still extremely high—thousands of degrees Celsius—and can be largely captured even though there is no sensible warmth. Highly selective absorbing surfaces, such as can now be made in foil form for $3.50/m^2$ with α/ϵ (visible absorptivity $\div$ infrared emissivity) $\sim$ 50 (K.-H. Raetz, *PTB-Mitteilungen* 89:217 (March 1979), Physikalisch-Technisch Bundesanstalt, Braunschweig, FRG), can heat water satisfactorily on a cloudy winter day in North Germany if the absorber to which they are bonded is in an air-filled flat-plate collector. In a hard vacuum, such a collector would provide under load a temperature around 500-600°C in such conditions, and if the coolant (presumably a liquid metal) should stagnate without suitable precautions having been taken, the absorber plate would melt.

[230]Technical progress is so dizzyingly fast that normal channels of publication cannot reflect the real state of the art. Up-to-date information requires great effort and a wide information network to collect; few analysts take the trouble. Further, fallacies abound in most official analyses. It is common to dismiss any one of a myriad types of soft technology, for example, as individually insignificant, or to fault it for its unattractiveness if irrationally used in the manner or at the scale of conventional large systems such as reactors, even though the strength of soft technologies is their immense *diversity* of type, scale, climate, integration opportunities, appropriate application, and level of technical sophistication and of accessibility to various users. Soft technologies work best when matched to a particular task, place, and user, and can easily be made to look bad by being misapplied or misdesigned. Another common fallacy is to assume a difficult energy storage problem when in fact the soft path avoids one. This is because cost-effective efficiency improvements smooth the heat loads of buildings, making

sources (each containing a vast array of subcategories and hybrids) varies between and within countries, but even countries poor in transitional fuels, such as Japan, appear to be amply rich in renewable energy if each kind is intelligently used to do the tasks it does best[231]. Indeed, Japan probably has the widest array of renewable energy options of any industrial country except Norway and New Zealand.

Given careful shopping for clever designs, efficient marketing structures[232], and cost-effective efficiency improvements done *first* (thus making renewable supply smaller, simpler, cheaper, and more effective[233]), soft technologies can be—

---

residual heat-storage requirements so small that storage is cheaper than backup (*Soft Energy Notes*[199] 2(1):16-18, May 1979); they reduce electrical loads so far [116] that grids are hydro-dominated (moreover, the main types of renewable electrical supply are statistically complementary: E. Kahn, *Annual Review of Energy* 4:313-52 (1979)); and liquid fuels for vehicles are readily stored, as is industrial heat or the fuel to make it. It is rather the hard energy path, with its extensive electrification, that has a formidable and very costly problem of energy storage.

[231] H.Tsuchiya, "A Soft Path Plan for Japan", Research Institute for Systems Technology (403 Taiyo Building 3-3-3, Misaki-cho, Chiyoda-ku, Tokyo 101), summarized in *Soft Energy Notes* 3(3):21-23 (June/July 1980), gives supply data for a nuclear-free and fossil-fuel-free Japan, assuming the present level of economic activity (corresponding very conservatively to a 38% primary demand reduction by 2010 via increased energy productivity[200]). Briefly, Japan has extensive low-latitude sun, vast onshore and offshore wind, enough hydro and geothermal capacity installed by 1985 to meet present electricity-specific needs, unexpectedly large biomass wastes (over two-thirds of Japan is forested), and—if desired in addition—a major wave and ocean-thermal potential. More refined calculations are in preparation in book form. See also A.B. Lovins, preface to Japanese edition of *Soft Energy Paths*, Jiji Press (Tokyo), 1979.

[232] For example, a "packaged" solar collector—manufactured, shipped to the site, and installed—often has an installed system price around $30-50/ft^2 collector area because it is marked up by the manufacturer, wholesaler, retailer, and perhaps installer. A fully equivalent "site-assembled" or "field-erected" collector, whose mass-produced components (glazing, absorber plate, etc.) are shipped to the building and there assembled directly into a collector, is only marked up once and therefore costs $10-15/ft^2. See e.g. *Proceedings of the First New England Conference on Site-Built Solar Collectors*, Dept. of Mech. Eng., Worcester Polytechnic Institute, Worcester MA, 1978.

[233] For example, the Saskatchewan Conservation House increases solar coverage of space and water heating from perhaps half or two-thirds to virtually 100% while decreasing solar-system size five- or tenfold compared with rule-of-thumb designs: *Soft Energy Notes, loc. cit.*[230]. When space-heating loads are small compared with water-heating baseloads, all fixed costs of an active solar system can be assigned to the latter, and only marginal variable costs to the former: *id.* and J. D. Balcomb *et al.* (Los Alamos Scientific Laboratory), "Hybrid Active-Passive Designs: Synergy or Conflict?", LA-US-79-1394, 1979. Further synergisms

though not all are—cheaper than today's oil. More important, they are consistently cheaper in capital cost[234], and several times cheaper in delivered energy price, than the power stations or synfuel plants which would *otherwise* have to be built to replace the oil and gas[235]. This comparison is conservative, is based on empirical cost and performance data, and omits all "external" costs and benefits: notably such soft-technology advantages as safety, environmental benignity[236], employment gains[237], avoidance of climatic[238] and proliferation risks, increased resilience[239], and low political costs[240]. Thus on the orthodox criterion

abound, e.g. if solar water-heating panels are installed in the top of a properly designed greenhouse[108].

[234]See e.g. the references in note 103. Further, a soft technology of the same capital intensity as a hard technology would typically require several times less working capital because of its shorter lead time and faster payback (no fuel costs).

[235]*Id.* This is not the economic test that governments traditionally make. They prefer to compare with each other in cost the systems they like to build (coal *vs* nuclear power stations *vs* synfuel plants) and then to compare soft-path investments instead with the dwindling, historically cheap, and often heavily subsidized fossil fuels which all these investments are meant to replace. The hard technologies would fail this test by a far wider margin. The advantage of the soft technologies over hard in delivered energy price is typically an average factor of three ("Soft Energy Technologies"[103], Table 2)—more without the multiple conservatisms there listed. For general background, see also B. Sørensen, *Renewable Energy,* Academic Press (NY), 1980.

[236]J. P. Holdren *et al.,* "Environmental Aspects of Renewable Energy Sources", ERG 80-1[130], 1980.

[237]See e.g. M. Schachter, "The Job Creation Potential of Solar and Conservation: A Critical Evaluation", USDOE Office of Policy Evaluation, 1979; S. Buchsbaum *et al.,*"Jobs and Energy", Council on Economic Priorities (NY), 1979; L. Rodberg, *The Employment Impact of the Solar Transition,* Joint Economic Committee, US Congress, USGPO 052-04915-4, 1978; B. Hannon, "Energy and Labor Demand in the Conserver Society", Center for Advanced Computation, U. Ill. (Urbana-Champaign IL), 1976 (which calculates by input-output regression that the capital requirements of an average 1-GWe power plant *reduce* total net employment by about 4000 jobs, directly and indirectly, by starving other sectors for capital). See also the publications of Environmentalists for Full Employment (1536 16th St NW, Washington DC 20036), notably "Energy, Jobs and the Economy", 1979.

[238]"Economically Efficient Energy Futures"[97].

[239]The authors are preparing a major report on this subject during 1980-81 for the President's Council on Environmental Quality, funded by the Federal Emergency Management Agency. See note 165 above and response to B. Wolfe, *Foreign Affairs,* Autumn 1980.

[240]See *Soft Energy Paths*[74], Chapters 2.9, 9, 10.

of lowest private internal cost, as the Harvard Business School
energy study recently found[241], the cheapest energy investments
are in general the efficiency improvements, then the soft
technologies, then synfuels, and last—costliest—power stations.
Most countries have so far taken these options in reverse order,
worst buys first.

In short, from the viewpoint both of immediate national
investment priorities and of long-term global energy requirements, technologies are available for increasing energy productivity and supply which have all the advantages claimed for nuclear
power and can do better everything it can do (except make
bombs). Since many of these technologies are but recently developed[242], many have been developed outside official channels,
few have strong commercial constituencies, and none has enjoyed decades of lavishly funded official support, it is not surprising that they are less well known than nuclear power[243]. But as
the word spreads that recent progress has rendered every technical and economic objection to a soft path obsolete, one concern
remains central: how can a soft path be implemented?

[241]R. Stobaugh & D. Yergin, eds., *Energy Future*, Random House (NY), 1979,
summarized in *Foreign Affairs* 57:836-71 (Spring 1979)—a good example of how
far soft energy strategies by any other name have become common coin.

[242]Even though in another sense most of them are centuries or millenia old,
awaiting only modern refinements in design and materials: K. Butti & J. Perlin, *A
Golden Thread: 2500 Years of Solar Architecture and Technology*, Cheshire
Books /Van Nostrand Reinhold (NY), 1980.

[243]Or than "hard" solar technologies—monocultural biomass plantations,
"power towers", ocean-thermal-electric conversion (OTEC), solar power satellites, etc.—which in general are neither economically nor environmentally attractive. Nor are they necessary if energy is used efficiently. If it is not, solar supply is
not precluded, but soft solar supply may no longer suffice. In general, the "supply
curve"—reflecting the cost, difficulty, or nastiness of supply as a function of how
much is required—rises steeply and often discontinuously for solar technologies.
They are relatively benign and attractive if used on the shallowly sloping soft-
technology lower portion of the curve: the region, happily, that expresses the
economically optimal balance between supply and efficiency-improving investments. Many solar studies, e.g. that completed in 1979-80 by IIASA[124], work
inefficiently on the upper part of the supply curve and naturally find the resulting
hard-technology-dominated mix unattractive.

Chapter Eight

Implementing Non-Nuclear Futures

The debate begun in 1976 over the technologies and costs of the soft energy path gave way by 1978-79, as critics verified the references, to a residual philosophical debate: Will people do it?[244] No analyst's view of what is important or tolerable to people can substitute for asking them[245], and not everyone shares our own view that a plutonium economy is more difficult to achieve, especially in a democracy, than well-insulated houses. But this is not a technical debate and cannot be settled on technical merits. The debate about implementation reduces to the Jeffersonian (and market economics) view that people are pretty smart and, given incentive and opportunity, can choose wisely for themselves[246], versus the Hamiltonian view that these complex issues must be centrally decided and the decisions enforced by a technocratic elite. Under the latter philosophy, energy policy requires massive central planning and intervention which, under the former, it cannot tolerate. For readers inclined to a Hamiltonian view, we plead at least for symmetry in comparing the rates, costs, risks, and difficulties of *all* policy opportunities; for a choice of easier problems even if they are less familiar; and for a suspension of disbelief about the efficacy of market forces: recent experience of what actually works is, we believe, empirically resolving the dispute in favor of the Jeffersonians.

A few examples give the flavor. Under a no-strings grant program, Nova Scotians weatherized half their houses in one year. In the winter of 1979-80, the people of Fitchburg, Mas-

[244]For collected critiques and responses, see H. Nash, ed., *The Energy Controversy: Soft Path Questions and Answers*, FOE [29] (San Francisco), 1979. Most can be found unedited in the US Senate Small Business and Interior Committees' voluminous compendium *Alternative Long-Range Energy Strategies*, 2 vols., USGPO, 1977-78.

[245]J. Ziman *et al*, "Deciding about Energy Policy", Council for Science & Society (3/4 St Andrew's Hill, London EC4), 1979; A. B. Lovins, *45 George Washington Law Review* 911-943 (August 1977); P. Junger, *Case Western Reserve Law Review* 3-335 (Fall 1976).

[246]Or can muddle through: for example, Leach's trebled British energy efficiency[114] can be achieved in fifty years, as he shows, if efficiency improvements can be implemented *more slowly* than they have been in Britain during 1973–79—a glacial pace indeed. (Efficiency advocates in Britain are still fighting for the level of roof insulation that Sweden had in 1945.)

sachusetts, without the grants but with door-to-door citizen action [247], did the same in seven *weeks*. By early 1980, Americans had built about two hundred thousand solar buildings, of which half were passive and half those were retrofitted greenhouses[248]: until the late 1970s, Federal publications had said that passive solar techniques could be only applied to existing buildings, but some fifty thousand householders who didn't know that were meanwhile building their greenhouses, in which they now bask in February munching fresh tomatoes and reflecting on the infirmities of government. By 1978-79, in the most solar-conscious communities, from a quarter to all of the new housing starts were passive solar designs, and by 1980, an estimated fifteen percent of all US commercial housebuilders were using passive design techniques. Leading solar areas, such as the San Luis Valley of Colorado[249] and the Taos area of New Mexico, had already achieved five to six percent solar heating penetration by 1980 and plausibly expected at least twenty percent by 1985. In the late 1970s, over one hundred fifty New England factories, and over half the

[247]The pilot program began less than two weeks after a team from ACTION (Washington DC) proposed it and cleared a few site-specific institutional barriers which had, for example, left low-income weatherization materials locked in a warehouse. Save for this initial impetus, however, the Federal officials wisely left local people, under their aegis of Fitchburg Action to Conserve Energy (FACE), to get on with the job and take the credit for it themselves.

[248]See note 108 and, for a compendium of specifics, B. Yanda and R. Fisher, *The Food and Heat Producing Solar Greenhouse*, John Muir Publications (PO Box 613, Santa Fe NM 87501), 1980. A recent survey for the Office of Technology Assessments obtainable from the New Mexico Solar Energy Association (Santa Fe; contact Scott Morris) of a sample of 150 of the estimated 1000 (mid-1979) retrofitted greenhouses in New Mexico shows generally fine performance, economic motivation, and information obtained by word of mouth or from popular publications rather than from official sources. The greenhouses seem to generate much enthusiasm, imitation, and interest in further renewable investments by their owners. Their design concept was invented by Day Chahroudi, prototyped by Tom Watson in the early 1970s, and popularized during 1973-77 by Bill and Susan Yanda in more than thirty "barn-raising" hands-on workshops.

[249]This cold, high-altitude rural area the size of Delaware contains some of the poorest (chiefly traditional Hispanic) communities in the United States. When fencing of common lands cut off fuelwood supplies, people had no choice but to heat with greenhouses, as they could not afford any commercial fuels. Starting with a few people who knew how to build simply from scrounged materials, they went in a few years from a few greenhouses to over 400 documented and over 800 estimated (as of spring 1980), mostly built for about $200 each, and including installations on trailers, a Post Office, and a mortuary. (There are also high-technology active solar systems on a Baskin & Robbins and on a Federally funded community center.) Many other renewable energy projects have now been spawned. Mainly responsible were Arnie and Maria Valdez (Rt 1, Box 3-A, San Luis CO 81152).

houses in northern New England, switched from oil to wood—a trend repeated by householders nationally, and not only in rural areas, as private woodburning increased sixfold during 1973-79. The number of stove foundries rose from a few to over four hundred. At the same time, over half the states, generally a year or two ahead of Washington, developed alcohol fuels programs. Small-scale hydro reconstruction is flourishing. More than forty manufacturers of wind machines are selling into a growing market whose two biggest commercial commitments in 1979, both for state governments, totalled some $230 million. The size, rate, and diversity of soft-path activities are now so great that national authorities are only dimly aware of how fast their own targets are being overtaken as thousands of communities—counties, cities, and towns—in the United States, and some abroad, begin to implement a soft path without waiting for anyone.

The reason for this grassroots ferment is easy to see. Conventional policies decided and implemented nationally require a prior consensus on matters which any pluralistic society is likely to find exquisitely controversial: price versus regulation, Hamilton versus Jefferson, capitalism versus socialism, the role of the oil companies, the future shape of society. A soft path cuts through these ideological disputes, commanding diverse loyalties for diverse reasons. An economic traditionalist, concerned with what's personally cheapest, can put up a greenhouse because it's cheaper than not doing it. A worker may wish to build it because it provides more and better jobs than building power stations. An environmentalist can build it because it's benign; a social transformationalist, because it's autonomous. But it's still the same greenhouse. People need not agree, before or after, about why they built it. In an era when both efficient use of energy and the use of appropriate renewable sources enjoy an overwhelming consensus, but other options do not and may never elicit any consensus, a soft path pushes hard on the things people agree about, because they're sufficient. It is then possible to forget about the things people don't agree about, because they have thus become superfluous. Societies have never tried before to design an energy policy around an existing, broadly based political consensus; but it seems long past time they started. If this is done at a sufficiently localized level so that the energy problem is concrete and fine-grained enough, people can recognize it as *their* problem—not abstract meaningless statistics that remote bureaucrats will worry about, but the cracks around the bedroom window. The immense latent energy and creativity of people solving their own daily problems in their own way can then be aggregated into solutions for the nation and the world.

So powerful, indeed, is the convergence between political and economic logic that it is hardly surprising how quickly a soft energy path is starting to implement itself through existing political and market processes. But the question remains whether a sustainable energy future will be achieved relatively smoothly by choice, or disruptively by necessity after the fossil-fuel bridge has been burned in a vain pursuit of other solutions that do not work. A transition as painless as can be achieved (bearing in mind the possibility of interruptions in oil supply or other unpleasant surprises no matter what we do) will depend on positive initiatives to allow the natural advantages of the soft path to show themselves: initiatives both to provide proper price signals and to permit people to act on them.

Paying what energy really costs

To begin setting their houses in order, all countries will first need to ensure that energy prices are not artificially depressed by subsidies. Despite short-term political attractions (at least until tax revolts begin), subsidies to supply lead to artificially inflated demand, bankruptcy of overcapitalized supply industries[250], inefficient allocation, absolutely intractable supply problems after the next election, and of course a mere transfer of the real costs to somewhere else such as taxes. The extent of subsidies is unknown in most countries[251], but where studied, has turned out to be unexpectedly large: the fifty-five percent solar tax credit in California, for example, is smaller than Federal tax subsidies to Alaskan gas or nuclear power, so solar heat that is actually cheaper than the gas is made to look costlier[252]. On this question it is clearly time to stop what Monte Canfield Jr called "nibbling

[250]See notes 137 and 138.

[251]Historic direct Federal subsidies have been authoritatively calculated for the US—B.W. Cone *et al. An Analysis of Federal Incentives Used to Stimulate Energy Production,* PNL-2410 Rev. II, Battelle Pacific Northwest Laboratory report to USDOE, February 1980 (the 1918-78 total was $252 billion in 1978 dollars, omitting various large but unquantifiable terms, and was allocated roughly half for oil, a quarter for electricity, 8% for nuclear and 0.15% for solar)—and for Japan[200]. Similar studies managed through BPNL are under way for France and FR Germany via Battelle offices in Geneva and Frankfurt respectively. An internal study has reportedly been done by the UK Treasury but is so sensitive that the UK Department of Energy has been unable to obtain it. Follow-on funding for this line of inquiry appears not to be available in the US, where direct subsidies on *current* account—investment tax credits, accelerated depreciation allowances, interest deductions, depletion allowances, etc.—are continuing at the rate of tens of billions of dollars per year. See also Lovins[105].

[252]D. Chapman[110], "Taxation and Solar Energy", 15 April 1978 report to Solar Office, Ca. Energy Commission (Sacramento).

at the bullet''. At the very least, while national and international[253] subsidies are being phased out, equal subsidies should be
passed through symmetrically to competing conservation and renewable investments[254]. The most defensible residual subsidies
would be those that tend to improve market structure, enhance
competitive choice, discourage consumption, and not be self-
perpetuating. Such subsidies will be few indeed—perhaps those
attempting to compensate for failure to internalize the external
social costs of new supply technologies. But in the absence of a
compelling rationale based on accepted economic principles, all
subsidies to supply are bad policy and lead to underinvestment in
measures to improve energy productivity—measures known to
be notably low in risks, inequities, and externalities.

Equally important is the rationality of tariff structures. Incremental consumption should attract true incremental costs. (In
the US in 1978 this failed to be the case by considerably more
than sixty-six billion dollars[255].) Promotional tariffs and cross-
subsidies[256] are especially common in selling electricity and
gas—holdovers from the era, ended a decade ago, when the next
unit of supply cost less than preceding units. Changing declining
(quantity-discounting) into flat or inverted tariffs can be designed
to be "revenue-neutral", not generating excess profits, but fairly
covering costs and discouraging increased demand by making it
pay its real supply costs[257].

[253]Export[145], aid-bank, and EURATOM loans on preferential terms, for example,
all of which are widely used to finance investments which could never be financed
in the capital market.

[254]Capital transfers as described above [139] would do this if set up so that the loan
obligation were considered an asset qualifying for Federal tax subsidies. This does
not seem unduly difficult in most states.

[255]This is the difference, as calculated by C. Bullard of USDOE using the conservative PIES model, between the rolled-in prices paid in 1978 and the prices corresponding to the costlier components of the 1978 fuel mix (Canadian gas, Alaskan
oil, recently commissioned power stations, etc.). The difference between rolled-in
and even short-run *marginal* prices (newly *ordered* power stations, etc.) would be
far larger. Bullard's $66.3 billion "price subsidy" consisted of $29 billion gas, $14
billion oil, $3.3 billion gas liquids, and $20 billion electrical—a sector in which the
PIES model is well known to underestimate costs.

[256] See note 105.

[257]In a few years, when people wanting an energy-efficient or solar house will be
able to get one properly built with Tennessee Valley Authority financing, TVA will
be tempted to start charging marginal costs for hookups to the grid: consumers
will be free to live in an electrically heated sieve and to pay what it costs TVA to
hook it up (probably at least $20,000).

Moving even gradually and fairly towards charging ourselves for depletable fuels what it will cost to replace them in the
long run—for example, by the severance royalty suggested
elsewhere[258]—can raise serious problems of equity[259]. Where
some people are poor, higher prices, however efficient, cannot be
fair, even when the mechanism that induces them is not significantly redistributive[260]. But this problem can be largely evaded
by a rather simple "investment balancing test"[261] to ensure efficient allocation of capital to major supply investments, notably by
gas and electric utilities. The test simply conditions permission to
construct new utility plants on the utility's first showing that the
proposed plant is the cheapest way to meet the incremental end-
use needs for which the extra energy would be used[262]. If this can
be shown, then the utility has a good argument for building the
plant. But if not—if, for example, improved energy productivity,
soft technologies, cogeneration, etc. can do the same tasks
cheaper — then instead of building the plant, the utility (or, if it is
nationalized, the government via the utility's billing system)
should instead loan out its money, on mutually fair and beneficial
terms[263], so that customers can do the cheaper things first, ensur-
ing the most efficient use of capital.

Such a decision mechanism has a profound and decentralized economic effect. It means that for the first time, the costs
of soft-path investments are directly compared with the replacement costs represented by new power plants or new synfuel

[258]A. B. Lovins, "How to Finance the Energy Transition", FOE[29] (San Francisco), from *Not Man Apart* 8-10, September-October 1978.

[259]See e.g. TransCentury Corp. (Washington DC), "The Impact of Rising Energy
Prices on Low Income Consumers", report to DOE Office of Consumer Affairs,
October 1979.

[260]As proposed in ref. 258—though revenues from the severance royalty could
and probably should be used redistributively. See also R. H. Williams [202].

[261]See ref. 258, Hutton paper [137], and CaPUC proceedings[137].

[262]This approximates present practice of the California PUC: see e.g. *NY Times*
editorial "Can 'Soft Energy' Save Hard Cash?", 11 August 1980. It entails redi-
recting present "need-for-power tests" from the cost of sending out kilowatt-
hours to that of providing delivered energy services (comfort, light, mechanical
work, etc.).

[263]See notes 115 and 139, ref. 258, Hutton paper [137], CaPUC proceedings [137], and
A. B. & L. H. Lovins, testimony to "Energy Conservation Initiatives" hearing,
24 October 1979, USHR Commerce Committee, Subcommittee on Energy and
Power. US investor-owned utilities have internally generated capital of about $11
billion in 1980 alone, of which probably at least $5-6 billion is real retained
earnings—a formidable capitalization for a revolving fund that nominally revolves
every few years.

plants, not with historically cheap fuels. Thus most of the capital going into the energy sector will be allocated *as if* energy were *already* priced at marginal cost, whether it is or not—without first having to achieve those unpalatably high prices[264]. The enterprises now responsible for typically four-fifths of all energy investments could thus buy the cheapest options for society independent of present prices, largely doing an end run around the difficult problem of finding prices that are both equitable and efficient.

From fuel bazaar to energy market

It would be an odd coincidence if the workings of the market always gave the same answer as the preferences expressed by the political system: in theory, democracies work by "one person, one vote", while markets, as Clark Bullard remarks, work by "one dollar, one vote". (Those possessing many dollars naturally try to remove this anomaly by making the former system work by the latter principle.) The market system is manifestly imperfect. But in its proper sphere—of mediating between diverse preferences for allocating resources in the short term—it is, as Churchill remarked of democracy, the worst system—except for all the rest. Whether freely or grudgingly, all but the most doctrinaire autarchists must admit that market allocation is preferable to the alternatives. It is therefore important to try to achieve some semblance of a market and of genuine competition in the provision of energy services. This requires the systematic identification and purging of market imperfections—"institutional barriers"—which prevent people from responding to market signals by using energy in a way that saves them money.

One of the most difficult barriers, especially for poor people, is inequitable access to capital[265]. For this we suggest a

---

[264]This can and should be done [263] without increasing utilities' monopoly power or placing unfair burdens on them or their customers. The "Oregon plan" of putting part or all of the loan into the utility's rate base is in nobody's financial interest (CaPUC[137] and USHR testimony[263]). See A. B. Lovins, testimony of 19 September and 9 October 1980 to New Mexico and Maine Public Utility Commissions respectively.

[265]Credit-card interest rates are common. Some investor-owned utilities have a still higher marginal cost of money (though generally a lower average or "imbedded" cost—the correct comparison if the faster cash flow[139] will let them avoid acquiring new capital at marginal cost). But most public utilities have a far lower cost even for new money: around 6-8%/y for rural electric cooperatives (most of whose cheap Federal loans go to bail out investor-owned utilities' big, mainly nuclear, construction projects that are otherwise unfinanceable), 2%/y for coops' lines in low-population-density areas, and well below general inflation rates for many tax-free municipals.

combination of utility capital transfers[266], outright grants to poor
people (perhaps as a distribution of severance-royalty proceeds),
innovative car-replacement programs perhaps like those described above, encouragement of innovative schemes in existing
banks[267] and other financial institutions[268], and, as a last resort,
perhaps complementary "solar banks", though these suffer unnecessary startup lags and transaction costs. These institutions
should all make revolving-fund money available to all classes of
borrowers, in order of their present difficulty of access to relatively cheap capital, on at least as favorable terms ("market parity") as it is now available for new conventional supply. The
lenders will then benefit from the highest rates of return available
anywhere, with relatively fast paybacks and low risks[269].

Specific regulations now in force in many countries pose
further barriers to rational investment decisions. Every country's
building codes are both technically and economically obsolete[270].
Many, along with some architectural fee structures[271], actively
inhibit efficient building design. Rigid and sometimes counter-

[266]See note 261.

[267]For example, San Diego Federal Savings & Loan Co., for a nominal transaction
fee, will add on a solar retrofit loan at the marginal cost of money to the back end
of an existing home mortgage, so the typical borrower does not repay it until the
house has been sold and the equity realized several times over. The bank benefits
because the borrower, relieved of unsupportable utility bills, becomes a better
loan risk, less likely to default and leave the bank stuck with foreclosure on a
house nobody can afford to live in.

[268]Several heating oil companies in North America operate conservation loan
schemes, and at least one major insurance company hopes soon to do the same. A
good deal of venture capital is going into private-enterprise energy-saving contractors.

[269]Including the removal of existing risks such as loss of utility assets owned by
the banks or insolvency of mortgage customers[267]: it was Susan Carpenter's comparison of future utility bills with future mortgage payments that induced some
Denver CO banks to start giving solar loans in their own self-interest.

[270]Even the proposed strict BEPS code in the US does not fully exploit the present
art of thermal efficiency nor fully invest to marginal supply costs. See the forth-
coming Summer Study book[210].

[271]Architects seldom have an incentive for energy-efficient design, and the custom
of splitting fees with consulting engineers in proportion to the cost of installed
equipment for which they are each responsible encourages the installation of, for
example, six blowers where one or two will do.

productive[272] standards are oriented too much towards prescription in a fast-moving technology and too little towards encouraging innovation for best performance. Minima are often misconstrued—even by the bodies that issue them—as optima or maxima. Most lending institutions' rules do not reflect the mutual economic advantages of conservation and solar loans, and many require the installation of costly backup systems even if they are patently unnecessary[273]. Many zoning regulations prohibit greenhouses or wind machines while allowing more obtrusive office blocks and television aerials[274]. Many electric utilities, despite new US legal principles prohibiting discrimination in supplying backup power to decentralized generators and requiring that their power output be purchased (if offered) at the utilities' own "avoided cost", still find ways to discriminate economically against dispersed sources[275], so denying themselves the mutual benefits of interconnection. Of course we must not be understood to say that all regulation *per se* is bad: indeed, in some areas, such as sun rights[276], more is needed, and in many, existing regulatory agencies captured by the regulatees badly need revitalization. But particular rules and habits left over from the cheap-oil era are unquestionably unjust, energy-wasting, unnecessary, and meant to subordinate the public interest to narrow private interests—as in the clothesline prohibitions promoted by some suburban utilities anxious to power more clothes-driers, or the building

[272]For example, the original form of the ASHRAE 90-75 building code adopted (under Federal pressure) by many US states counted windows as a heat loss regardless of their orientation, and had the practical effect of prohibiting many passive solar designs. One of its accounting rules may also require the use of electric resistance heating in hydropower areas.

[273]In some communities, a single electric baseboard heater circulates from house to house for this purpose, being installed whenever the bank inspector is due and then handed on to the next project.

[274]Silly rules of this kind are generally evaded by e.g. putting a TV aerial on a wind machine, or by semantic devices: a 40-m² underground walk-in greenhouse was built as a "cold-frame" in an area whose zoning barred greenhouses, and a passive solar house got a mortgage by being described—truthfully if incompletely—as heated by a "forced-hot-air" system.

[275]For example, Consolidated Edison (NY), as part of its escalating war with small self-generators, persuaded municipal authorities to tax a Seal-Kap cogeneration system as real property: B. Feder, *NY Times*, 24 August 1980.

[276]G. B. Hayes, *Solar Access Law*, Environmental Law Institute (Washington DC), 1979.

regulations that entrench the monopoly power of some sectors of
the building industry. It is also not too soon to worry that in trying
to solve some genuine problems, such as solar quality control in
the face of dishonest or (more often) inexperienced vendors,
legislators may seek new regulatory solutions that are simple and
wrong[277], such as equipment "standards" whose main effect is to
prohibit simple, clever, and cost-effective designs or small-
business participation without protecting the public.

    Lack of information is an all but complete bar to action, and
is most pervasive in government policy circles, where hier-
archies—described by Kenneth Boulding as an "ordered ar-
rangement of wastebaskets designed to prevent information from
reaching the executive"—compound the difficulties of keeping
up with dispersed, fast-moving, mainly unofficial developments.
It is common to find lags of several years in merely reading literature that is itself several years out of date. Officials fire-fighting in
the capital and used to getting their information from traditional
sources find themselves unknowingly cut off from most of the
exciting news. Still worse is *wrong* information, often propagated
by governments and by competing energy industries, whether
through bad faith or simple ignorance. Especially common and
pernicious are economic comparisons whose tendentious conclusions depend on obscure assumptions opaque to non-experts. It is
striking, for example, that virtually every official study of the
economics of active solar space heating assumes costly, high-
technology packaged collectors, large collector areas to compensate for an inefficient building, and no economic integration with
water heating—methodological errors that can easily increase the
apparent price of such a system by a factor of between ten and
one hundred[278].

    Information is implicit, too, in price signals; but who gets
the signals? The incentive to make an energy-saving investment
may be split off from its cost. Why should a landlord retrofit a
building whose tenants pay the utilities, or a cab company fix an
inefficient taxi whose driver buys the gasoline, or a builder or
lessor invest up front in measures that will save money for later

[277]TVA solar loans provide that the contractor is not entitled to payment until
TVA (or, we would prefer, some other competent inspector of the customer's
choice) has certified that the job was done in a workmanlike way. Another good
alternative to standards and licensing is simple information feedback so that customers can assess contractors' and vendors' past performance—and so that the
suppliers know their faults will be publicized to deter future buyers.

[278]See notes 232 and 233 (and, for hot-water loads themselves, *Solar Age*[107]).

tenants? The ways to address these awkward problems exist[279], but must be tailored to local conditions. In every community, in virtually every walk of life, institutional barriers remain to be tackled, whether as obvious as a split incentive or as subtle as a quirk of the tax code[280].

Creatures of habit

The information/action problem afflicts governments as seriously as individuals: some institutional barriers flourish only in cozy bureaucratic niches. A government wanting a reactor need only call Bechtel, KWU, Framatome, or Mitsubishi to have hundreds of technocrats soliciting in the corridors. The centers of excellence in soft technology are scattered, unprestigious, impecunious, all but unknown. That the New Alchemy Institute, Volunteers in Technical Assistance, the Intermediate Technology Development Group, the Institute for Local Self-Reliance, the Small Farm Energy Project, the Farallones Institute, the Land Institute, and their improbably named journals can offer better buys than Bechtel is unlikely to occur to most governments[281]. Historic patterns of reward and prestige, too, make bureaucracies safe for incompetence, bypass vision, and scorn technologies that are sophisticated not in their complexity but in their simplicity. It is difficult to admit that one's career has been misdirected, or that grand gestures—Atoms for Peace, the Apollo Project, rural electrification, the Aswan High Dam—showed more flair than foresight. It is difficult for some to see counterflow heat exchangers as sexier than fast breeders: to get excited about solutions that are not thousand-megawatt, computer-designed with exotic materials, and studded with numerous brass knobs. Much of our

---

[279]The landlord/tenant split incentive can be attacked in cities with rent control by allocating mainly to the landlord any excess of heating bills above a level reasonable for an efficient building, but providing capital transfers[261] to pay for the retrofit. Minnesota uses a different approach, unfortunately lacking the capital transfers: mandatory point-of-sale retrofit after a five-year grace period. Rented housing is one of the few cases where mandatory retrofit may be necessary.

[280]For example, the way energy bills are a deductible business expense while conservation investments must be capitalized. A comprehensive energy policy must overhaul many indirectly energy-wasting tax rules: for example, it should seek to increase the durability and recycling of goods—perhaps e.g. by excise taxes on cars, and on other major goods bearing them, that are inversely proportional to the length of the warranty—provided, of course, that this will not increase the turnover time of presently energy-inefficient capital stocks.

[281]The invasion of solar markets by some of the world's largest corporations may reduce this problem but risks substituting another—abuse of market power.

species' energy prospect depends on our ability to bring both persuasiveness and compassion to these real human problems within the community of energy technologists and administrators.

Yet against this array of internal and external barriers to change, governments must weigh the unpleasant and all too familiar types of social change entailed by the hard-path, and especially by the nuclear, alternative [282]. The emotional overtones and deep moral divisions inspired by the nuclear issue have already destabilized politics more in FR Germany and Switzerland than any other issue for decades, more in Sweden than any since World War I. We do not know what degree of consensus is necessary to run a significant nuclear program, but suspect it has not been achieved so far in any democracy[283]. Soft technologies, in

---

Though the purchase of e.g. most photovoltaic companies by major oil companies is contrary to public policy, and vigorous antitrust enforcement is highly desirable, it is nonetheless encouraging that with isolated exceptions, those corporations flocking to their place in the sun are tending to lose their market battles with unknown small businesses that have smarter ideas, lower overheads, and far greater ability to tailor devices to local conditions for best performance. Most soft technologies lend themselves very badly to natural monopoly—unlike fossil and nuclear fuels—and competition in soft-technology markets favors the local and adaptive, not the big.

[282]For example[225], increased concentration of economic and political power, abrogation of market forces (e.g. the Synthetic Fuels Corporation, meant to finance by corporate socialism investments which the market wisely refused to finance), more technocratic and less accountable decision-making (Lovins[171]), authoritarian measures needed to impose unwanted policies and facilities on increasingly restive populations, specific risks to civil liberties[59], allocation of energy and its social costs to different people at opposite ends of the transmission lines (Lovins[171] and Gerlach[171], who analyzes the 60-odd "energy wars" now going on in the US for this reason), and greatly increased vulnerability[165].The question of perceived legitimacy (Aga Khan[171]) is especially important: it is revealing that *Pravda* has lately had to resort to front-page editorials assuring Soviet citizens of the safety of reactors built e.g. in Leningrad with no containment shell—and that such shells will, though allegedly unnecessary, be added to *future* reactors.

[283]Many senior civil servants in Whitehall share our suspicion that if Prime Minister Thatcher pursues her intention of a major LWR program in Britain—long regarded as the most tolerant and stable of the parliamentary democracies—it will be the end of the whole nuclear program. Siting and licensing will require procedures as openly farcical as motorway inquiries (R. Grove-White, "A Motorway Threat to Nuclear Democracy", *New Scientist,* 13 March 1980) became in the late 1970s, so the regulatory process and institutions will lose whatever legitimacy they have left, and the tolerance hitherto extended by many to the gas-cooled reactors will be withdrawn. See also W. C. Patterson & J. Greenholgh, "The Impact Abroad of the Accident at the Three Mile Island Nuclear Plant: March to September 1979," Congressional Research Service, for US Senate Committee on Governmental Affairs, Subcommittee on Energy, Nuclear Proliferation & Federal Services, 1980.

contrast, are correctly perceived as relatively benign; their impacts are in general directly sensible and susceptible of commonsense judgments; they are chosen in the marketplace by individual action and at a democratically accountable political level; and they give their costs and benefits very nearly to the same people at the same time, enabling them to judge for themselves how much is enough. This seems a formula for low political costs.

Some governments will not be disposed to give due weight to these arguments of political and economic efficiency. Some will not be ready even to imagine that non-nuclear energy policies, implemented by the most conservative market orthodoxy, can offer the national security advantages—speed, cheapness, sureness, and flexibility—claimed for nuclear power, but without its risks. After all, the contrary assumption is endorsed by the major international energy agencies (OECD, IEA, IAEA) and is being continuously ratified in new institutional arrangements. But it is possible to respect such countries' choice without encouraging it; to honor diversity without inviting opportunists to *accomplir* their *faits*; to help those lacking up-to-date assessments to obtain them. Countries unwilling even to explore in good faith the possibility of alternative policies should not be rewarded by further political or economic support for their nuclear programs, nor insulated from the political effects of more flexible countries' reassessments[284].

It is also critically important to devise mechanisms for the orderly recycling of the human and technical resources previously committed to the nuclear industry—a recycling already well under way at considerable cost, as in the past dispersal of aerospace and military technologists[285]. Industrial conversion

[284]This will mean curbing the US tendency to ancestor-worship, expressed in a peculiar fondness for grandfather clauses. It is time to bring nuclear proponents face-to-face with Lew Perelman's thesis ("Social Dynamics of the Nuclear Power Program", 1979 typescript, CalTech Jet Propulsion Lab., Pasadena CA 91103): the fatalistic attitude that nuclear commitments are already too great to be reversed or redirected, and "the unwillingness to consider objectively whether nuclear power is either necessary or socially acceptable, are the principal reasons for the nuclear power program's acknowledged failure to achieve its proponents' goals."

[285]The Institute for Energy Analysis, in *Economic and Environmental Impacts of a U.S. Nuclear Moratorium, 1985-2010*, notes (Ch. 10) that "probably no more than about 50,000 workers [gross, not net] in the [US] nuclear power industry would lose their jobs as a direct result of a moratorium. Although tragic for those involved, the effect would certainly be small compared with the 350,000 who lost their jobs in the aerospace industry between 1968 and 1970." (Interestingly, some companies reported that shedding their nuclear activities would improve their profitability.) Much of this shakeout—perhaps half or more—has already occurred[141].

legislation in the key countries[286] would greatly reduce that cost. Most nuclear technologists are broad-gauge engineers who moved sideways into nuclear power from other fields and can as well move out again (the number of good ex-nuclear solar engineers is growing rapidly). The few highly specialized and dedicated people —radiochemists, core physicists, and the like—who would find such a transition more difficult will still be needed to look after the wastes already made: a business with a long future. But people who, in good faith, committed their careers to an abortive product deserve more active social support in switching to fields where their talents are more needed.

Cutting our losses

Recycling the nuclear industry: surely, some will say, this is a drastic gamble with our energy future, prematurely sacrificing an insurance policy which we may desperately need if alternatives do not work. But the real insurance policy lies in the well-proven, completely conventional efficiency improvements and transitional fossil-fuel technologies (such as industrial motor retrofits and cogeneration) which can each unquestionably provide more electricity faster and cheaper than nuclear power but were left out of the official projections on which, a decade ago, today's nuclear enterprise was predicated. This is ignored, and the whole burden placed on renewables, in typical official statements of the supply-oriented "insurance-policy" argument:

It is too early to be categoric about which energy sources will prove to be dominant by the middle of the next century. Governments should indeed go ahead with major development of solar and other renewable energy sources. But at a minimum, governments would be unwise to deprive themselves of the nuclear option during the early part of the [next] century when the transition from oil and gas is likely to occur. A rapid transition to renewables is likely to be costly and to involve unforeseen problems. A judicious energy policy, like any major social policy, should have flexibility and redundancy to protect against failures. On this basis, nuclear energy has a major role to play in relation to the long run problem in the U.S. *even if* solar optimism proves to be justified. This is even

---

[286]Senator George McGovern has long advocated and drafted such legislation in the US, and formal policies to the same end exist in some European countries. It is not clear, however, whether the US unions concerned with nuclear-industry job loss will join with the growing number backing a soft path (Machinists & Aerospace Workers, Sheet-Metal Workers, United Auto Workers, et al.) to form a united constituency for conversion legislation: sectionalism may again prevail.

more true for other countries with less access to fossil fuel resources to help buffer the transition to renewable energy technologies[287].

Such a statement embodies, characteristically, seven fallacious assumptions:

- that adequate solar technologies remain to be developed[288];
- that in their putative absence nothing else is left to fall back

[287]See note 96.

[288]Ironically, it is in nuclear power's very arena—in the supply of electricity—that renewable sources are most mature and most unquestionably competitive (wind, microhydro), and that technical developments in the 1980s are likely to be most dramatic. Cheap solar cells (photovoltaics) will very probably be on the market before anyone knows how best to use them, and long before a recently ordered power station can be built. Though our analysis conservatively omits this option, the best conventional (Czochralski silicon) photovoltaic components already in pilot stage and scheduled for marketing in 1982-83, if combined into a single unit, would yield electricity comparable to or cheaper than that delivered by newly ordered conventional stations in developed countries[216]. Even at 1980 array prices ($6/W peak), photovoltaics are very attractive in most developing countries, which tend to have costlier electricity and little distribution grid: sunlight is distributed free. For example, at a 0.l/y real fixed charge rate, 0.2 capacity factor (many developing countries may exceed this—Atlanta is 0.19, Phoenix 0.25) $3\times$ optical concentration, and $2\times$ markup for clever installation, molded-plastic Winston concentrator, and interface, delivered power will cost about 23¢/kW-h—about twice present New York City rates, but a bargain in isolated sites, even with a surcharge for battery storage. Several US firms are now gearing up to market arrays at $2-3/$W_p$ in 1982-83. Many lines of development now proceeding with unexpected speed and success, mainly with amorphous, polycrystalline, and multilayer cells, promise at least a good chance of 0.3-0.5 $/$W_p$ array prices by the mid-1980s—in which case even a fancy installation could compete not only with grid electricity but arguably with direct fuels! But even in less ambitious prospects lies a snag. Utilities in, say, the US now face marginal delivered prices around 8-10¢/kW-h. With cheaper options now on the market—wind at about 3-6¢ and microhydro and cogeneration[117] often in a similar range, let alone the imminent arrival of photovoltaics—there is an incentive for utility customers to install them. The utilities are compelled by PURPA (the 1978 Public Utilities Regulatory Policy Act) to buy back customers' excess power at their own "avoided cost". This generation will *combine* with price-induced efficiency improvements to increase supply as demand stagnates or decreases[116], leading to still more idle utility generators, higher fixed costs, higher prices, and more incentive to customers to generate their own power. This positive feedback loop may imply no less than the rapid technical and economic obsolescence—in perhaps a decade—of one or two hundred *billion* dollars' worth of utility investments. This will certainly complicate the utilities' struggle against insolvency[137] and may lead them to press for legislative or regulatory countermeasures that enforce their franchise monopoly (effectively deregulated by PURPA as to generation) or reduce self-generators' advantage: Con Ed's fight against highly competitive cogenerators in New York [275] may be a taste of this future institutional fight for survival.

upon (the enormous stretching of all fossil fuels by efficiency improvements being neglected), so that the need for nuclear power for the next fifty years is established if there are any doubts about the ability of renewables to take over quickly;
• that the transition to a post-petroleum energy system should take place in the next century rather than at the margin starting now;
• that renewables are costly and unproven compared to equivalent nuclear programs[289];
• that their deployment will probably hit sociopolitical snags more severe than those of equivalent nuclear programs[290];
• that the extent of need for transitional nuclear power depends on the availability of transitional fossil fuel, begging the question of what countries lacking such fuel will use during their even longer transition to nuclear dependence: in fact, whether a country has indigenous fossil fuels, or which ones, or how much of them, has nothing whatever to do with whether nuclear power or soft-path investments can displace that country's oil use faster;
• that the US and other countries need *every* available energy option—a holdover from the inflated demand forecasts made before 1973. It is like saying that someone who wears both a belt and suspenders should buy a gross of safety pins and go about holding up his trousers.

In view of the trivial potential contribution of nuclear power compared to alternatives which are already implementing themselves far faster (despite remaining barriers), and which are empirically known to be much cheaper and more attractive, the nuclear "insurance" argument smacks of insurance fraud.

It is neither necessary nor possible to do everything at once, and some options exclude others. Keeping the nuclear industry alive, even in a semi-comatose state, is not like offering vitamin tablets to a healthy athlete; it demands heroic measures to resuscitate and artificially sustain the victim of an incurable attack of market forces. Not "depriving ourselves of the nuclear option" would require dramatic intervention—a rescue operation costing

[289]They are empirically cheaper, even in capital cost[103] (and especially in working capital required[234], typically several times less for equivalent capital-intensity because of shorter lead times and faster paybacks), and are arguably more technically mature than nuclear power.

[290]This suggestion is especially ludicrous when enunciated by a government that for thirty-five years has proven unable to manage the timely deployment of its own nuclear fuel cycle.

a substantial fraction of the world's energy investment budget, starting with an emergency transfusion approaching one hundred billion dollars and continuing with ten or twenty billion dollars per year indefinitely. Of our finite resources, only crumbs would remain[291].

Countries wanting to shift to reliance on renewable sources—both the adequate ones already available and the improved ones being rapidly developed—must do so before the relatively cheap fossil fuels, and the relatively cheap money made from them, are gone. They are going fast. In this historically unique transition, nuclear power does not complement but devours its rivals. It is a long, irreversible step in the wrong direction.

[291]Such enormous commitments do not complement but foreclose[225] softer options:
•by cultural conditioning, a hard-path and soft-path approach each make the other harder to imagine—just as today many people cannot imagine any approach to the energy problem except what they have been doing for the past few decades;
•by accreting thick layers of laws, customs, and organizations, each approach inhibits the other—just as institutional barriers are inhibiting change today;
•by committing scarce resources—money, work, skills, political and managerial attention, and (most precious) time, each path slows the realization of the other—risking that its implementation will fade so far into the future that the transitional fossil-fuel "bridge" to it will have been burned.

Chapter Nine

Nuclear Power and Developing Countries

The International Atomic Energy Agency was established in 1957 to promote the spread of nuclear energy for peaceful purposes, especially in developing countries, and to see that this was "not used in such a way as to further any military purpose"[292]. The IAEA's promotional zeal, however, conflicts with the practical difficulty of finding any *exclusively* peaceful nuclear technologies[293]. This tension is mirrored in the Non-Proliferation Treaty, whose primary obligation[294] is the promise of weapons states in Article I (reciprocated by non-weapons states in Article II) not to transfer bombs or "in any way to assist [or] encourage" others' acquisition of bombs. Yet in Article IV, all parties undertake "to facilitate", and have a right "to participate in, the fullest possible exchange of equipment, materials and scientific and technological information for the peaceful uses of nuclear energy", and have an "inalienable right" to peaceful uses "without discrimination"—subject to Articles I and II. This ambiguous compromise does not resolve but embodies the underlying dilemmas of classical nonproliferation policy: reconciling national sovereignty with world order and the promotion of reactors with the prohibition of bombs[295].

[292]The IAEA thus combined promotional with regulatory duties. Unlike the national nuclear regulatory bodies in the US, France, Britain, Canada, and Japan, it has not so far felt compelled to separate the two functions in order to avoid the appearance of a conflict of interest.

[293]The legislative history of the IAEA Statute confirms the unambiguous commitment to *exclusively* peaceful uses (a category which, on our analysis, is vanishingly small). See Wohlstetter *et al*[35] at 41-42, 58-61, and A. Steiner, "Article IV and the 'Straightforward Bargain' ", Pan Heuristics[8] report 78-832-08 to ACDA.

[294]So described by the Director-General of the IAEA: S. Eklund in *Atom* 258:107-09 (1978), reprinted in *Reader*[20] 127-29.

[295]As first drafted by US and Soviet negotiators in Geneva, the NPT did not contain this ambiguity: it was a simple treaty in which states having bombs promised not to spread them and states lacking them promised not to seek or acquire them. It was to make this draft more saleable to certain other countries, and to buy time in which, for example, it was hoped that anti-bomb members of India's Congress Party could strengthen their hand, that provisions for nuclear technology transfer (for electricity or explosive excavation) were added as a "sweetener". At the time, of course, the military implications of nuclear power,

Conflicting commercial and military interests, spurred by the world nuclear industry, have amply exploited the ambiguity. Some nations, for varying reasons, adopt the industry's view that Article IV legitimates or even mandates the supply to all NPT adherents of plants that yield pure bomb materials, or of those materials themselves, so long as they have some civilian use: in short, that a treaty against proliferation encourages or requires that non-weapons states be placed days or hours away from having bombs, provided that they promise (quite revocably and unenforceably) not to make them. Supplier nations' unilateral and multilateral declarations of "restraint" in transferring "sensitive" (code for "unsafeguardable in principle") equipment, technologies, and materials have not said, however, that such transfers would breach the Article I obligation "not...in any way to assist"; they have on the contrary reaffirmed the suppliers' commitment (conveniently for famished reactor vendors at home) to export still more thermal reactors and their fuel. (To remove awkward hitches in this process, Ambassador Gerard Smith has sought to remove the USNRC's export review powers.) Article IV alludes to "sensitive" transfers only implicitly, by its requirement—either universally inclusive or eliminatively restrictive, depending on one's viewpoint—of conformity to Articles I and II.

As Albert Wohlstetter has remarked[296],

The contention was made by many...delegates to the [1977] Iran Conference on Transfer of Nuclear Technology at Persepolis...[that Article IV's] "inalienable right" includes the stocking of plutonium or other highly concentrated fissile material and was therefore violated by President Carter's [and Ford's] proposal to delay commitment to unrestricted commerce in plutonium....[Their] declaration to that effect...has been characterized as a Rebellion of the Third World against this violation of the NPT. This particular third world rebellion might have been a little more convincing if the President of the American Nuclear Society had not played a leading role in the writing of the declaration, and if some of the countries complaining most bitterly about a supposed violation of a most sacred part of the NPT had not themselves neglected ever to sign or ratify the NPT.***Some help and certainly the avoidance of *arbitrary* interference in peaceful uses...[are involved in Article IV]. However, the main return for promising not to manufacture or receive nuclear weapons

---

especially of once-through thermal reactors, were perceived more dimly than today[4], and often through the rose-colored spectacles of "denaturing" theories [37] not finally debunked until the late 1970s.

[296]Wohlstetter *et al*[293,80].

is clearly a corresponding promise by some potential adversaries, backed by a system to provide early warning if the promises should be broken. The NPT is, after all, a treaty against proliferation, not for nuclear development.

Yet this common-sense reading is far from universally accepted[297]. Any attempt to resolve the ambiguity in Article IV seems to some parties a discriminatory abrogation of their own hallowed interpretation and, often, an insult to their sovereignty. Tempers are running high[298]. But the impasse results from misstating the problem.

Rethinking the NPT Article IV obligation

Denial—of bombs to states lacking them—is the central purpose of the NPT. The compensatory rewards to non-weapons states, however, were stated in terms of nuclear power because of an historical artifact—the nuclear context and background of the negotiators—*not* as an expression of the essential purpose of Article IV.

As conventionally construed, Article IV is an obligation to

[297]For example, the expansive view that Article IV positively obliges "all advanced countries to transfer any civilian technology except ['peaceful nuclear explosives'] . . . no matter how far such transfer might carry the recipient country toward [bombs]"[296] was gleefully embraced by Mr Justice Parker in his Windscale report[42]—to the thinly disguised embarrassment of the British Foreign Office, whose efforts in the London Suppliers' Group were impliedly a conspiracy to breach the NPT. The US has ducked this issue by saying simply that "all states that meet basic non-proliferation conditions have the right to access to the benefits of nuclear energy for peaceful purposes without discrimination"[185], without specifying how this can be *exclusively* peaceful[293]. As Commissioner Gilinsky notes[35], calling attention to the unsafeguardability of bomb materials violates a taboo against "undermining" the IAEA by realistically assessing its limitations—even though in practice some states, like the USSR, have never been willing to export sensitive fuel-cycle facilities even to their closest satellites, and the London Suppliers' Group, which included some principal technology-importing nations, has adopted this policy. Apparently it is all right to note the limits of the safeguards regime by deeds but not by words.

[298]The emotions raised by this issue, and to some extent the issue itself, are reminiscent of the US debate over the inalienable right to bear handguns. So harsh is the Article IV conflict, assiduously fanned by the nuclear industry, that according to D. A. V. Fischer of the IAEA (*Reader*[20] 151-56),

...under the leadership of Yugoslavia, Pakistan and Nigeria–two NPT and one non-NPT country–there will be a major effort to convene another international conference...similar to that which was held in Geneva in 1968 and which would be political in character. It would seek to reaffirm Article IV...and codify, expand and articulate–perhaps in a convention or other legal instrument–the "inalienable right" of every country to advanced [Code for "Plutonium-based"] nuclear technology.

facilitate the transfer of nuclear power. That transfer, on our analysis, is in fact a liability for its ostensible purpose of providing energy[299], but is singularly useful for its forbidden purpose of providing bombs. Nuclear power is something which under Article I the givers mustn't give and under Article II the recipients shouldn't ask for. The time is therefore ripe to reformulate the bargain in the light of new knowledge. Instead of denying or hedging their obligation, the exporting nations should fulfill it—in a wider sense based on a pragmatic reassessment of what the recipient nations *say* their real interests are. When Eisenhower spoke in the fading glow of FDR's rural electrification program, and when the NPT was negotiated at the zenith of cheap oil, nuclear power was expected to be cheap, easy and abundant. Now that everyone knows better, recipients should insist on aid in meeting their declared central need: not nuclear power per se, but rather *oil displacement and energy security*.

The arguments that efficiency improvements and available soft technologies can displace oil and meet energy needs better than nuclear power are in fact strongest in developing countries[300], where capital, delivery systems, infrastructure, and income are most limited. By enhancing resilience, self-reliance, and economic strength, a soft path aids national security. It can serve equally well, we shall suggest, another legitimate motive: prestige. It does not serve the illegitimate motive which NPT adherents have disavowed: getting bombs. It thus isolates legitimate from illegitimate motives and makes proliferators explicitly reveal their intentions.

Prestige and national welfare

To the extent that developing countries seek reactors for prestige, the West's bad example is to blame. The West's motives

[299]Or, in President Eisenhower's extravagant phrase (in his 1953 Atoms for Peace UN speech), providing "abundant electrical energy in the power-starved areas of the world". This ambitious concept appears to have received virtually no prior analysis within the Administration, and the whole history of the origin of the Atoms for Peace concept is surprisingly obscure.

[300]See references in notes 146 and 224. Even studies by nuclear-oriented USDOE aid teams have found major scope for *industrial* energy savings in Egypt and Peru. Of each ten kW-h generated by a new power station in, say, India, about eight will go typically to urban industry, one to rich urban households, and one to rural areas (distribution to which is often astronomically costly). Considerably less than one kW-h—probably less than one-tenth—will end up helping the destitute villagers in whose name it was installed, as most of them cannot afford it, and have no way to use it. See also H. Gustaffson, "Electricity in Development", *Economic & Political Weekly* (Bombay), 7 July 1979, and K. S. Parikh, "India in 2001—Fuels or 'Second India' and Energy", Indian Statistical Unit (New Delhi), 1979.

for starting nuclear programs at home—largely psychological and
political, not economic or energy-related—are understandably
contagious in countries lacking the West's (and the North's) advantages of money, technology, fuels, and world recognition. But
prestige, a consuming interest for any politician, is normally defined in terms of an accepted theory of national welfare. Reality
has debunked the fantasy that nuclear power would make deserts
bloom, cities boom, and villages prosper. The difficulties of fish-
ing for spent fuel with bamboo poles at Tarapur, the distressing
link between electrical and political centralization[301], the minis-
cule impact of enormous resources on national energy needs[302],
and the simple cost of a $3500-per-kilowatt reactor (the latest, but
surely not the last, estimate for Brazil's Angra II—at least four
times the cost of local central-station power alternatives) must
now strike national planners as less seductive. Heroic diversions
of national resources for pitiful ends may comfort nuclear
bureaucrats, but not a finance minister facing massive oil debts, a
district commissioner fighting deforestation, or a prime minister
whose people still cannot cook their rice. Clay stoves, biogas
plants, and cogeneration may lack sex appeal for technocrats, but
a practical politician has more to gain from thousands of small,
successful projects than from a single ribbon-cutting. Romantic
images can have a long half-life[303], but ultimately market forces
will work, and investment in pyrolyzers and windmills, solar cells
and solar stills, will become commonplace and "respectable".
How fast this happens depends on the good sense of both developed and developing countries. To hasten the demise of decisions based on bad economics and false glamor, the industrialized
countries for their part need simply to ask that buyers of nuclear
power pay for it[304]—and to provide a psychological lead, as when
seventy-eight percent of Swedes voted in 1980 to stop reactor

[301]Z. Khalilzad, "Pakistan and the Bomb", *Bulletin of the Atomic Scientists* 11-16
(January 1980), and Hayes *et al*[146]. The link has already destabilized Iran, Brazil,
and the Philippines.

[302]To his credit, a leader of India's reactor development program agreed several
years ago that if they had it to do over again, investment in clay stoves, biogas
plants, etc. would have produced vastly more improvement in national welfare;
but he is unlikely to say so in public.

[303]Though the IAEA has withdrawn its embarrassingly inflated (and US-inspired)
estimates of developing countries' nuclear prospects, it actively fights other UN
agencies' efforts to counterbalance its continuing nuclear promotion: all the UN
development agencies follow the World Bank's lead (at least to date [316]) in reject-
ing nuclear projects for development, on purely economic grounds.

[304]See notes 146 and 178.

ordering and to phase out nuclear power altogether within about twenty-five years[305, 306].

Some leaders may see short-run glamor in bombs. But as the Vietnam debacle showed a decade ago, prestige comes from a

---

[305]D. Abrahamson and T. B. Johansson (the latter is Vice Chairman of the Swedish equivalent of the USNRC) noted in a letter to *The New York Times*, 30 April 1980:

> ... *The results of [the 23 March 1980] referendum have been erroneously reported as showing approval for a general go-ahead for nuclear power. In fact, the meaning of that referendum is that there will be no more nuclear power plants built in Sweden, and within about 25 years no nuclear power plants will be operating.*
>
> *Three alternatives were on the ballot, plus the choice of casting a blank ballot. Options 1 and 2 both stated that the six currently operating reactors, the four that are ready to operate and the two that are under construction should be allowed to operate for about 25 years. No additional reactors would be built. The formal difference between options 1 and 2 was that the second option included full nationalization of reactor operation.*
>
> *Option 3 stated that the six operating reactors should be shut down within 10 years and that the other six should not be allowed to operate. Option 3 received 38.7 percent of the vote. The turnout was over 74 percent of eligible voters, 3.3 percent of whom cast blank ballots.*
>
> *During the pre-referendum campaign, the supporters of the first option did not make a strong commitment to a stop of reactor construction after completion of the two that are being built. Option 1 was therefore interpreted by voters as being an open-ended nuclear option. It received 18.9 percent of the votes.*
>
> *The supporters of option 2, on the other hand, strongly emphasized that the 12 reactors would be the end of the nuclear program.*
>
> *They presented a detailed, 37-point program to demonstrate how this would be done. That program stressed the aim of replacing both oil and nuclear power, e.g., "The nuclear power industry is to be transformed and made to focus on other, primarily renewable, forms of energy. . . . Direct electric resistance heating will be forbidden in new construction. . . . Electricity charges and taxes will be designed to facilitate conservation and the introduction of new energy sources." It was clear that phasing out nuclear power within 25 years was not just wishful thinking. Option 2 received 39.1 percent of the vote.*
>
> *A large majority of Swedish voters (the 77.8 percent who supported options 2 and 3) thus advise that future energy supply will come from solar energy captured through hydropower, biomass and solar heating. Sweden already gets over 20 percent of its energy from hydropower and biomass; several additional biomass systems are under construction, and there is a large renewable-energy research, development and demonstration program.*
>
> *Sweden has embarked on the route to replace oil and nuclear over the next several decades with solar energy and more efficient energy use. This is the meaning of the Swedish referendum.*

[306]The essential process here is the evaporation of legitimacy—a process which, once its time has come, can run its course in a surprisingly few years. The loss of legitimacy that largely eliminated overt colonialism by the Western powers, and that may now be threatening some multinational corporations, is well under way for nuclear power too.

leader's ability to influence events, not from mere technology or troop strength. In the long run, a policy of self-denial, recognizing the near-irreversibility of a peek over the nuclear threshold, has often been a policy of shrewd self-interest. Nehru, for example, chose Indian nonalignment not from Gandhian idealism but from common-sense realization that the security of his young nation depended on others' rivalries. His avoidance of entangling alliances established moral leadership, helped to confine the risks posed by the Superpowers to others and to each other, and bought time for India's military and economic growth.

Nehru's policy had a more troublesome aspect: while denouncing bombs, he carefully designed and brilliantly pursued a civil nuclear program to provide a bomb option. While repudiating the discriminatory controls of Atoms for Peace, India took advantage of its huge subsidies and open laboratories. Nehru garnered a Canadian reactor "for peaceful purposes", American heavy water, other resources from many countries, and USAEC training programs not only in dual-purpose plutonium technologies but in specific techniques for nuclear explosives. He adeptly played off against the supplier states' foreign ministries their own autonomous nuclear agencies. He succeeded; and for our argument, his success in acquiring bombs poses a difficult question: why should a major developing country forego such an opportunity, accept superpower hegemony, and live within the innately discriminatory restrictions of the NPT? We cannot address this question as citizens of a non-weapons state, nor can we know the ultimate consequences to India of its pursuit of bombs. The valid argument about discrimination we must postpone until Chapter Ten. But we can suggest that the "option" strategy, if it was so meant, backfired badly by creating not only the means but the bureaucratic pressures and the ultimately irresistible political impetus to exercise the option. The bomb technologists, as Lord Zuckerman has remarked, "have become the alchemists of our time, working in secret ways which cannot be divulged, casting spells which embrace us all." Save in exceptionally open societies (Sweden is the only obvious historical example), there seems to be no turning back. Bomb proponents, such as Dr Bhabha, may become so powerful that they can override internal dissent and become virtually a government unto themselves: only recently, the atomic energy commission of one near-weapons state reportedly reversed a top-level political decision to accept international safeguards.

Despite the course that India took in approaching too near the edge of the nuclear pit, Nehru's understanding of the limits of nuclear deterrence looks sounder with each passing year. Today,

US moves toward China and, to some extent, Pakistan push India closer to the USSR; a more strongly nuclear-armed India elicits a similar response from Pakistan and (more likely) China, raising the stakes in any Indian conflict and discouraging allies or potential supporters from intervening. Nehru understood the benefits of nuclear "weakness" and maximized them. It is not so clear that his daughter understands that the costs of nuclear "strength" (more nervous and better-armed generals—at home and abroad—and more reluctant allies) are less than the putative "benefits"[307] (deterrence, and distraction from internal problems). One can well imagine Indian strategists a few decades hence, like their Western counterparts today, wishing they had never heard of nuclear bombs.

Bomb programs have probably always decreased their patrons' security from within and without. The first act in the worldwide nuclear arms race began, chillingly, with the misperception that a rival (Nazi Germany) was about to develop bombs. A nuclear force possessed by, say, India or even Japan cannot deter neighbors' nuclear attacks (which may arrive anonymously by oxcart, fishing-boat, or Railway Express); and far from deterring first strikes by the great powers, it is an attractive nuisance inviting them[308], as when the US and USSR each sounded out the other about a preëmptive strike against nascent Chinese nuclear capacity. That those who begin to seek security through bombs persist in their fruitless quest, apparently unable to stop, does not mean that, if they had to do over again, they would choose to restart.

[307]The US is doing almost nothing to address these perceived benefits—countries' motivation to get bombs. Nosenzo[185], emphasizing "the important role that fission can and must play in meeting energy demands into the next century", stated:

> Our policy initiatives to reduce motivation have focused primarily on major efforts to promote universal adherence to the NPT and similar binding international commitments coupled with supporting and improving the technical safeguards of the IAEA.

(See also Comptroller General of the US, General Accounting Office, ID-80-41, 31 July 1980.) At the same time, US plutonium policy has clearly implied the inadequacy of the NPT/IAEA regime; so though the steps stated may slightly increase the risk and political cost of detected diversions, they can hardly relieve non-weapons states' anxieties about regional rivals or the weapons states. Thus those steps have very little to do with motivation. The real motives are being handled inconsistently, as when Secretary Kissinger, in August 1976, sought to discourage proliferation by simultaneously threatening to ship arms to the Shah and no arms to Mr Bhutto. Such measures as urging Japan to remilitarize could easily backfire.

[308]For an analysis of the Japanese case, see Ch. 5 of Wohlstetter *et al*[13]. As for conventional military attack, especially by saboteurs, one can hardly imagine a more tempting target than a single reactor whose containment can be breached and core melted by various low-technology means, simultaneously crashing the national electrical supply and releasing a substantial fraction of a radioactive inventory equivalent to the fallout from thousands of Hiroshima bombs.

Nonviolent energy strategies

Many developing countries are eager to avoid these costs and to advance their people's welfare by indigenous, appropriate, nonviolent energy policies. Though the precondition for such policies—an energy establishment not run by electronuclear bureaucrats—is even harder to achieve than the staple ingredients—imagination, innovation, and hard work—the advantages are obvious enough. Whether at the scale of virtually zero-cost clay stoves that quadruple or quintuple the efficiency of burning scarce firewood[309] (cooking fuel for some one and a half billion people; a further billion cook with dung and crop wastes), sailwing pumps, solar driers and cookers, or sophisticated efficiency-boosting and solar technologies in major urban industries, a soft path has just the strengths a developing country seeks. It can save capital and foreign exchange, use abundant local resources, retard urbanization, provide clean energy equitably at relatively low cost, protect soil fertility, avoid the clutches of technological colonialism, and nurture indigenous innovation. Amulya K. N. Reddy of the Indian Institute of Science in Bangalore has neatly encapsulated these advantages by comparing, using empirical mid-1970s Indian data, two ways to make two hundred thirty thousand metric tons per year of fixed nitrogen in fertilizer:

Characteristic	Western-style coal-fed fertilizer plants	Indian-style gobar biogas plants[a]
number of plants	1	26,150
total capital cost (10^6)	140	125[b]
total foreign exchange (10^6)	−70	0
direct employment (10^3 jobs)	1	131
net energy balance (10^{15} J/y)	−0.4	+23

[a]Digester fed with human and animal wastes and with crop residues to balance C/N ratio. Each plant produces 142 m^3/d (5000 ft^3/d) of high-quality methane plus 8.8 t/y of enhanced-availability nitrogen in residual fertilizer. The capital cost of each plant is equivalent to about $4825 and the value of the nitrogen output to about $510/t (1.1-y payback if no value is assigned to the methane). About 10^4 plants are installed annually in India.
[b]Chinese-design plants normalized to the same output cost about half this much, require no metal, and can yield a considerably higher gas pressure for village distribution. See *Soft Energy Notes*[199] *1*(1):10–12, *1*(2):27–29, *1*(3):45–46, *1*(4): 81–83 (1978); *2*(8):80–81 (1979); *3*(2):10–13 (1979), for comparisons.

[309]See references in note 224 and, for a less elaborate example, *Soft Energy*

Besides their obvious economic advantage as fertilizer producers, the gobar gas plants provide enough net methane to meet virtually all the lighting, cooking, and pumping needs of the village—about half India's total energy needs today. Currently, dung is burned in open fires for cooking, so all the nitrogen and most of the heat goes up in smoke (which blinds people). The gobar gas plants yield an improved fertilizer plus a clean and efficient fuel, and help to break the devastating cycle of firewood shortage/ deforestation/erosion/loss of fertility. Clearly, in an Indian context, this is an example of a powerful development tool if handled with sensitivity for the cultural context (so that all actors share the benefits and incentives, rather than creating new inequities by allowing a few capital-rich people to turn dung from a free good into a commodity). That is why the People's Republic of China has reportedly installed some *nine million* biogas plants since 1972.

An impressive literature[310] attests to many developing countries' interest in capturing these benefits. Some, like China in biogas and microhydropower or like Brazil in biofuels for transportation, are already world leaders. Even oil-exporting countries are finding soft-path logic compelling, whether in saving more oil for export (Indonesia) or boosting internal development for a sustainable post-oil economy (Kuwait, Saudi Arabia). It is not unusual today to find a more sophisticated understanding of the benefits of soft technologies in developing than in developed countries—and even no less knowledge of technical opportunities. But despite vast differences of resources and cultures, the task of deployment is teaching broadly the same lesson in most countries: that the most useful role of central government is to remove institutional barriers, provide psychological leadership

Notes[199] 2(8):89-90 (1979). Denis Hayes estimates that two percent of one year's world military budget would buy every rural Third World Family an efficient wood stove. A further option is to pyrolyze wood, crop wastes, etc. to far more efficiently burnable char and fluid fuels: the better burning efficiency far more than covers the energy losses in pyrolysis (heating with little air). Quite serviceable pyrolyzers have been built from old oil drums and rocks in Ghana, Indonesia, and Senegal by J.W. Tatom (4070 Ridge Rd, Smyrna GA 30080).

[310]See references in note 224; *Soft Energy Notes*[199] 3(1):8-11 (1980); J. W. Howe *et al.*, "U.S. Energy Policy in the Non-OPEC Third World", Overseas Development Council (Washington DC), 1979; UNCTAD (Geneva), "Energy supplies for developing countries: issues in transfer and development of technology", TD/B/ C.6/31, 17 October 1978; and for the flavor of recent work in biotechnologies, M. Slesser *et al.*, "Self-Reliant Development", Report TC1, IFIAS (Ulrikdals Slott, 17171 Solna, Sweden), 1979, and *Journal of the New Alchemists* (NAI, Box 432, Woods Hole, MA 02543).

and selective, short-term help to grassroots efforts, then get out of the way while human diversity and ingenuity go to work. In a problem as fragmented and heterogeneous as energy, even the countries with the most elaborate communication and control systems are discovering that central management can be more part of the problem than of its solution: rediscovering, as Lao-Tse said some two and a half millenia ago, that

Leaders are best when people scarcely know they exist, not so good when people obey and acclaim them, worst when people despise them. Fail to honor people, they fail to honor you. But of good leaders who talk little, when their work is done, their aim fulfilled, the people will all say: "We did this ourselves."

Tools for a new development

Experience in a wide range of countries suggests that centrally aided decentralized action toward a soft energy path can benefit enormously from a few simple tools:

• "Classic designs" that can spread rapidly and attract local refinements, like Chinese biogas plants, New Mexican greenhouses[311], Indian bamboo tubewells, Saskatchewan superinsulation[312], and the integrated food/energy systems of South and East Asia: all success stories that owe little if anything to central planning. Word spreads in the industrialized countries by telephone, broadcast media, and photocopiers; in China, by word of mouth (which spreads throughout the country at the pace of a person walking eight hours a day) and by simply printed illustrated pamphlets. The mechanism does not matter; the process does. The incredibly rapid flowering of clever, accessible designs worldwide is a tribute to the most powerful known tool in the universe: four billion minds wrapping around a problem.

• Fieldworkers, extension services, wandering gossips/minstrels/Jane and Johnny Appleseeds/cross-pollinators, staff exchanges, networking newsletters. The network is a far more fruitful and adaptive form of social organization than the hierarchy.

[311]See notes 248 and 249.

[312]See the first three references in note 211.

• Appropriate-technology and self-help groups[313]. There are already many able and experienced fieldworkers who know what mistakes to avoid. They need modest but adequate amounts of cash and freedom to disburse it at discretion with no red tape.

• Small-grants programs at national and regional levels. With low unit cost, low overheads, high volume, high dispersion, and willingness to take risks, these have been among the richest sources of rapid innovation. The US Federal program of Appropriate Technology Small Grants (there are also independent programs in some states) is oversubscribed with worthwhile proposals (i.e. is underbudgeted) by a factor of twenty to fifty: in the most recent round, one Alaskan household in *ten* asked for information, compared with one in twenty-eight thousand in California the previous year. The principle—let a thousand flowers bloom—is straightforward. The money needed to build a single reactor, if spread among a million groups and individuals (several thousand dollars each), could hardly avoid dispersing a hundred thousand successes where people can see and imitate and improve them. Thousands would probably yield innovations *each* more important to national welfare than the initial foregone reactor.

• Reliance less on specialized technical institutions, high technologies, and credentials than on smart people, who are to be found everywhere. Technical skills and facilities are valuable but have been overrated as prerequisites. Many of the best soft technologies can be made in any vocational high school or by a good blacksmith or "Mexican mechanic". One little-educated Alaskan bush homesteader who wrote to us recently had invented many useful energy devices, including a biogas plant which he had wished would digest paper. He noticed a moose eating a willow tree, seeded his digester with moose gut (doubtless recycling the rest of the moose), and found that his digester would then chew up not only paper but even pieces of wood. He discovered something important, but he is not Exxon. Similar cases abound. Who is doing the best anti-desert reforestation in the world? By all accounts, not a high-powered academic or industrial team, but Mongolian peasants. Perhaps it is time that those of us raised to appreciate the power of Western technostructure learned some humility. Some of the world's best energy projects bear witness to the value of avoiding educated incapacity.

---

[313]Worldwide networks including many of these groups are maintained by IP-SEP[199], TRANET (PO Box 567, Rangeley ME 04970), and VITA (3706 Rhode Island Ave, Mt Ranier MD 20822).

- Small-business soft-energy credit systems and marketing infrastructures analogous to farm credit systems and coöps. An Indian family might save upwards of three dollars a year in kerosene with a ten-dollar stove, but a thirty percent annual return on capital is not compelling for people with no capital[314]. There is seldom a marketing structure for indigenously manufactured energy devices as there is for corresponding imports.

- Soft-path lending by national energy development banks oriented toward farming, forestry, small-business, and household needs. Utilities, national fuel companies, and existing public and private banks should provide complementary finance mainly in industry and help to ensure that fledgling industries buy the most energy-efficient technologies.

- Investment balancing tests[315] by international lending agencies, which now fund hard technologies generously while funding cheaper, softer ones penuriously[316]. They should make comprehensive, fair comparisons and fund the best buys. Through force of habit, the export banks and EURATOM pay for reactors, the World Bank for oil, state enterprises for gas—but nobody seems to want to pay for ways to replace them all. Even in countries (Philippines, Indonesia) where there is clearly a major, cost-effective geothermal resource, it remains untapped because development agencies are inattentive, lines of credit are already frayed, and international oil companies are more interested in large fields of oil and gas that can extend their own corporate lifetimes. The World Bank's soft-energy programs are modest—a small fraction of hydropower and oil expenditures— and despite increased rhetorical attention, the Bank has apparently not even studied industrial energy saving, a major opportunity in many developing countries. When the 1978 international economic Summit meeting asked the Bank to explore and promote renewable sources, the Bank doubled its staff of one halftime professional. (There are now a few more.) Until four years after the 1973 oil embargo, the Bank was resisting suggestions to lend for large-field oil exploration in developing countries. The doubling of energy-for-development funding announced in August 1980 is to go mainly to giant electric projects and to oil and

[314]The World Bank eventually started a stove program, but it is apparently meant to stay relatively small and ineffectual.

[315]See note 262 and accompanying text.

[316]The World Bank's non-hydro renewables disbursements to date are in the region of $20 million: about enough to pay the interest on Brazil's foreign debt for one day. The Bank's August 1980 policy commitment to a vast central-electric program could even reverse its previous non-nuclear position.

gas. At this rate it could easily take a decade or more before cost-effective soft technologies get the Bank's attention and significant funding.

 • Soft-technology transfer concessions, including mutual exchanges, licensing of public-sector patents for home and regional markets[317], and international financing of local production and marketing. Unfortunately, many developed countries, including the US, are schizophrenic about soft technologies for development, viewing them in large part as a further market for domestic vendors—the same faulty logic[318] that led to nuclear export subsidies.

 • International ad hoc advisory networks, preferably organized by biogeographical province (like the emerging ad hoc coalition of researchers in Scandinavia, northern Canada, and Alaska), to help plug the gaps and propagate the successes of indigenous workers in locally appropriate technologies. Following the pattern of the most successful international scientific collaborations, the networks should on no account be allowed to fall into the hands of existing intergovernmental bodies.

 • Willingness by developed countries to learn from countries they have long considered backward, many of which are actually far ahead of them—leaders on a world scale in truly advanced technologies for meeting human needs.

We cannot presume to tell developing countries what to do— there has been far too much of that already—but we do venture to suggest that these are some of the tools which experience has shown useful in addressing the real and pressing needs of energy for development, the needs at which Article IV was aimed. Some developing countries are already ahead of these ideas and now lead the world, technically and institutionally, in deploying the soft technologies appropriate for themselves.

International institutions

Currently there are many fora for Northern nations to exchange energy data and views, none for Southern. The International Energy Agency's oil-sharing arrangements exclude the South. New global and regional energy and financial institutions will undoubtedly be emerging during the 1980s, and NPT adher-

---

[317]See UNCTAD[310]. Such a "Sunbeams for Peace" program could be overtaken by events, since many of the best soft-technology designs are so simple that patents on them, if obtainable, are absolutely unenforceable. The best things in life are free.

[318]See *Interagency Report*[145].

ents, especially non-weapons states, deserve substantive preference, a strong voice, and preferably a guiding role in them. To
reinforce success in energy policies that make the NPT effective,
or ultimately unnecessary, countries displacing oil most effectively with inherently nonviolent technologies should be entitled
to special financial or interim oil guarantees by weapons states.

Pessimism about new international organizations is well deserved. If nuclear and other kinds of conventional energy were
not objects of faith, hope, and charity; if the world oil crisis were
not a potential source of war and economic collapse; if capital
markets and governmental bureaucracies were prepared to finance a least-cost energy system; if the NPT were universal and
secure; if, in short, there were world enough and time to allow a
slow transition to renewable energy in developing countries, then
there would be no plausible case for a new financing institution—perhaps a Fund for Renewable Energy Enterprise (FREE),
somewhat analogous to the International Fund for Agricultural
Development. But conversion of the world energy system away
from oil and uranium is a project of the same urgency as the
post-World War II reconstruction that gave rise to the Marshall
Plan, World Bank, IMF, and OECD: institutions whose very success is now paradoxically used as an argument for *laissez faire*
energy policy. Expecting the present international financial institutions to reverse their energy priorities forthwith would be like
relying on the Kellogg-Briand Pact to ensure the security of con-
temporary Europe. We therefore see a case, as did many Third
World delegates to the 1980 NPT Review Conference, for
FREE—a substantial fund, financed perhaps by a tax on oil sales,
oil or fossil-fuel use, uranium mining, arms budgets, or megatonnage of bomb inventories (Chapter Ten). FREE would aggres-
sively finance opportunity identification, distribution, site testing,
training, and institution-building for soft technologies[319], especially those targeted on oil-sensitive uses. It would complement
existing institutions, work closely with appropriate nongovernmental organizations, substitute broad social accounting
for narrow profitability tests, take risks, be at least half controlled
by recipient states, and operate via semi-autonomous regional
centers maximizing their dispersion of staff, decisions, and
money. As one of the many complementary mechanisms needed
to address the full spectrum of developing-country energy needs
at different scales, so as to satisfy the real interest at which Arti-

---

[319]Limited by charter to decentralized systems, lest it become a vehicle for more
giant dams, power towers, monocultural biomass plantations, solar power satellites, etc. These should be left to meet their fate in the market.

cle IV was aimed, this concept could be explored and refined at the 1981 Nairobi UN Conference on New and Renewable Sources of Energy.

But we have not yet addressed the asymmetry of interests reflected in the NPT's attempt to balance Article IV entitlements against non-weapons states' acceptance of a morally and pragmatically superior, but in perceived Realpolitik and prestige terms perhaps inferior, status. We therefore turn next to the unenforceable, idealistic sentiments of the NPT's Article VI: the formidable question of nuclear disarmament.

Chapter Ten

The Nuclear Arms Race

The Preamble and Article VI of the Non-Proliferation Treaty call for a comprehensive nuclear test ban, cessation of the arms race, "effective measures in the direction of nuclear disarmament", and good-faith negotiations toward "a treaty on general and complete disarmament under strict and effective international control." These provisions have been utterly ineffectual, used cynically by both the weapons states and their imitators. The nuclear weapons states, having conducted more than eleven hundred nuclear test explosions, continue their race to build another twenty thousand bombs or so during the next decade. It is indeed curious that a single test explosion in 1974 by India— which presumably has from none to a couple of bombs today— "jarred the nuclear [weapons] states awake to the catastrophic dangers of nuclear weapons; and once awake, they launched with enthusiasm—not a painstaking review of disarmament possibilities—but rather an ambitious global non-proliferation effort."[320]

Such inverted priorities are nothing new. Upon signing the Partial Test-Ban Treaty of 1963, which bound the weapons states to seek "to achieve the discontinuance of all test explosions of nuclear weapons for all time", the USSR and US did not even seriously discuss an underground test ban for more than a decade[321]: they were too busy testing exciting new designs unabated, ignoring many annual General Assembly requests to desist. The Threshold Test-Ban Treaty of 1974 allowed as unlimited an underground test program as the parties could possibly wish for their qualitative bomb improvements (150 kilotons) and removed even that size limit for "peaceful" explosions. The US and USSR, convergently protective of their hegemony, have rejected all attempts to link the issues of vertical and horizontal proliferation, as when they rejected an ingenious protocol (suggested by nineteen nations in the first NPT Review Conference in 1975) calling for increasingly stringent mutual strategic-force ceiling re-

---

[320] H.A. Feiveson & J. Goldemberg, "Denuclearization", PU/CES-99²⁰², 1980.

[321] W. Epstein, "The Proliferation of Nuclear Weapons", *Scientific American* 18-33 (April 1975). See also *SIPRI Yearbook 1975*, Almquist & Wiksell International (Stockholm) and MIT Press (Cambridge MA), 1975, at 517-520.

ductions for each additional ten NPT adherents[322]. Such states as China and India, while vocal about the Superpowers' unwillingness or inability to do more than focus their arms race into the most militarily advantageous channels[323], to "institutionalize and regulate it"[324], are themselves NPT nonadherents and bomb-builders. China and France say their bombs are intended to eliminate the world's nuclear arsenals[325]. The atomic bombings of Hiroshima and Nagasaki were rationalized as life-*saving*. There are as many rationalizations as aspirants. Conversely, the US had the gall to lecture India on exploding a bomb in the week in which the US and USSR had exploded seven far larger ones, and in the decade in which the USSR tested one hundred ninety-one bombs, the US one hundred fifty-four, France fifty-five, China fifteen, and Britain five. The US Congress rejected as a sham India's claim of a "peaceful" explosion (a distinction not recognized by the NPT) two months *before* the US and USSR signed a Threshold Test-Ban Treaty explicitly reaffirming the research legitimacy of "peaceful" bombs[326].

Further, pervasive militarization (the real US military budget, for example, has for twenty years fluctuated about the peak Korean War level, an unprecedented continuous wartime economy) has combined with advanced technologies to produce a nuclear arsenal capable of destroying every city in the Northern Hemisphere inside thirty minutes. The US Polaris and Poseidon submarines on station at any one time have the MIRV capacity to devastate all two hundred eighteen Soviet cities of over one hundred thousand population approximately twenty times over. Any *one* of the thirty-one Poseidon submarines can have the approximate capacity to do so once [327]. Yet apparently dominant

[322]C. Whalen, at 3 in "The Second Nuclear Nonproliferation Treaty Review Conference: Implications of Recent Nuclear Developments", 16 July 1979 hearing, USHR Foreign Affairs Committee, committee print, 1979. The weapons states had apparently agreed in a confidential memorandum before the Review Conference to resist any NPT amendments.

[323]G. Kistiakowsky & H. York, *Science 185*:403-06 (1974).

[324]Epstein [321], likewise characterizing the SALT process (though it is better than nothing).

[325]H. York, *op. cit.*[22].

[326]Via a new bilateral agreement on data exchange about them: hardly a good way to support the Congressional argument—however true it was—that the supposed benefits of "peaceful" bombs had been shown to be illusory.

[327]This MIRV capacity does not appear to be fully used, but each submarine's sixteen missiles are each capable of carrying ten to fourteen warheads, a total of 160-224 per submarine, each independently targetable within broad limits, and

forces in the US attribute recent political reverses—Vietnam, Iran, Afghanistan—to a lack of military power, construed as a lack of strategic nuclear armaments, even though more power of that kind would not have helped at all to prevent those reverses and has proven an unusably blunt instrument in thirty-five years of warfare: indeed, the more terrible the retaliation threatened by the nuclear "deterrent", the less credible it is that that deterrent will ever be used[328]. As massive investments accelerate for still more bombs, largely aimed at each other, and as the US Senate ratifies neither SALT II nor the Treaty of Tlatelolco's First Protocol, the suspicion grows that the meek are in no way intended to inherit the earth. The political fallout of that suspicion "could lead to the unraveling of the NPT"[329].

Building blocs

The political obstacles to nuclear disarmament are daunting and may prove insuperable. Obfuscation, jingoism, fear, and simple momentum are so strong and pervasive that lucid efforts to rethink from first principles can hardly penetrate a dazed public consciousness[330]. But some possible approaches have not yet

each with a nominal average yield of about forty kilotons (three times that of the Hiroshima bomb, and causing major destruction killing roughly half the people present in an area of the order of fifteen square miles). For lucid surveys of effects, see e.g. K. N. Lewis, "The Prompt and Delayed Effects of Nuclear Weapons", *Scientific American* 35-47, July 1979, and J. C. Mark, Annual Review of Nuclear Science 26:51-87 (1976).

[328]H. A. Feiveson, "Tactical Nuclear Weapons", PU/CES-100[202], 1980, to be published in *World Politics,* discusses this problem, which J. Schell, in *The Time of Illusion* (Vintage, NY, 1976) has cogently argued leads to requirements in the selection and behavior of national leaders that are fundamentally at odds with democratic principles.

[329]C. Van Doren, at 17 in ref. 322. At the 1980 NPT Review Conference, hints or outright statements that some states were considering withdrawal from the NPT in protest at the nuclear arms race were dismissed by a US delegate as "wild talk" (D. Cook[177])—hardly a diplomatic response to a concern so deeply felt that many delegates expect the NPT to fall apart if Article VI is not taken more seriously before the 1985 Review Conference. Meanwhile, many major nuclear technology suppliers have continued to offer concessionary technology transfers to nonadherents—originally to FR Germany, Japan, and Italy, now to Argentina and Brazil—on terms equivalent or superior to those available to adherents: a clear incentive for nonadherence, as some resentful adherents pointed out at the 1980 NPT Review Conference.

[330]Thus Feiveson[328] suggests that the Boston Study Group's admirably clear analysis *The Price of Defense* (Times Books, the New York Times Book Co., NY, 1979) is likely to be dismissed because it is so simple as to seem—wrongly—to be simplistic. (Likewise, no doubt, the Group's "Call to Halt the Nuclear Arms Race", 1980, available from Moratorium, Institute for Defense & Disarmament Studies, 251 Harvard St., Brookline MA 02146.) For another stimulating effort at

been tried—particularly by the non-weapons states, for they have not fully grasped their potential collective influence nor organized themselves to exercise it. It was nonweapons states (Ireland, Sweden, India) that first proposed the NPT concept; yet there is now no coherent coalition lobbying for substantive disarmament measures or linking their fiscal savings to development aid. Despite the efforts of such groups as the Stockholm International Peace Research Institute, there is no effective International Arms Control and Disarmament Agency to act as an activist secretariat. Such lobbying has worked in the past—NPT, test-ban treaties—when it was in nonweapons states' interest, but today, when the interest in avoiding universal catastrophe is all the stronger, a few stalwarts (notably, through the efforts of Inga Thorsson, Sweden) are left to pursue their lonely campaign for the whole bloc. It is the nuclear midgets who should be collectively admonishing the giants for their bombs' threat to the world, not the reverse. Respected, nonaligned nonweapons states have a critical collective role in any raising of world consciousness about bombs, and many nations whose vital interests are threatened by a nuclear arms race they abhor—Mexico, Papua-New Guinea, and Denmark, for example—are also the same ones that might be most ready and able to help lead a consortium of diverse states promoting the soft-energy development measures mentioned in Chapter Nine.

Some possible initiatives are fairly conventional:

• balanced force reductions;

• test bans, either comprehensive (such as the US, USSR, and UK have been talking about since 1977) or incremental[331];

• international control of all enrichment facilities (under NPT Article I conditions and with provision for technological secrecy);

• no-reprocessing pledges;

• freezes on additional bomb or delivery-vehicle production;

• no-first-use pledges (such as China has consistently given and sought since 1964), whether to NPT parties, nonweapons states, or everyone.

• declarations by weapons states that they will treat as hostile any state first using bombs.

---

fundamental rethinking, see F. Dyson (Institute for Advanced Study, Princeton NJ 08540); "The Quest for Concept", draft typescript, September 1980.

[331]For example, the longstanding proposal[323] to reduce allowed tests to one per year. Another possible incremental approach would be to lower the threshold from the present 150 kT to 15 kT: a level which would overcome all the technical objections (verification, confirming stockpile reliability, etc) raised to a comprehensive test ban. It is, however, discriminatory, in that it would permit the testing of some advanced bomb designs and components while severely restricting any testing by first-generation weapons states.

But some new ideas are also emerging about the principles of possible new instruments for denuclearization[332]. And the Brandt Commission's proposal to tax arms expenditures suggests the intriguing possibility of a heavy and steadily rising international tax on the megatonnage of bomb inventories—as an annual ritual of penance, a vehicle for helping to finance nonviolent oil-displacing programs, and a small compensation for imposed insecurity.

The missing link

In military as in energy policy, the key missing ingredient is the same: promoting a psychological climate of denuclearization, in which it is comes to be seen as a mark of national immaturity to have or want reactors or bombs, requires above all the *political example* of the "fallen" states' desire for redemption[333]. At least four US presidents have apparently brandished the nuclear threat on at least ten occasions[334], or, by a 1976 Brookings Institute count, thirty-three times during 1945–75—an average of more than once a year. The leaders of weapons states need not only to eschew such loose talk but also frequently, publicly, prominently,

---

[332]For example, Feiveson and Goldemberg's first stab at a nondiscriminatory successor to the NPT[320], or A. McKnight's proposed instrument focusing on the institutional mechanisms for eliminating nuclear arsenals (*World Disarmament Draft Treaty with Introduction and Explanatory Notes*, UN Association of the UK (3 Whitehall Court, London SW.1), 1978). Various denuclearization theories and scenarios are starting to be more widely considered than was fashionable a few years ago: see e.g. J. H. Barton's (and to some extent R. Garwin's) contributions to D. C. Gompert *et al.*, *Nuclear Weapons and World Politics*, 1980s Project of the Council on Foreign Relations, McGraw-Hill (NY), 1977; and R. A. Falk's early discussion "Nuclear Policy and World Order: Why Denuclearization", World Order Models Project Occasional Paper #2, 1978 (Institute for World Order, 1140 Ave of the Americas, NYC 10036), 1978, expanding on *International Security* 1:79-93 (1977).

[333] There is a psychological as well as a military dimension to Candidate Carter's remark[176] that

> ...by enjoining sovereign nations to forego nuclear weapons, we are asking for a form of self-denial that we have not been able to accept ourselves. I believe we have little right to ask others to deny themselves such weapons for the indefinite future unless we demonstrate meaningful progress toward the goal of control, then reduction and, ultimately, elimination of nuclear arsenals.

Unfortunately, President Carter's short-lived early call for major bilateral force reductions failed to link them with Article VI obligations or with his efforts for horizontal nonproliferation; a potential synergism fell through the cracks. The later internal debate in the Carter Administration over neutron bombs (which were new politically but not technically) apparently never considered the political effect of that decision on horizontal proliferation: it was deemed a purely domestic (or Alliance) decision whose only relevant political effects would be in the Kremlin. In fact, it badly undermined the Administration's simultaneous nonproliferation initiatives—as if the two policies had been made by separate committees that never happened to meet together.

and sincerely to regret their possession of bombs, emphasize the insecurity that bombs bring, and pray for their speedy elimination. Despite occasional rhetorical gestures in this direction, most political signals are just the opposite[335]. Weapons states almost daily proclaim the prestige they feel their bombs merit for them. They consider themselves the mighty at whose councils others should beg to sit. They apparently expect permanent membership of the Security Council as of right. The first state to announce that its acquisition of bombs had shown its moral unworthiness for such a post would certainly make a stir. Lacking that courage, the weapons states are reinforcing a habit of thought they should be disparaging: that it is legitimate not only to have and even to use bombs, but to rely upon violence, including nuclear violence, as a central instrument of foreign policy.

What is the alternative to reversing this perception? As the world system fragments, many countries may come to see themselves as beleaguered, and bombs as much cheaper than armies. Bombs or the means of making them may become the new opium poppies, the most valuable potential export or the highest-return investment. If France, FR Germany, and Switzerland today cannot resist the temptation of exporting surrogate bombs, can India, Pakistan, and Israel resist tomorrow the temptation to do so more directly[336]?

[334]D. Ellsburg is compiling detailed documentation of these figures. The Brookings count was cited by G. B. Kistiakowsky at the 1980 Harvard symposium organized by Physicians for Social Responsibility. The US has explicitly left open the option of nuclear first use in Europe and Asia (Defense Secretary's *Annual Report,* FY 1980, at 86). Making the refusal of any weapons state to give a no-first-use pledge (only China has done so unambiguously) a subject for wide debate could help to clarify the limits of military, and especially of nuclear military, force in conventional disputes. Even if it were true that current imbalances of conventional forces might require interim local expansions of non-nuclear armaments, and if all efforts to substitute mutual non-nuclear force reductions had failed, the resulting risks seem smaller than those created directly and psychologically by casually running about the world with nuclear six-shooters at the ready.

[335]Near the top of the list must be NATO's continued emphasis on forward nuclear deployment in Europe, which the Boston Study Group[330] argues
> . . . impels nuclear proliferation, by appearing to provide a rational purpose for the acquisition and deployment of nuclear weapons by non-nuclear states through its insistence that nuclear weapons play an important part in international politics.[328]
Alternative defenses against Warsaw Pact tanks, notably by the highly dispersed deployment of miniaturized anti-tank ordnance, seem to have received relatively little attention, and it is not clear whether either the Soviets or many American strategists find it credible that the US would devastate its principal middle European allies in order to defend them. (Using neutron bombs instead of older models would not prevent such devastation.)

[336]The inadvertently published 4 September 1974 CIA memorandum "Prospects

"Let us be the last"

What will happen the next time bombs are used in anger? If the victims are relatively few or, equivalently, remote, nonwhite, and unpublicized (as in Biafra),the world audience—or at least its affluent and bomb-laden minority—may become desensitized and suppose nuclear war is not so bad after all. Already, apologists are redefining the threshold of proliferation, suggesting that it really means having many, diverse, high-yield, miniaturized bombs carried by sophisticated missiles[337]. But the opposite possibility is even worse. The next use of bombs could remind insecure governments of the forgotten lesson of 1945: that one or two crude bombs in the low kiloton range can abruptly end a large war. To protect themselves from real or imagined enemies, dozens of states might then rapidly make *very large* numbers of bombs if the tools to do so—notably reactors—are at hand. Human nature and human fallibility being what they are, the risk of those bombs' use would then rapidly approach unity.

Many analysts believe bombs will before long be used

---

for Further Proliferation of Nuclear Weapons" remarked:

France, India and Israel, while unlikely to foster proliferation as a matter of national policy, probably will prove susceptible to the lure of the economic and political advantages to be gained from exporting materials, technology and equipment relevant to nuclear weapons programs. And most potential proliferators are on good terms with one or all of them.

Some countries appear already—in Laos, Yemen, and Afghanistan—to be resorting to poison gas, the "poor country's A-bomb", and if the bombs themselves become widely available, they will eventually be used too. As Baruch noted in 1946,

. . . terror is not enough to inhibit the use of the atomic bomb. The terror created by weapons has never stopped man from employing them. For each new weapon a defense has been produced, in time. But now we face a condition in which adequate defense does not exist.

[337]The rationalization—e.g. by D. Avery of British Nuclear Fuels Ltd at the Windscale Inquiry—that a few low-kiloton weapons deliverable by, say, light plane or by car does not amount to a "genuine nuclear force" is "unlikely to be accepted by a country without nuclear weapons facing an adversary with such weapons." (Wohlstetter[35] at 39.) Indeed, the aim of the Manhattan Project "was to get a yield of one kiloton, and...seven months before the first nuclear test, its leaders expected the yield to be considerably less, and nevertheless did not consider the project would then be a military failure...." (*id*) Of course, the *n*th-bomb problem *is* real, and is just starting to be explored by analysts conscious of their failure to solve the 1st-bomb problem. Very little attention has yet been paid to the second-tier problem of inhibiting the spread of *advanced* bombs (fusion designs, miniaturization, advanced guidance and delivery systems, etc.). In general, the limiting ingredient for fission bombs is not knowledge but materials; for fusion bombs, whose manufacture is a very high technology, the opposite—hence the concern over the knowledge spread by laser fusion energy research programs[25], at least one of which in a major non-weapons state is apparently already being turned to military lines of inquiry.

again, whether deliberately or by accident. Yet nobody is preparing[338] to grasp that psychological opportunity for new initiatives to raise the perceived cost and lower the perceived benefit of having bombs. Military ways to do both—such as a pact of all weapons states to bomb any state using bombs, especially against a nonweapons state—have been toyed with in part[339], but present obvious practical difficulties. The most potent tools may rather be psychological, not military. In 1945, bombs came as a shattering surprise. Their effects seemed awesome but remote. Electronic mass media were in their infancy, and censored news reports referred mainly to destruction of Japanese industries, not incineration of people. Today, when napalm raids can be brought into the living-room, it would be very different. The reaction to the recent FR German screening of the film *Holocaust* suggests the value of broadcasting as widely as moonwalks and Olympics, and perhaps starting in the US and USSR by agreement, documentaries of what bombs do, so that the horror of them becomes more than a vagueness in a dark recess of the mind, and the necessity of eliminating them can start to grow into a globally shared moral imperative: as Theodore Roethke remarked, "In a dark time, the eye begins to see." New rituals to this end are needed, new symbols. For example, it should become customary for each incoming head of state in every country (and for as many other people as possible) and especially for heads of weapons states to make a pilgrimmage to the A-Bomb Museum at Hiroshima[340], to learn at first-hand the meaning of the survivors' plea: "Let us be the last."

Bombs are a common problem—getting them may seem to offer benefits mainly to oneself and costs mainly to others—but television brings the commons nearer home. At the next opportunity, fictional or real, seeing as if at firsthand who gets what sorts of costs and benefits could be psychologically searing. A detailed, exact, and universal understanding of what bombs really do may be the most effective way to eliminate them.

The anthropologist Mary Catherine Bateson recently offered the parable of a man who has the habit of drinking himself

[338]Though some have urged it: B. Stewart, "Some nuclear explosions will be necessary", *Bulletin of the Atomic Scientists* 51-54, October 1977.

[339]As in the 1968 US, UK, and USSR pledges in connection with Security Council Resolution 255: see C. Van Doren[329] at 10-ll.

[340]Failing that, a remarkably vivid substitute would be to read the *Barefoot Gen* comic books (especially the second [1979] of the two volumes translated into English from the six originals of the *Hadashi no Gen* series by Keiji Nakazawa), available from the War Resisters League (339 Lafayette St, NYC 10012).

nightly into oblivion, and who, perhaps once a year, gets out his revolver and plays solo Russian roulette. He is killing himself in three ways: the annual gamble with instant death, the slow death of cirrhosis, and the daily rejection of the reality of his being. But these three modes of death are mutually reinforcing. When the revolver fails to fire, he thinks he is all right and continues to drink himself to death. He doesn't think too much about what the alcohol is doing to his body because of his overwhelming fear that the Russian roulette will kill him first. The daily oblivion that this fear compels him to seek keeps him from noticing the creeping cirrhosis or resisting the temptation of the revolver. And so the three go round and round, despair feeding on itself. In our culture, perhaps once a year, various nuclear alerts are proven false and the nuclear gun doesn't quite go off. We kill ourselves slowly with chronic pollutions and privations, to which we deaden ourselves with the electronic oblivion and "entertainment" to which our fears drive us. These too feed on each other, and the steady revolving of the insane merry-go-round can be jammed only by minute particulars of work and hope[341]. But first, like the alcoholic, we must recognize the depth of our addictive predicament. Bombs, like alcoholism decades ago or cancer today, are taboo in polite society. Breaking the numbed silence of dread, facing the reality, must precede any attempt at healing.

---

[341]And by appreciating the cultural and human dimensions of our plight: see e.g. G.F. Kennan, "US-Soviet Relations: Turning from Catastrophe", *Christianity and Crisis* (NY) *40*(9): 155-58 (26 May 1980), and G. Blaine, *The Causes of War*, Macmillan (NY), 1973.

Chapter Eleven

A Once-In-a-Lifetime Opportunity

It is very late; perhaps too late. The Hopi prophesy the scattering of a gourd of ashes on the earth; the think-tanks prophesy that thousands of small stars may be kindled here and there on its surface. The continuity of three billion years of biological evolution may falter in a few incandescent hours.

The proliferation problem has seemed insoluble primarily because vast worldwide stocks and flows of bomb materials were assumed to be permanent. Policy never looked beyond the nuclear power age because there was no beyond. But the proffered end of that age may—given pragmatic planning—make it possible to arrest proliferation just short of total unmanageability.

Alwyn Rees remarked that when you have come to the edge of an abyss, the only progressive move you can make is to step backwards. We seek rather to turn around and step forwards. The world is instinctively beginning to turn around, and needs some guides to navigation.

Three tasks

To abandon nuclear power and its ancillary technologies does not require any government to embrace anti-nuclear sentiment or rhetoric. It can love nuclear power—provided it loves the market more. As a first step toward nonproliferation—the step of civil denuclearization—governments need merely accept the market's verdict in good grace and design an orderly terminal phase for an unfortunate mistake. That should include the least unattractive and most permanent ways[342] to eliminate from the biosphere (via interim internationally controlled spent-fuel storage under an unambiguous pledge not to reprocess) the hundreds of tons of bomb materials already created[343]. Phasing out reactors

[342]Virtually no analyst has yet considered how best to do this. Packaging and disposal of intact spent fuel in some geological medium will have to be done in any event (the marine and extraterrestrial options look obviously unsafe or impracticable or both); though legitimate doubts can be raised about any scheme proposed, some least-evil scheme will have to be found. How to dispose of already separated fissile material, including the stock already in bombs, is a more interesting puzzle. It may even be worth building special low-power-density reactors (probably akin to Magnox) to fission the materials in a non-fertile matrix, since there is no other way to get rid of them and they are arguably less dangerous as fission products than as bomb materials (most of which are even longer-lived radiotoxins, independent of their explosive properties).

[343]Formally planning a schedule for phasing out reactors should enormously

by the means suggested in Chapters Four, Seven, and Eight would probably take of the order of a decade, and should reduce both political tensions and electricity prices. Its fundamental requirement is merely that national energy policies be realigned to conservative economic principles—to meeting each end-use need at least cost.

While collective leadership by other countries is desirable and would be sufficient, the US example alone would promptly deprive non-cooperating countries of the domestic political support that an exorbitantly costly bailout of their nuclear industries would require: support that they cannot muster in the face of a coherent US alternative model[344]. Interdependent political illusions would quickly unravel. In a period of tight budgets and narrow electoral margins, explicit US recognition that the market has cut short the nuclear parenthesis in favor of more effective means of oil displacement would focus the accelerating swing of public and professional opinion worldwide. The unwinding of the spiral of nuclear promotion, like the nuclear arms race, can widen as it runs backwards. The alternative—allowing the nuclear industry to die without noting and politically capitalizing on its passage—would be a signal failure of international leadership and a loss of an historically unique opportunity for nonproliferation.

The demise of nuclear power has been ascribed to a misperception to what conditions the technology must satisfy and how this must be demonstrated:

When the history of the nuclear controversy comes to be written, those who killed nuclear technology will be seen to have been its most avid promoters, who systematically mistook hopes for facts, advocacy for analysis, commercial zeal for national interest, expertise for infallibility, engineering for politics, public relations for truth, and the people for fools.[345]

---

simplify problems already unavoidable, such as managing nuclear wastes: many people who oppose schemes for the disposal of unlimited, open-ended quantities of wastes would feel better about responsible measures to deal with a known and limited quantity. See A. B. Lovins, "Comments on X.78 draft IRG Report to the President (TID-28817 draft)", 10 December 1978, available from IPSEP[199].

[344]This political judgment, based on thirteen years' residence and close involvement in European energy and nuclear politics, is shared by most careful students of such matters (e.g. by Bupp[33] for France). Other judgments may of course differ; but it would be a grievous error to mistake for a balanced assessment of political reality the statements of a government's or industry's official position[169-72].

[345]A. B. Lovins, letter to Carl Goldstein (Atomic Industrial Forum), 5 January 1978.

The nuclear industry thought that if it could claim vigorously enough that it had made a safe, economic, and necessary product, acceptance was assured. But society is more discriminating. Societies have various political mechanisms which rigorously test such assertions and reject technologies found to be unsafe, uneconomic, or unnecessary—especially all three at once. In a sense, those nuclear advocates who now attribute the collapse of their dreams to "political problems" are right, but they are only identifying the last step in a long sequence of events: the falsity of their initial claims is now being expressed through the wisdom of mechanisms hidden in the political process. Having so long denied the existence or the relevance of those mechanisms, let us now acknowledge and use them.

Second, as efforts to make the market more efficient (Chapter Eight) hasten the recycling of nuclear resources into the soft path, the United States unilaterally and interested states (especially nonaligned nonweapons states) multilaterally should freely, unconditionally, and nondiscriminatorily help any other country that wants to pursue a soft path—especially developing countries (Chapter Nine). Nuclear fuel security initiatives should be turned into energy security initiatives.

Third, these efforts must be psychologically linked to the slower and more difficult problem of mutual strategic arms reduction—and, even more fundamentally, of the delegitimization of international violence (especially by bombs) and of the demilitarization of the security concept—treating them all as interlinked parts of the same problem with intertwined solutions. All bombs must be treated as equally loathsome, rather than being considered patriotic if possessed by one's own country and irresponsible if by others. A vigorous coalition of nonweapons states to this end is urgently needed (Chapter Ten). But most needed is a reversal of the bad political example now set in word and deed by the weapons states. A propitious beginning would be for at least one weapons state—again, preferably but not necessarily the United States—to begin reacquiring some moral authority by declaring that its bombs are a cause for national shame. In the same spirit, the US should declare that Atoms for Peace, though well meant, was a serious error, based on technical and political miscalculations which were perhaps understandable in the light of 1953 knowledge of energy options but are no longer, and which the US is willing now to go to considerable trouble and expense to correct. Getting the world into this mess took unilateral US action on a grand scale. Getting it out may take more. As the senior author of most proliferative trends and of virtually every major nonproliferation initiative, the US has an overriding obligation to try to rebottle the genie it released and nourished. And absolute symmetry in this effort—expecting nothing of others that one does not do oneself—is imperative. For example, weapons states cannot expect to achieve either shutdown or internationalization of sensitive fuel-cycle plants if they maintain such plants under their own control for their bomb programs: a logic that dovetails neatly with verifiable proposals for freezing the production of further bombs[346].

It is important to note that regional rivals or anxiety-partners could advantageously use a similar sort of aikido politics on each other. Soft-technology aid can be targeted at countries becoming uneasy about nuclear costs and risks, or at countries threatening to develop ambivalence in their nuclear goals. A country facing a neighbor's reactor buildup could consider inviting the neighbor to join in a bilateral or regional soft-energy program in lieu, or, failing that, pursuing such measures unilaterally while pointedly announcing their advantages to maximize their influence on the neighbor's domestic constituencies. (The Brazilians and Germans learned to hate each other, and the Brazilian military government split over the nuclear issue, without any help from Argentina. What if Argentina had suggested a joint soft-energy program to meet the same energy needs at a lower economic and social cost? What if Brazil, now ahead on soft energy and behind on bombs vis-à-vis Argentina, does the same in reverse?) Is it even too naïve to imagine a "Bombaholics Anonymous" in which thoughtful officials and private citizens from current and aspiring weapons states meet privately to share insights on the difficulties of having—and kicking—the habit?

These combined actions may succeed only if they are taken together and *explicitly linked* together. Our thesis is certain to be misrepresented as "trying to stop proliferation by outlawing reactors [or uranium mining]". We have not said that. We have presented three main elements, and many sub-elements, of a coherent market-oriented program. We emphasize that they have a mutually reinforcing psychological thrust—a synergism—that rises from their logical and political connections and is essential to their success. Their linkage is also directly pragmatic, as illustrated by the common and valid argument that if one phased out nuclear power and did nothing else instead (Chapters Four and Seven), oil competition could worsen. Although the fight against vertical proliferation—the nuclear arms race—will be far more difficult than against the horizontal spread of bombs, their inter-linkages with each other and with nuclear power are so inextrica-

---

[346]E.g. ref. 320 and the "Call"[330], which offers various incremental options.

ble that they must be pursued jointly and thought of jointly if either is to succeed.

Pakistan: a case study

Pakistan may offer a laboratory for creative approaches to interlocking security, energy, and development problems. The political signals sent to Pakistan have been muddled for a decade. The Indian explosion caused a further US tilt toward India, fostering Pakistan's earlier sense of insecurity. Wide popular support for a Pakistani bomb stems substantively from fear of the Indian bomb. It does not loom large in Pakistani consciousness that a Pakistani bomb would not deter India, that it invites preëmptive strikes by several nations, and that the very unreliability of conventional alliances that motivates an independent "deterrent" is itself a recognition of the limits of nuclear armaments owned by anyone. Western complicity in and apparent acceptance of the Indian bomb[347] was supplemented in summer 1979 by an "abandonment" of Pakistan couched in such vehement terms that some observers think it encouraged the Soviet invasion of Afghanistan: it suggested that to the US State Department, a Soviet Pakistan was preferable to a nuclear-armed Pakistan.

What is most needed here? Military aid, even if evenhanded, heightens Indian concerns and the risk of Soviet intervention. Greater Chinese moderating influence on India will be slow in coming. A World Bank development program, initially of several billion dollars, for basic needs in Pakistan (food, water, energy), aimed above all at Baluchistan, seems a prerequisite for easing legitimate Pakistani concerns. It would make a greater contribution to real security, provide more domestic political benefits, and offer more chance of encouraging political liberalization and less of spooking India, than any number of advanced fighter planes. Such a program bears the risk of seeming to reward a bomb program (the Indian precedent is hard to live down here too). But the formidable logistical problems which infrastructure-poor Pakistan faces in building even one bomb[348], let

---

[347]Only Pakistan, Canada, Japan, and Sweden took a strong public stand against the Indian test itself (a few others, like Australia and the Netherlands, took weaker ones). Yugoslavia and France sent congratulations.

[348]Though Pakistan's announcement in mid-1980 that it now has uranium enrichment capacity may be correct, the key issue is how much uranium (which Pakistan can get from an indigenous mine) can be enriched how fast. Highly efficient centrifuges are a considerable technical challenge even to the most advanced nations; crude centrifuges, which Pakistan would find easier to build and operate,

alone matching India's technical capacities, must give the bomb
program (at least in the 1980s) more a psychological than a major
military value—like the laboratory-scale Pakistani plutonium
separation facilities which offered fruitful ground for seeking
safeguards parity from India while the equipment itself sat for
years in unopened crates. The inference that can fairly be drawn
so far from Western words and actions—that Pakistani bombs are
anathema, Indian bombs tolerable, and Western bombs admir-
able—must surely bear much of the blame for our present plight;
and the solution lies far nearer Washington than Islamabad.

Neither this specific approach nor our broader recommendations can be guaranteed fully effective. A coherent approach to
nonproliferation, in the face of so many deeply rooted myths, will
not be easy. It will take a few years to get up to speed, and
decades to pursue most of the way. Meanwhile, some pockets of
metastasis—the day-to-day concerns of those professionally concerned with nonproliferation, notably India, Argentina, South Africa, Taiwan, Iraq, and Israel—may remain worrisome. We do
not claim perfection; only that nobody has yet come up with a
more internally consistent approach, or one better matching
economic and political realities.

The wider agenda

Nonproliferation policy addresses the increase of bombs,
not their existence. If human life, and perhaps any life, is to
persist on this planet, the *present* level and dispersion of bombs
cannot be tolerated. We have no special insight into how the
underlying political problems of the world can be solved, nor
special optimism that they can be. Yet we place some small hope
in the gathering portents of a fundamental transformation of
human values such as not been seen for centuries[349]. As terrible
global pressures—oil, a half-trillion dollars' uncollectable debts,
ecological constraints, North-South and East-West tensions, the
failure of the old development concepts, tyranny, poverty, the
numbing weight of military spending—all converge to crush us, a
greater spiritual energy that can inwardly rework human attitudes
is starting to be pressed out of the cracks. In the next decade it

---

are much slower. The rates likely to be achieved in practice are no doubt known to
various intelligence services but have not been published. Pakistan may achieve a
plutonium bomb before a uranium bomb. See also Khalilzad[301].

[349]Many futurists and social theorists with a broad historic perspective assert that
a transformation of Renaissance-like proportions and significance is probably now
beginning and will run its course through at least the remainder of this century.
See e.g. W. Harman, *An Incomplete Guide to the Future*, Stanford Alumni Association (Palo Alto CA), 1976.

may become a flood, profoundly extending the ways we care for the earth and for each other. No one can say if this will happen, nor whether the new symbols and moods now emerging are evanescent or prophetic; but knowing that it might be starting to happen can alert us to grasp the lifelines of new awareness that our increasingly cornered psyches may throw out. The ego is strong, but the love of life may yet prove stronger.

Nor can we long survive if that hope proves illusory. On 15 November 1945, President Truman and Prime Ministers Atlee and Mackenzie King declared:

We are aware that the only complete protection...from the destructive uses of scientific knowledge lies in the prevention of war. No system of safeguards that can be devised will of itself provide an effective guarantee against production of atomic weapons by a nation bent on aggression. Nor can we ignore the possibility of the development of other weapons, or of new methods of warfare, which may constitute as great a threat to civilization as the military use of atomic energy.

Many nuclear physicists, in reflective moments, have wished for a magic wand that would make all nuclear fission impossible: they would wave it instantly. Yet if such a wand were waved, but if we did not also reverse the psychic premises of eons of homocentric, patriarchal, imperial culture, then the time bought might only be used to devise other ingenious ways of killing each other: as the nuclear industry soothingly reminds us, there are lots of others, and more invented all the time. The United States dropped on and around Vietnam the explosive equivalent of one Nagasaki bomb per week for seven and a half years. There are nerve gases, napalm, fuel-air explosives, submunition clusters, cruise missiles, germ warfare, now high-powered lasers. What next? Nonproliferation, however successful, can only buy time before some other holocaust unless we also come to grips with the central problems: power without purpose, tribalism, human aggression, injustice. A soft energy path would foster a social framework in which to address these problems, but it cannot solve them. It is not by itself enough of a vehicle, though it can be one component, to carry that vision without which the people perish. Indeed, Carl-Friedrich von Weizsäcker suggests that as artillery made city walls and hence the city-state obsolete, so nuclear weapons have made both the nation-state and the institution of war obsolete—a necessity so alien, so inconsistent with the whole cultural history of our species, that governments turn to the diversion of "deterrence" to avoid having to face it squarely.

On that yes the future of the world depends

Bernard Baruch's choice between the quick and the dead is still before us, with a new potential resolution that has every justification in rational calculations of cost, of security, of economic and political interest. But people and governments are not purely rational—as Baruch found when his 1946 plan fell victim to the cold war. Our idea, or the refinements we solicit, may work—if many decisions now made irrationally are brought expeditiously within the confines of the criteria which are claimed to guide them, or if political instincts at least rest on a wise perception of self-interest. This will require, however, that governments abandon cherished fantasies, accept the disquieting likelihood of error, and reconcile themselves to the more narrow boundaries of power and ambition consistent with survival. Whether this happens soon enough will "pose a supreme challenge to the adaptability of democratic institutions and to the vitality of our spiritual life."[350] If we fail, it may be left to the cockroaches to speculate about how we could have done better.

Need we have proliferation without nuclear power? Not if we do it right. The methodical collapse of the greatest cause and facilitator of proliferation offers, briefly, the chance to start nearly afresh, to start to unravel the web of hypocrisy and doublethink that has stalled arms control and nonproliferation alike. Perhaps the same promotional skill that spread reactors around the world can now nurture alternatives to them and so place prohibitive political obstacles in the way of making bombs. The same ingenuity and goodwill that managed, against all odds and inconsistencies, to obtain the small measure of international nuclear agreement we have today can now, freed from commercial imperatives that have proven vacuous, find ways to divert trend before it becomes destiny.

In 1946, the Acheson-Lilienthal report proposed a technological monopoly to prevent proliferation in an inevitably nuclear-powered future: mere treaties and policing, it reasoned, would prove weaker than the rivalries of nation-states and the imperfections of human institutions. In 1980, with nuclear power no longer inevitable or even pragmatically attractive, the same political logic leads to quite a different policy prescription. Yet as we frame our different answers to different questions, the same prescient Acheson-Lilienthal conclusions seem apposite still:

We have outlined the course of our thinking in an endeavor to find a solution to the problems thrust upon the world by the development of the

[350]Quoted from the last reference in note 225.

atomic bomb—the problem of how to obtain security against atomic warfare, and relief from the terrible fear which can do so much to engender the very thing feared.

As a result of our thinking and discussions we have concluded that it would be unrealistic to place reliance on a simple agreement among nations to outlaw the use of atomic weapons in war. We have concluded that an attempt to give body to such a system of agreements through international cooperation holds no promise of adequate security.

And so we have turned from mere policing and inspection by an international authority to a program of affirmative action....This plan we believe holds hope for the solution of the problem of the atomic bomb. We are even sustained by the hope that it may contain seeds which will in time grow into that cooperation between nations which may bring an end to all war.

The program we propose will undoubtedly arouse skepticism when it is first considered. It did among us, but thought and discussion have converted us.

It may seem too idealistic. It seems time we endeavor to bring some of our expressed ideals into being.

It may seem too radical, too advanced, too much beyond human experience. All these terms apply with peculiar fitness to the atomic bomb.

In considering the plan, as inevitable doubts arise as to its acceptability, one should ask oneself "What are the alternatives?" We have, and we find no tolerable answer.

About the Authors

Amory B. Lovins, born in Washington DC in 1947, is a consultant physicist who has lived in England since 1967. After two years each at Harvard College and at Magdalen College, Oxford he became a Junior Research Fellow of Merton College, Oxford in 1969, but resigned in 1971 to become full-time British Representative of Friends of the Earth, Inc. (and, in 1979, Vice President of Friends of the Earth Foundation). He received an Oxford MA degree by Special Resolution in 1971 and a DSc degree *honoris causa* from Bates College in 1979. Twice appointed Regents' Lecturer in the University of California (Berkeley, energy policy, spring 1978, and Riverside, economics, spring 1980), he was 1979 Grauer Lecturer in the University of British Columbia. In 1980 he was appointed to the Energy Research Advisory Board of the US Department of Energy.

A consultant experimental physicist since 1965, Mr. Lovins has concentrated on energy and resource strategy since about 1970. His current or recent clients, none of whom is responsible for his views, include several United Nations agencies, the Organization for Economic Cooperation and Development (OECD), the MIT Workshop on Alternative Energy Strategies (WAES), the International Federation of Institutes for Advanced Study (IFIAS), the Science Council of Canada, Petro-Canada, the US Energy Research & Development Administration, the US Congress's Office of Technology Assessment, the US Solar Energy Research Institute, Resources for the Future, the governments of California, Montana, Alaska, and Lower Saxony, and other organizations in the US and abroad. He is active in energy affairs at a technical and political level in about fifteen countries, and has published seven earlier books, several monographs, and many technical papers, articles, and reviews. In September 1979 he married L. Hunter Sheldon Esq., and they now work as a team on energy policy.

L. Hunter Lovins, born in 1950 in Vermont, is a lawyer, forester, sociologist, political scientist, and cowboy. Her 1972 BA degree from Pitzer College and was a double major in political studies and sociology with an environmental emphasis. Her law degree (JD) from Loyola University School of Law (Los Angeles) concentrated on land use, administrative and environmental law, and was granted in 1975 with the Alumni Award for Outstanding Service to the School of Law. She is a licensed member of the

California Bar Association and a partner of Hirschtick & Sheldon in Los Angeles.

From 1974 to 1979 she served as co-founder and Assistant Director of the California Conservation Project ("Tree People") in Los Angeles. In this capacity she supervised the planting of thousands of smog-tolerant trees in forest and urban areas of Southern California, designed and implemented the Project's holistic environmental and energy education programs, coordinated community participation in urban forestry, wrote and edited the Project's publications, and served periodically as photographer, firefighter, and emergency logistics and disaster relief coordinator. She has served as a consultant in environmental education, urban forestry, and community energy education and participation, has lectured and written widely on energy policy, and served in 1978-79 on the City of Los Angeles Energy Management Board.

Earth
Needs More
Friends

And so does Friends of the Earth. Not that the friends we've got haven't performed near miracles. They have. They've enabled FOE to play a leading role in unmasking the "peaceful atom," in espousing a soft energy path, in strengthening the Clean Air Act, in getting (after lo, these many years) stripmine control legislation through Congress, in rallying support for endangered marine mammals, in debunking the SST, in developing and pushing proposals to save Alaskan wilderness, in opposing public works boondoggles, in exposing the undesirability (not to mention the impossibility) of incessant material growth, and in striving for the preservation, restoration, and rational use of Earth and its resources.

FOE has never been large, as membership organizations go. This has made it easier, no doubt, for us to be quick-reacting and maneuverable. But there are times when there's no substitute for sheer muscle—and organizational muscle, in the view of many politicians and publicists, is strictly proportional to membership size. More members, more muscle. (More money, too, a fact we can't afford to ignore.) So one of the most crucial ways you can help FOE defend our planetary habitat is by helping us to enroll new members. Please bring the membership coupon, below, to the attention of someone who shares our concerns. Thank you.

FRIENDS OF THE EARTH   124 Spear Street, San Francisco, California 94105

Please enroll me as checked, at the old rates, including **Not Man Apart** and discounts on selected FOE books.

☐ Regular, $25 a year;   ☐ Contributing, $60 a year;   ☐ Life, $1,000;   ☐ Retired, $12 a year;
☐ Supporting, $35 a year; ☐ Sustaining, $250 a year;   ☐ Student, $12 a year;   ☐ Patron, $5,000 or more
☐ Sponsor = $100   ☐ Spouse = add $5 to any membership

(Name) _____

(Address) _____

(City, State, Zip) _____

(Contributions to FOE are not tax-deductible.)